"Thirty years ago, Ron Sider prophetically challenged the evangelical world with *Rich Christians in an Age of Hunger*. Now he raises the bar with a new challenge: to develop a holistic, biblically grounded political philosophy. If you're wondering what it means to say Christ is Lord of our political life, Sider has, as always, credible and compelling answers. This book again establishes why Ron Sider is one of our most important public theologians."

Jim Wallis, president, Sojourners; author, *God's Politics*

"For decades now, Sider has been the evangelical Christian world's clearest, sanest, and most biblically faithful voice on politics and public policy. Now, in *Just Politics*, Sider serves up his most compelling statement ever on how Christians can and should influence American government to promote the common good, both at home and abroad. It would be a scandal for anyone who truly cares about the subject not to read and heed this marvelous book by the evangelical thinker who puts the fact-based in faith-based and practices what he preaches. Sider is a civic and intellectual treasure."

John J. DiIulio Jr., first director, White House Office of Faith-Based and Community Initiatives; author, *Godly Republic*

"Ron Sider could well be our nation's best professor of Christian social activism. He not only equips us to understand the Bible's teaching on current issues, he also trains us for loving and effective political involvement. *Just Politics* should be a guidebook for Christians who want to be a voice for Jesus in shaping social policy. This book is becoming a part of my personal discipleship process."

Joel C. Hunter, senior pastor, Northland, A Church Distributed; executive committee member, National Association of Evangelicals

"*Just Politics* is in some ways a culminating achievement of Ron Sider's remarkable life of service to God's kingdom. The fulfillment of a dream he has long cherished, Sider here offers a mature, balanced, well-informed, richly biblical Christian political ethic for a broad audience.

"Far less a work of critique than of constructive thought, the book reflects Sider's commitment to both/and rather than either/or thinking, his hopeful spirit, and his wide reading and dialogue both nationally and internationally.

"This is a significant contribution to the emerging evangelical center in Christian political ethics."

David P. Gushee, Distinguished University Professor of Christian Ethics, Mercer University; president, Evangelicals for Human Rights; author, *The Future of Faith in American Politics*

"For decades now, Ron Sider has been a rare voice in the public square calling believers to both a broader agenda that includes the poor and to an approach to public life that is less sectarian and more grounded in principled pluralism and love of neighbor. Here, Sider systematically offers a badly needed public philosophy to ground that work, one reflective of biblical ethics and history, and one that points to both the promises as well as the limits of the State in settling the great moral and social issues of society.

"Reflecting well his own Anabaptist history, Sider consistently brings a quiet, thoughtful yet compelling voice to the policy table. Ron's work has undoubtedly helped usher in an era in which fewer believers rush to embrace the secular ideologies of either Left or Right—and even less the rancorous behavior associated with them—and instead embrace a deeper biblical ethic as a guide to political positions as well as public conduct."

Don Eberly, author; White House aide to presidents Ronald Reagan and George W. Bush

"This is vintage Sider: an abundance of biblical texts to ground and inspire the kind of civic action Christians should take to serve God and neighbors. American evangelicals should read and discuss this book and think hard about the kind of organizing that will be needed to fulfill genuine political responsibility."

James W. Skillen, former president, Center for Public Justice

"This is the book that we've been waiting for Ron Sider to write for years. In *Just Politics* he persuasively brings the Bible to bear on the major issues of our day. In so doing he provides a road map, a guide to help Christians of all political persuasions to develop a relevant and just political philosophy. This work shows how political philosophy should ultimately result in civic responsibility."

Tony Hall, United States ambassador, United Nations, Rome

JUST
POLITICS

JUST
POLITICS

A Guide for Christian Engagement

RONALD J. SIDER

BrazosPress
a division of Baker Publishing Group
Grand Rapids, Michigan

© 2012 by Ronald J. Sider

Published by Brazos Press
a division of Baker Publishing Group
P.O. Box 6287, Grand Rapids, MI 49516-6287
www.brazospress.com

First edition published in 2008 by Baker Books as *The Scandal of Evangelical Politics*.

Printed in the United States of America

Library of Congress Cataloging-in-Publication Data

Sider, Ronald J.
    Just politics : a guide for Christian engagement / Ronald J. Sider. — [2nd ed.].
       p.   cm.
    Rev. ed. of: The scandal of evangelical politics.
    Includes bibliographical references (p.   ) and index.
    ISBN 978-1-58743-326-9 (pbk.)
    1. Christianity and politics. I. Sider, Ronald J. Scandal of evangelical politics. II. Title.
BR115.P7S5155 2012
261.7—dc23
                                          2012017950

In keeping with biblical principles of creation stewardship, Baker Publishing Group advocates the responsible use of our natural resources. As a member of the Green Press Initiative, our company uses recycled paper when possible. The text paper of this book is composed in part of post-consumer waste.

12   13   14   15   16   17   18   7   6   5   4   3   2   1

green press INITIATIVE

Contents

Acknowledgments

I want to thank the many, many people who contributed to this book. Most cannot be named because their specific contribution—at numerous conferences, in vast numbers of personal conversations, and in many books read over more than four decades—has faded from conscious memory. A large portion of those interactions happened in one or another program of Evangelicals for Social Action or my teaching at Palmer Seminary at Eastern University, which have provided wonderful places for my thinking on this topic to develop over more than thirty years.

The several-year process that Diane Knippers and I cochaired for the National Association of Evangelicals was an especially significant time for me. That time of vigorous interaction with key evangelical thinkers on public policy, which led to "For the Health of the Nation: An Evangelical Call to Civic Responsibility" (unanimously approved by the NAE's board of directors in October 2004), helped crystallize my thinking about an evangelical political philosophy.

I want to thank Timothy Shah and Daniel Philpott, who provided crucial assistance on short notice for chapter 12. I am also especially grateful for two graduate research scholars. Regina Downing (my Ayres Graduate Research Scholar) did research and typed the vast bulk of the manuscript (slowly learning how to decipher my handwritten original). Peter Sensenig (my Wilberforce Graduate Research Scholar) helped Regina with some of the research and typing. Many thanks for their careful work over many long hours.

For this second edition, Heather Biscoe (my Wilberforce Graduate Research Scholar) provided excellent help typing the manuscript and Rachel Lesher (my Sider Scholar) did valuable research.

Preface

Human experience proves that politics profoundly impacts billions of people. Bad political choices lead to dictatorship, starvation, and death for hundreds of millions. Good political decisions nurture freedom, life, justice, and peace. Politics matters.

Christian faith teaches that all authority on heaven and earth has already been given to the risen Lord Jesus. He is now King of kings and Lord of lords. Christians, therefore, must act politically in ways that are faithful to Christ the Lord.

Tragically, Christian political activity today is a disaster. Christians embrace contradictory positions on almost every political issue. When they join the political fray, they often succumb to dishonesty and corruption. Even when they endorse good goals, they too often promote their political agenda in foolish ways that frighten non-Christians, thus making it more difficult or nearly impossible to achieve important political goals.

At the heart of the problem is the fact that many Christians, especially evangelical Christians, have not thought very carefully about how to do politics in a wise, biblically grounded way. This book seeks to develop an approach, a methodology, for doing that. It attempts to show how to integrate a thoroughly biblical normative vision with a careful study of society in a way that develops a conceptual framework—a political philosophy—that can guide Christians into more thoughtful and effective political activity.

Both because I am an evangelical and because evangelicals have done less work than other Christians on this topic, this book is addressed primarily to evangelicals and Pentecostals. I pray, however, that growing evangelical reflection on political engagement will lead to more dialogue and greater cooperation among all branches of historic Christianity as we pursue the important task of shaping political life.

Preface to the Second Edition

In the first edition of this book, I lamented the fact that evangelicals have not engaged in the kind of extensive systematic reflection on political life that has been done for decades by Catholics and mainline Protestants. That is beginning to change. In the four years since that first edition, there has been a flood of books on politics by evangelical authors. Some are scholarly volumes, some are the reflections of political practitioners, some are popular manifestos, some are good introductory textbooks, and some are partisan screeds. Here I comment on some of the more important books that have appeared, either since 2008 or too late in 2007 for me to mention them in the first edition.

Michael Lindsay, recently named president of Gordon College, published a superb book called *Faith in the Halls of Power: How Evangelicals Joined the American Elite* (Oxford: Oxford University Press, 2007). He shows how a growing evangelical elite has become influential, not just in politics, but also in business, athletics, Hollywood, and the academy. Based on massive research and many personal interviews, Lindsay helps us understand how evangelicals are shaping American life.

In 2010, James Davison Hunter published a controversial book titled *To Change the World: The Irony, Tragedy, and Possibility of Christianity in the Late Modern World* (Oxford: Oxford University Press, 2010). As a distinguished professor of religion, culture, and social theory at the University of Virginia and a widely read and highly respected scholar, Hunter himself is an illustration of Lindsay's point that evangelicals have joined the American elite. Hunter challenges all of the political strategies that evangelicals have used in the last few decades, recommending an approach of "faithful presence." His thesis probably places too much emphasis on elitist, "top-down" strategies, but he certainly offers a brilliant challenge to all Christians, and evangelicals in particular, to rethink how best to change society.

Eric Gregory, assistant professor of religion at Princeton University, draws on his mastery of the thought of St. Augustine to develop an argument for Christian engagement with contemporary liberal democratic societies. His *Politics and the Order of Love: An Augustinian Ethic of Democratic Citizenship* (Chicago: University of Chicago Press, 2010) is a significant scholarly contribution to Christian political engagement.

In *The Future of Faith in American Politics: The Public Witness of the Evangelical Center* (Waco, TX: Baylor University Press, 2008), David P. Gushee (distinguished university professor of Christian ethics at Mercer University) argues that an emerging evangelical center is slowly replacing the Religious Right as the dominant evangelical political voice. Abandoning a largely exclusive preoccupation with the two issues of abortion and marriage, the emerging evangelical center (especially younger evangelicals) also cares deeply about economic justice, creation care, and peacemaking.

In *Jesus and Justice: Evangelicals, Race, and American Politics* (New Haven: Yale University Press, 2009), Peter Goodwin Heltzel argues that Martin Luther King Jr. and evangelical elder statesman Carl F. H. Henry provide a good deal of the inspiration for four of the major evangelical networks today: The Christian Community Development Association and Sojourners on the one hand, and Focus on the Family and the National Association of Evangelicals on the other. A year earlier, Heltzel (assistant professor of theology at New York Theological Seminary) and his coeditor, Wheaton College Professor Bruce Ellis Benson, published *Evangelicals and Empire: Christian Alternatives to the Political Status Quo* (Grand Rapids: Brazos, 2008). In it, a distinguished, diverse group of thinkers challenge American evangelicals to reevaluate their understanding of and relationship to the "American Empire."

Calvin College's Corwin E. Smidt and a circle of evangelical political scientists have been doing sophisticated statistical analysis of American (especially evangelical) political engagement for several decades. In *The Disappearing God Gap? Religion in the 2008 Presidential Election* (Oxford: Oxford University Press, 2010), Smidt and several other political scientists analyze, using sophisticated polling data, the extent to which Democrats in 2008 managed to attract deeply religious voters. J. Daryl Charles attempted to reintroduce evangelicals to the long Christian tradition of natural law in *Returning to Moral First Things: The Natural-Law Tradition and Its Contemporary Application* (Grand Rapids: Eerdmans, 2008).

Yale theologian Miroslav Volf published *A Public Faith: How Followers of Christ Should Serve the Common Good* (Grand Rapids: Brazos, 2011), an excellent contribution to the discussion of the proper relationship between religious faith and public life.

These and other important new books indicate that evangelical scholars are now engaged in a more sophisticated analysis of politics. But evangelicals have also become deeply engaged in politics itself, and a number of practitioners have provided probing reflections on political life.

Don Eberly has served in both the Reagan and George W. Bush administrations and has written widely on civil society. His *The Rise of Global Civil Society: Building Communities and Nations from the Bottom Up* (New York: Encounter, 2008) is a brilliant book reflecting his years of experience both in Washington, DC and on the ground in places like Iraq. Michael Gerson was President George W. Bush's brilliant speechwriter and respected advisor. After leaving the Bush administration, he published *Heroic Conservatism: Why Republicans Need to Embrace America's Ideals (And Why They Deserve to Fail if They Don't)* (New York: Harper, 2007). A key advisor in President Bush's major initiative to greatly expand US economic foreign aid in order to combat AIDS and malaria in Africa and elsewhere, Gerson makes an impassioned case for "compassionate conservatism." In *City of Man: Religion and Politics in a New Era* (Chicago: Moody, 2010), Gerson and his coauthor Peter Wehner (also a veteran of the Bush White House) articulate their vision of the proper relationship between politics and religion. In *Prisoner of Conscience* (Grand Rapids: Zondervan, 2011), long-time Republican congressman Frank R. Wolf reflects on his thirty years in Congress where he struggled to apply his evangelical faith by successfully becoming a powerful champion of human rights around the world.

Prominent evangelicals are also engaged as activists, popularizing ideas and organizing Christians for political engagement.

Jim Wallis's *God's Politics: Why the Right Gets It Wrong and the Left Doesn't Get It* (San Francisco: HarperSanFrancisco, 2005) became a New York Times best-seller and propelled Wallis into heightened national visibility and influence. As an evangelical political activist and the president of Sojourners, Wallis has more recently published other widely read books: *The Great Awakening: Reviving Faith and Politics in a Post-Religious Right America* (San Francisco: HarperSanFrancisco, 2008) and *Rediscovering Values on Wall Street, Main Street, and Your Street* (New York: Howard, 2010).

Long-time staffer for InterVarsity Christian Fellowship and now director of mobilizing at Sojourners, Lisa Sharon Harper articulates an activist Christian vision in her *Evangelical ≠ Republican . . . or Democrat* (New York: New Press, 2008). More recently, she joins coauthor D. C. Innes (conservative columnist and political scientist) in *Left, Right, and Christ: Evangelical Faith in Politics* (Boise, ID: Russell Media, 2011) in a vigorous, controversial dialogue on current political issues. Adam Taylor, former White House fellow and Sojourners staffer and now vice president of advocacy at World Vision, issues a strong call for vigorous Christian political activism in his *Mobilizing Hope: Faith-Inspired Activism for a Post-Civil Rights Generation* (Downers Grove, IL: InterVarsity, 2010).

Counselor to former president Clinton and member of the platform committee for the Democratic party in 2008, Tony Campolo (professor emeritus at Eastern University) is one of the most dynamic evangelical speakers today. His 2008 *Red Letter Christians: A Citizen's Guide to Faith and Politics* (Ventura, CA: Regal Books) reflects Campolo's lifetime of speaking about politics. Campolo's student Shane Claiborne has become a powerful young evangelical voice for engagement with the poor. In *Jesus for President* (Grand Rapids: Zondervan, 2008), Claiborne and his coauthor Chris Haw question the importance of politics and call for a much greater emphasis on Christian community and grassroots engagement with poor people.

From a much more conservative perspective have come books by prominent evangelicals identified with the Religious Right. For more than a couple of decades, Richard Land has been the articulate public policy voice of the Southern Baptist Convention. His *The Divided States of America? What Liberals and Conservatives Are Missing in the God-and-Country Shouting Match!* (Nashville: Thomas Nelson, 2007) develops a Christian argument for a conservative political agenda. Prominent evangelical pastor D. James Kennedy and coauthor Jerry Newcombe do the same in *How Would Jesus Vote? A Christian Perspective on the Issues* (New York: WaterBrook, 2008). Charles W. Colson, Richard Nixon's tough advisor and later founder of Prison Fellowship, played a key role in evangelical conservative politics for three decades. His *God and Government: An Insider's View on the Boundaries Between Faith and Politics* (Grand Rapids: Zondervan, 2007) illustrates the thoughtful, probing analysis he brings to every political discussion.

Evangelical scholars have also written several recent textbooks on politics. Former state senator and longtime professor of political science at Calvin College and Pepperdine University Steve Monsma published a balanced, thoughtful introduction to politics titled *Healing for a Broken World: Christian Perspectives on Public Policy* (Wheaton: Crossway, 2008). Also useful in sorting out differing evangelical political perspectives is the book edited by P. C. Kemeny: *Church, State and Public Justice* (Downers Grove, IL: IVP Academic, 2007). Wheaton College political scientist Amy Black has written a helpful guide to the "nuts and bolts" of American politics in her *Beyond Left and Right: Helping Christians Make Sense of American Politics* (Grand Rapids: Baker Books, 2008).

From the pen of prominent evangelical theologian Wayne Grudem, we have a huge textbook: *Politics according to the Bible: A Comprehensive Resource for Understanding Modern Political Issues in Light of Scripture* (Grand Rapids: Zondervan, 2010). Now professor of theology and biblical studies at Phoenix Seminary, Grudem provides his usual masterful assembly of relevant biblical texts on a wide range of foundational questions and concrete issues. In many instances, evangelicals would agree with his discussion of foundational principles. But it is less clear why or how his preference for a flat tax rather than a "progressive" income tax (where the rich pay a higher percent than the poor) flows inevitably from the Bible. Or why politics according to the Bible leads to a constantly negative critique in virtually all references to President Obama. Grudem even rejects the view of the vast majority of scientists on global warming, and suggests that the "underlying cause" of fears of global warming comes not from science but from "rejection of belief in God."[1] (For a detailed summary of the scientific evidence, see below 233n1.)

This brief overview of recent books on politics by evangelicals is by no means exhaustive, but it shows that vigorous evangelical political reflection has entered an exciting, more extensive, more sophisticated phase. In the short span of five years there has been a flood of new books on politics by evangelical authors. Some contain groundbreaking scholarship, others the thoughtful reflection of political practitioners and popular activists, and still others are helpful textbooks. One can only hope that this flowering of evangelical political reflection will grow and deepen in the next few decades in a way that nurtures a more thoughtful, more biblical, more sophisticated evangelical political engagement. My prayer is that this present volume will make its own contribution to that important task.

PART 1

The Scandal of Evangelical Political Engagement

For thirty years, evangelicals around the world have been rushing into politics. Occasionally, we have been wise and effective. More often, we have floundered and failed. Too frequently, our political activity has hindered our evangelistic witness and disgraced our Lord. We must face what we have done wrong so that we can do better.

1

Tragic Failure, New Opportunity

Evangelicals today are up to our ears in politics. After decades of with-drawal, we are now vigorously engaged in political activity all around the world. The opportunities are enormous. But the lack of thoughtful preparation is creating tragic failure.

The evangelical return to politics in the last three decades has been strikingly rapid. As late as 1965, Jerry Falwell sharply condemned the clergy engaged in civil rights marches and issued a sweeping rejection of politics.

> Believing the Bible as I do, I would find it impossible to stop preaching the pure saving gospel of Jesus Christ and begin doing anything else—including fighting communism, or participating in civil rights reforms. . . . Preachers are not called to be politicians but to be soul winners. . . . Nowhere are we commissioned to reform the externals. The gospel does not clean up the outside but rather regenerates the inside.[1]

Just fifteen years later, Rev. Falwell's name was everywhere in public debate as the leader of a new "Religious Right" political movement called the Moral Majority, widely credited with helping elect Ronald Reagan as president of the United States in 1980.

Many fundamentalists and other theologically conservative leaders followed Falwell into vigorous political activity, urging their followers to register, vote, and lobby their representatives. Prominent fundamentalist author and pastor Tim LaHaye went so far as to declare that "the only way to have a genuine spiritual revival is to have legislative reform."[2] What an incredible reversal of the earlier, standard evangelical view that evangelism and spiritual revival, *not* political reform, are the way to change society.

In the decade before the so-called Moral Majority burst on the scene, a number of younger evangelicals had called for evangelicals to reengage in political life.[3] Many of the specifics in Falwell's Moral Majority were not exactly what they had in mind, but there is no doubt that Falwell's Moral Majority and then the Christian Coalition organized by charismatic TV preacher Pat Robertson drew millions of formerly disengaged evangelicals (especially fundamentalists and charismatics) into the political arena.

During this same time, evangelicals in Latin America and Asia also joined the political fray in dramatic new ways. There have been at least eight evangelical presidents in developing countries in the 1980s and 1990s. Among the best known are Obasanjo in Nigeria, Chiluba in Zambia, Ramos in the Philippines, Kim Young Sam in South Korea, and Ríos Montt in Guatemala. In Spanish-speaking Latin America alone, well over twenty evangelical political parties have emerged.[4]

In a recent book by Brazilian evangelical scholar Paul Freston, the author surveys and analyzes this sweeping new evangelical political engagement in the Third World. In spite of important positive developments, Freston found widespread confusion, ineptitude, misguided policies, and considerable corruption. Brazil experienced a flood of new evangelical (especially Pentecostal) political activity after 1986, but vote selling and outright corruption "have characterized Protestant politics since 1986."[5] Lacking any carefully developed Christian political philosophy to guide his politics, one evangelical politician announced the principle that "everything that is praised in the Bible should be prescribed [i.e., enacted as public law], everything that is condemned should be proscribed [i.e., prohibited by law]."[6]

Frederick Chiluba, widely known as an evangelical Christian, was elected president of Zambia in 1991. He appointed several evangelical pastors to his cabinet and pronounced Zambia a "Christian nation." When he issued this declaration, Chiluba announced: "I submit the Government and the entire nation of Zambia to the Lordship of Jesus Christ. I further declare that Zambia is a Christian nation that will seek to be governed by the righteous principles of the Word of God."[7] (Chiluba's statement is reminiscent of the decades-long attempt by some American evangelicals to pass an amendment to the US Constitution declaring that Jesus Christ is Lord.)[8]

Unfortunately, Chiluba violated human rights, tortured opponents in custody, bought votes, and allowed widespread corruption so he could run for a third term. He even used tear gas on groups who opposed him. Eventually, more than half of Zambia's members of parliament voted to impeach Chiluba.[9]

Freston blames these and other failures on a lack of systematic evangelical reflection on the nature of political engagement.[10] "A community that goes from apoliticism to political involvement without teaching on biblical political ethics will be susceptible to the prevailing political culture."[11]

Ralph Reed, the brilliant strategist who led Robertson's Christian Coalition for many years, provides a striking illustration. In his book *Active Faith*, Reed reflects on what changed when he became a committed Christian and began attending an evangelical church: "My religious beliefs never changed my views on the [political] issues to any degree because my political philosophy was already well developed."[12] If one assumes that a biblically informed and balanced political agenda was identical with the conservative platform of the Republican Party in the 1990s, then one can understand why Reed's new evangelical faith did not change any of his politics. But if that was not the case, then Reed offers a classical example of how Christians often uncritically embrace inherited political perspectives of Right (or Left) without reflecting in a systematic, biblical way on what should be a uniquely Christian political agenda.

Ed Dobson, Falwell's vice president in the early years of the Moral Majority, has subsequently lamented the movement's lack of a coherent, developed political philosophy. Their approach, he says, was "ready, fire, aim."[13] Their lack of careful reflection, Dobson now believes, contributed to many failures: thinking America had a "favored-nation status with God," neglecting what the Bible teaches about the poor, unfairly attacking enemies, and using manipulative fund-raising techniques.[14]

Many thoughtful commentators—both evangelical insiders and friendly outsiders—agree with Dobson's lament about the failure of evangelicals to develop a comprehensive political philosophy. Michael Cromartie, who has spent years in Washington nurturing evangelical political reflection, notes that evangelicals have "become involved in politics for cultural reasons without seeking theological justification for that involvement until after the fact."[15] In a letter inviting evangelical leaders to a Washington gathering in early 1997 to discuss Christian faith and public life, Don Eberly pointed to "the absence of an evangelical theology." In fact, Eberly suggested that the lack of a solid political philosophy had led evangelicals to use language in their political work that prompted non-evangelicals to view them as "intolerant," dangerous people with theocratic designs. Eberly concluded that unless evangelicals developed an "orthodox public theology," they would soon revert back to a separationist mentality and a new withdrawal from politics.[16]

Prominent evangelical Republican politician Paul Henry lamented as early as 1977 that "the evangelical community . . . seeks to leap from piety to practice with little reflection on guiding principles."[17]

Evangelical historian Mark Noll has written several important pieces analyzing evangelical political engagement throughout American history. That engagement was vigorous up until the early twentieth century when evangelicals reacted one-sidedly against the liberal theology of the Social Gospel movement and retreated into separatist, fundamentalist enclaves. But Noll argues that even earlier, when evangelicals *were* politically engaged, they did very little theological reflection on their politics. Grounded in an emotional fervor characteristic of the revivalism that so powerfully shaped evangelicals, their political activity was populist—based on intuition and simplistic biblical proof texting rather than systematic reflection.

The situation grew even worse as premillennial dispensationalism, preoccupied with the details of the last times surrounding Christ's return, swept through many evangelical circles in the first half of the twentieth century. Apocalyptic speculation about whether Mussolini, Hitler, or Stalin might be the antichrist reached fever pitch in the 1930s and 1940s as evangelical political engagement plunged to an all-time low. Even as biblical a leader as Donald Barnhouse, famous Philadelphia pastor, editor, and radio preacher, declared that Christians who study the details of the end times in Ezekiel knew more about current political developments than those who read the best secular newsmagazines.[18] At a time when end-times novels are by far the most widely read evangelical books, we need to hear Noll's warning that if evangelicals continue to be influenced by the kind of historicist dispensationalism that tries to identify current events as the detailed fulfillment of biblical prophecy, "there is little intellectual hope for the future" of responsible evangelical political reflection.[19]

According to Os Guinness, there has been "no serious evangelical public philosophy in this [the twentieth] century."[20] Not quite that negative, Noll has detected signs of renewed evangelical political reflection in several evangelical traditions, especially among Dutch Reformed, theonomist, and Anabaptist thinkers.[21] Unfortunately, he concludes, "Their diverse approaches to the Bible leave evangelical political thought scattered all over the map."[22]

Evangelical failure to develop a comprehensive political philosophy contrasts sharply with what other Christian traditions, especially Catholics, have done. Roman Catholics benefit from over a century of papal encyclicals that have carefully developed and articulated a Catholic approach to public life.[23] Mainline Protestants—both through church declarations and the work of brilliant individuals like Reinhold Niebuhr—have also developed a substantial collection of careful thought on politics.[24] The evangelical community has simply failed to develop anything comparable.[25]

The absence of any widely accepted, systematic evangelical reflection on politics leads to contradiction, confusion, ineffectiveness, even biblical unfaithfulness in our political work.

Consider the evangelical community's inconsistency with regard to the sanctity of human life. Almost all evangelicals agree with the principle. But many highly visible evangelical pro-life movements focus largely on the question of abortion—as if, as one wag commented, life begins at conception and ends at birth. But what about the millions of children who die every year of starvation or the millions of adults killed annually by tobacco smoke? Are these not also sanctity-of-life issues?

Senator Jesse Helms provides one of the most stunning illustrations of this problem. For many years, Senator Helms was one of the most prominent pro-life leaders in the US Congress, pushing for restrictions on abortion. But Helms happened to represent the largest tobacco-growing state in the country, so he also supported government subsidies for tobacco growers—even using tax dollars to subsidize shipping American tobacco to poor nations under the Food for Peace program! Hardly a pro-life use of public tax dollars.

Most evangelicals believe that widespread moral decay threatens the future. Some evangelicals argue that restoring public Bible reading and prayer at the beginning of the school day in the public schools would help reverse the moral decay. Other evangelicals believe that would violate the constitutional separation of church and state.

Evangelicals have disagreed sharply on the faith-based initiatives of President George W. Bush and the earlier legislation on charitable choice signed by President Clinton. These new measures strengthen the ability of deeply faith-based organizations to receive federal funds to expand their social programs serving the poor and needy, without having to abandon the religious character of their programs. Many evangelicals enthusiastically support these measures as a reversal of several decades of radically secularized misinterpretation of the First Amendment on religious freedom. Other evangelicals argue that the faith-based initiatives, especially charitable choice, violate the First Amendment and threaten to destroy both church and state.

Evangelical pronouncements on the role of government are often contradictory. Sometimes, when attacking government measures they dislike, evangelical voices use libertarian arguments that forbid almost all government programs that help the poor. ("Helping the poor is a task for individuals and churches, not the government," some argue. "Government should provide a legal framework, fair courts, and police protection but then leave almost everything else to the free choice of individuals.") But, when the issue changes from the poor to the family, the definition of marriage, abortion, or pornography, the same people quickly abandon libertarian arguments that maximize individual freedom. Instead they push vigorously for legislation that involves substantial government restriction of individual choices. It is possible that there are valid intellectual arguments for adopting libertarian arguments in the first case and non-libertarian arguments in the second, but a careful argument would have to be made. Without such an argument, flipping from libertarian to non-libertarian arguments looks confused and superficial.

The agenda of many Christian political movements is also problematic. One sees a great deal on abortion, euthanasia, and the family, but hardly ever do they push for public policy to combat racism, protect the creation, or empower the poor. If the Bible says that God cares *both* about the family *and* the poor, about the sanctity of human life *and* racial justice *and* creation, then should not evangelical political movements be promoting *all* these things? Does not a one-sided focus on the issues that happen to be favored by either the Left or the Right suggest that one's political agenda is shaped more by secular ideology than careful biblical, theological reflection? Fortunately, as prominent evangelical ethicist David Gushee has recently argued, a new evangelical center is emerging that embraces a broader, more balanced biblical agenda.[26]

Consider also the tough question: What should we legislate? Should public law, as the newly engaged evangelical politician we quoted earlier said, support everything the Bible says is right and outlaw everything the Bible says is wrong? Should public law allow divorce only in the narrow circumstances under which Jesus permitted divorce?[27] Or should the state's law on divorce differ from the church's teaching? If one believes that adultery and homosexual practice are sinful, does that mean that the law should make such activity a crime? If not, why not? Answering the complex question of what to legislate and what not to legislate requires a lot of thinking about the proper, limited role of the state, the nature of human freedom, and the purpose and limitations of laws. In short, it requires sophisticated thinking about a biblically grounded, factually informed political philosophy.

All this may sound so complicated that some conclude, "Forget it. We don't need all that highfalutin intellectual stuff." But those who take that route are doomed to continue the present pattern of political engagement: contradiction, confusion, ineffectiveness, and failure. They are likely to despair of achieving anything significant through politics—and drop out. (That's basically what Falwell's two former vice presidents, Cal Thomas and Ed Dobson, recommend in their book *Blinded by Might*.)[28]

Would that be so bad? After all, politics is certainly not the most important activity in the world. It is not as important as evangelism. Being good parents, church members, neighbors, school teachers—none of these things are politics, but they are enormously important and help build good societies.

So should faithful Christians just forget about politics? No, for two reasons—one practical, the other theological.

It is a simple historical fact that political decisions have a huge impact—good or bad—on the lives of literally billions of people. Think of the devastation and death the world might have avoided if German voters had not elected Hitler to public office. Think of the freedom, goodness, and joy that followed for tens of millions from the fact that evangelical member of Parliament William Wilberforce labored for more than thirty years and eventually persuaded his colleagues in the British Parliament to outlaw first the slave trade and then slavery itself in the British Empire.

It is through politics that country after country has come to enjoy democracy. It is through politics that nation after nation has stopped jailing and killing "heretics"—thousands of my ancestors in the sixteenth century were burned at the stake or drowned in the rivers by fellow Protestants who disagreed with our belief that the church should be separate from the state. It took centuries, but eventually more and more politicians in more and more countries decided that religious freedom for everyone is a necessary mark of a just political order. It is through politics that Marxist-Leninist totalitarianism first conquered and developed and then waned and disappeared in Eastern Europe and the Soviet Union. It is through politics that we develop laws that either restrict or permit abortion, allow or forbid "gay marriage," protect or destroy the environment. Politics is simply too important to ignore.

The theological reason for political engagement is even more compelling. The central Christian confession is that Jesus is now Lord—Lord of the entire universe. The New Testament explicitly teaches that he is now "ruler of the kings of the earth" (Rev. 1:5). "All authority in heaven and on earth" *has been* given to the risen Jesus (Matt. 28:18). Christians who know that must submit every corner of their lives to their wonderful Lord.

Since we live in democratic societies where we have the freedom to vote, our votes—or even our failure to vote—shape what happens in important areas of politics. If Christ is my Lord, if Christ desires the well-being of all, and if my vote has the potential to encourage political decisions that will promote the well-being of my neighbors, then the obligation to vote responsibly follows necessarily from my confession that Christ my Lord calls me to love my neighbor. One way Christians must live out our belief that Christ is Lord, even of political life, is to think and pray for wisdom to act politically in ways that best reflect Christ our Lord.

That is the basic task of this book. How do we acquire the wisdom to act in politics in a way that truly reflects Christ? How do we move from a commitment to Jesus Christ and biblical authority to concrete political decisions that lead us to support or oppose specific laws and candidates? Is there an approach, a method, a framework that will help us do that? I hope the following chapters succeed in articulating an evangelical political philosophy that will do just that.

Some may ask: Why call it an *evangelical* political philosophy? My friends David Gushee and Dennis Hollinger have recently argued that what we call evangelicalism is really a series of revival movements designated to call Christians who are straying from historic Christianity back to orthodox Christian faith and practice. Therefore there is really no such thing as evangelicalism per se, or an evangelical ethic, or an evangelical political philosophy. There are simply a number of orthodox Christian political philosophies articulated by persons who stand within one of the several orthodox Christian theological traditions (whether Lutheran, Reformed, Pentecostal, Anabaptist, Wesleyan, Eastern Orthodox, or Roman Catholic).[29]

We need not decide whether Gushee and Hollinger's basic thesis is valid in order to note one problem: their argument obscures the fact that there are more than 600 million Christians, living in virtually every country on the planet, whose leaders identify in some important ways with the label "evangelical." They know they are Protestant, not Roman Catholic or Eastern Orthodox. Many of them also see themselves as Pentecostal or Wesleyan or Anabaptist or Reformed or Anglican. But most (although not all) also see themselves as part of the broad family that identifies with the label "evangelical Protestant." This family shares a common passion to share the gospel of Jesus Christ with those who have never heard, to submit their whole life to the lordship of Jesus Christ, and to embrace the Bible as God's authoritative, revealed word and as the final authority for faith and practice.

In spite of the many specifics of their theological traditions that still divide them, they sense that all those who identify with the label "evangelical" have important things in common that enable them to work together, not only in evangelism but also in political life, to move their societies toward wholeness. As we have seen, their first steps in the past couple decades have often been confused and imperfect. But evangelicals are ready to try again. All around the world, evangelical thinkers and politicians are wrestling at a deeper level with how to act politically in faithfulness to Christ.[30] If even a modest fraction of that rapidly growing number of 600 million evangelicals and Pentecostals would develop a commonly embraced, biblically grounded framework for doing politics, they would change the world.

A Better Approach

The failures of recent evangelical political engagement flow, at least to a significant degree, from the fact that we failed to develop a biblically grounded, systematic approach to the complicated task of politics. Our approach was "ready, fire, aim." We failed to do our homework before we took the test.

We need two things: a wise methodology for engaging in politics, and a solid biblical foundation that guides and shapes our politics. In part 2, we take up these tasks.

2

Developing a Faithful Methodology

How do we begin?

Our basic goals are fairly clear. As Christians we want to whole-heartedly submit our politics to the lordship of Christ. We want to be un-compromisingly biblical. We also want to be grounded in "the facts"—in an honest and accurate reading of history and the social sciences. Finally, we want a comprehensive framework that helps us make consistent, faithful, and effective political decisions about very concrete questions: Should I oppose or support this law? Should I vote for this or that candidate for Congress or the presidency?

Furthermore, we need to be able to communicate our political ideas to an enormously diverse group of fellow citizens in our highly pluralistic society. In fact, we need to have a language that will enable us to persuade a majority of citizens that our proposals are wise. If we cannot do that, we will never succeed in persuading our democratic society to adopt any of the political ideas we think are so wonderful and good.

So how do we get to where we want to go? What methodology will enable us to reach these goals? Christians have been thinking about politics for two thousand years. We need to listen carefully to their wisdom to see what we can learn from Christian history. We also need to listen to and interact with contemporary secular thinkers who profoundly shape the current debate. Out of this dialogue will emerge a methodology that enables evangelicals to think carefully about politics.

Christian History

One part of one chapter cannot begin to do justice to a vast body of Christian reflection on politics stretching over two thousand years. Here I can only point briefly to a few of the most important ideas and thinkers.

Almost certainly the most significant political declaration of the early church was that Jesus, not Caesar, was Lord. The Roman emperors claimed to be divine. People throughout the empire worshiped them. Christians refused. In the late second century, Theophilus of Antioch explained why he gladly prayed for and honored the emperor but refused to worship him: "He's not God but a man appointed by God, not to be worshiped—but to judge justly."[1] By insisting, with the blood of many martyrs, that they would obey their Lord Jesus when the emperor's demands contradicted those of Jesus, the early Christians articulated the profoundly important and practical claim that human government is limited and must answer to a higher authority. By insisting on the right of the church to define itself independently of the state, Christian faith transcended the Greco-Roman world with its view of society as a single, homogeneous unit.[2]

Much changed in the early fourth century when Constantine allegedly had a vision directing him to conquer his military opponents with the sign of the cross and declared Christian faith a legitimate religion throughout the empire. Within one hundred years the great theologian St. Augustine would defend the government's right to coerce, even execute, Christian "heretics." Thus began a union of church and state that denied religious freedom to dissenters: it would be the norm in Christendom for almost fifteen hundred years.

Augustine's *City of God* (finished in AD 426) is perhaps the most famous of all Christian writings on politics.[3] In it he describes two cities, each defined by what they love and the peace they provide. The earthly city is controlled by the love of earthly things (food, houses, money, power, fame) and at its best produces temporary, limited, but still significant earthly peace, social order, and political justice. The heavenly city is focused on love for the true God and offers a vastly more important peace—eternal, heavenly peace. The most important purpose of the earthly city is to serve the heavenly city by restraining evil and thereby offering Christians a temporary home during their short life so they may live in peace, have the freedom to worship God, and spread the gospel. Christians appropriately serve in the institutions of the earthly city (whether as soldiers, judges, or politicians) to nurture its limited, temporary goods of imperfect peace and justice. However, they never lose sight of the fact that all socioeconomic, political achievements in the earthly city are vastly less important than the eternal peace of the heavenly city.[4]

Augustine's Platonic thought undoubtedly led him to undervalue the goodness and worth of earthly life. But his powerful insistence on the inevitable imperfections of the earthly city and the fact that persons are designed by God for a future that transcends every humanly shaped political order contributed to the developing Christian understanding that politics is not all-important and government must be limited.

Thomas Aquinas (ca. 1225–1274), the most influential Catholic philosopher and theologian of the Middle Ages, articulated an approach to politics that remains influential to the present. Two of his ideas are especially important here: the positive role of the state, and natural law. Aquinas integrated important ideas from both the Bible and Aristotle to emphasize that human beings are made for community. Therefore, political rule that leads and guides persons in community is a natural, necessary outcome of the communal nature of persons. The state is not merely a post-fall necessity needed only to restrain sin. It follows naturally from our communal nature and promotes the common good, not just by restraining evil but also by promoting things like a sufficiency of material goods.[5]

God is the source of all law, but we become aware of that law in two ways: we learn of divine law through God's special revelation; we learn of natural law through human reason. All persons are rational beings and therefore have some insight into natural law. Through human reason, we can understand that people ought to keep promises and children ought to respect and obey parents.

In fact, Aquinas and the Thomist tradition that developed from his thought argue that people in general (whether Christians or not) can discern the shape of a good society and fashion just laws simply by a growing perception of natural law through human reason. Thus the great twentieth-century Roman Catholic theologian John Courtney Murray would insist: "The Catholic assumes that 'religion,' for all its indispensability as the basic energy of civilization, is not a force directive of public affairs, except in so far as its truth and imperatives are translated to society and to the state through the medium of the public philosophy that has been elaborated by human reason over centuries of reflection and experience."[6] Murray believed all the pillars of American political life—the role of law, democratic process, and religious freedom—could be deduced from natural law by rational persons regardless of their specific religious beliefs. To the extent that concrete human laws are just, they are valid, rational applications to society of the underlying natural law.

Later, we will have to consider the many criticisms leveled against this understanding of natural law. But one of its greatest strengths is certainly the way that it grounds concrete law, not in the arbitrary whim of rulers or the self-interest of the powerful, but in the universal moral order embedded in creation.

The Protestant Reformation in the sixteenth century produced new, creative Christian reflection on politics. We will explore three of these traditions: the Lutheran, Calvinist, and Anabaptist.

In his work *On Secular Authority*, published in 1523 in the early years of the Protestant Reformation, Martin Luther argued that God rules the world through two kingdoms or governments. The spiritual government rules Christians through the gospel and love. The secular government (which includes not just the area of the state but also culture, economics, education, etc.) rules the world through law and sword.[7] Luther wants to keep a sharp distinction between these two kingdoms. At times he even goes so far as to say that Christians have no need for secular government.[8] Partly to guard against works-righteousness, Luther insists that the gospel has no connection with secular government and the kingdom of this world. The Sermon on the Mount and other gospel principles should never be applied in secular government.

> God made the secular government subject to reason. Nothing is taught in the Gospels about how it is to be maintained and regulated. . . . Therefore the heathen can speak and teach about this very well. . . . Whoever wants to learn and become wise in secular government, let him read the heathen books and writings.[9]

The Christian lives in both kingdoms and submits to both governments but follows radically different norms in each kingdom. As a Christian, one trusts in justification by faith alone and lives out a radical love, abandoning any claims for one's self. The same individual, as a member of the kingdom of this world, uses the sword as executioner or soldier to forcibly restrain evil.

From this perspective, the only purpose of secular government is to restrain evil. Indeed, the state, Luther insists, is a "kingdom of sin" because "its theme is nothing but sin and the checking of sin." It is merely a "remedy required by our corrupted nature."[10] Thus, Lutheran theologian Helmut Thielicke describes the state as an "emergency order in a fallen world, not an order of creation."[11]

Luther's insistence that the state operates by its own norms without any interference from the gospel opened the door for those who later would argue that Christians should blindly obey whatever the state commands. That was the response to Hitler on the part of many Lutheran Christians, and it provoked a vigorous critique by Karl Barth, who rejected the claim that the justification of the sinner through faith in Christ has no connection with the issue of law and justice in society.[12]

Luther's negative view of the state left no room for Aquinas's claim that the state plays a positive role in nurturing the common good. But at least Luther's view underlined the reality of pervasive imperfection and sin in human society. Taken seriously, it could have helped us avoid the kind of naïve optimism of the last few centuries that often believes earthly society is rapidly moving toward a glorious utopia produced by human effort. Luther's perspective would also have helped us see that not everything that is normative for the church ought to be legislated by the state.

John Calvin (1509–1564) was far more hopeful than Luther about the ways in which society could be transformed to reflect God's will. The purpose of "secular government" is "to foster and protect the external worship of God, defend pure doctrine and the good condition of the church . . . mould our conduct to civil justice, reconcile us one to another, and uphold and defend the common peace and tranquility."[13] The state's responsibility includes the positive task of nurturing human "flourishing" and cultivating "upright conduct and discovery."[14]

Two sets of leaders ruled Calvin's Geneva: church government managed worship and moral discipline in the city; secular government oversaw practical life. Working closely together, secular and religious structures enforced a rigid discipline: compulsory church attendance, the execution of heretics, the banning of improper books, and the prohibition of jewelry, luxurious clothing, and extravagant banquets. Every area of society was to be reformed and transformed so that it conformed to the will of the sovereign God.

This powerful Calvinist drive to legislate God's will in order to create a renewed social order was to have a major influence on American political life: English Puritanism in New England; Dutch, German, and Scottish Calvinists in the Middle Colonies; and Anglicans of a Reformed bent in the South were, as historian Mark Noll points out, the dominant influence in American culture for the first two centuries. They and the more populist evangelicals of the nineteenth century "assumed it was necessary to move directly from passion for God and the Bible to passion for the renovation of society."[15]Calvin and his American descendants provided a model of reforming zeal that H. Richard Niebuhr later called "Christ transforming culture."[16]

The sixteenth-century Anabaptists offered a starkly different approach to the state. They embraced the Reformation's principle of *sola scriptura* but taught that the other Reformers were ignoring several central biblical teachings. Believing that only adult believers should be baptized, they rejected more than a millennium of infant baptism. Believing that only believers and not secular government should rule in the church, they rejected twelve hundred years of Constantinian union of church and state and championed religious freedom. Most radical of all, believing that Jesus taught his followers not to kill, they insisted that true Christians could not serve in the army or the government.

The Anabaptists recognized that God orders and uses the state to punish evil and protect good. "In the law, the sword is established to punish and to kill the wicked, and secular authorities are established to use it." But Christians must follow Christ's clear teaching not to kill. "The sword is ordained by God *outside the perfection of Christ.*"[17] Non-Christians may serve in the army or the government, but not Christians.

Not surprisingly, the majority of their Christian contemporaries vigorously attacked these radical Anabaptist ideas. Lutherans, Calvinists, Anglicans, and Catholics slaughtered thousands of these "heretics." Hunted from country to country, a minority (now called Mennonites) managed to survive in isolated enclaves, first in Switzerland and Holland, then in Russia and America. Grateful simply to survive and to model faithful Christianity in their withdrawn communities, they seldom engaged in political life.

The Anabaptists' call for the separation of church and state spread slowly in the following centuries, eventually becoming the consensus of the modern world. But their rejection of the sword has remained very much a minority view in the Christian church. For the first three centuries after Christ, to be sure, every known Christian writing that deals with war or killing teaches that Christians should not kill.[18] But since the time of Constantine, only a minority of Christians has continued that belief: Mennonites, Quakers, and small groups of pacifists in Catholic, Lutheran, Reformed, Pentecostal, and Wesleyan circles.

In the latter half of the twentieth century, Mennonites rejoined the Christian conversation about politics. John Howard Yoder's *Politics of Jesus* (1972) was read widely in many Christian circles. Yoder abandoned the earlier dualistic view that although Christians dare not kill, God wants the state to use lethal violence.[19] God can and does act to bring good out of war, but it is never God's will. Yoder argued that most Christians simply set Jesus aside rather than ask what it would really mean to obey him in the area of politics. The first task of the church in politics, Yoder insisted, is simply to be the church modeling the radical new social order of Jesus's new community.

In an important book on politics, another contemporary Mennonite argues that Christians' political engagement should have three universal characteristics. First, it identifies primarily with the church, not with the nation, and it asks not what seems right or permissible to national political leaders but rather what Christian faith obligates Christians to do. Second, its identity is primarily as a citizen of the world, not as a citizen of a particular nation. And third, its primary question is how policies and progress affect the least and poorest.[20]

Whether or not one agrees with the Anabaptist claim that Jesus taught his followers not to kill, all Christians can agree that obedience to Christ must transcend the summons of any secular government and that a Christian's identity with the worldwide body of Christ outweighs every nationalistic loyalty.

All the main streams of Christian political reflection we have explored—Augustinian, Thomist, Lutheran, Calvinist, and Anabaptist—have flowed into Christian dialogue about politics in the last century. Aquinas especially, but also Augustine, has influenced the large number of sophisticated, carefully argued papal encyclicals, starting with *Rerum novarum* (1891), that have fleshed out a Catholic political philosophy.[21] And that Catholic stream has inspired tens of millions of Christian political activists around the world—not least in the several Christian Democratic parties in Western Europe.[22] America's greatest political theologian, Reinhold Niebuhr, writing in the middle of the twentieth century, embraced Augustinian, Lutheran, and Reformed themes in his brilliant articulation of political realism.[23] Subsequent mainline Protestant thought has been deeply shaped by Niebuhr's long shadow.[24] Dutch Calvinist philosopher and politician Abraham Kuyper (1837–1920) has inspired a significant number of important books on politics by evangelical Reformed thinkers in the last few decades. Especially important are books by Richard Mouw, Stephen Monsma, Paul Marshall, and James Skillen.[25] Liberation theologians weighed in with a powerful call to develop a political philosophy that started with the poor and oppressed.[26] And evangelical scholar Stephen Mott articulated a political philosophy shaped by the Wesleyan tradition.[27]

In the last two decades, evangelicals have begun to think about political life in a renewed, careful way. There is not yet any substantial body of evangelical political reflection comparable to that in Catholic or mainline Protestant circles, although, as we saw in the preface to the second edition, there has been a flood of new books on politics in the last few years. Furthermore, what there is, is often contradictory, lacking widespread agreement across a broad range of evangelical traditions. Some are near libertarians.[28] Others are theonomists.[29] Several promote a modification of Dutch Reformed thought.[30] Others promote a Wesleyan[31] or Anabaptist approach.[32] To the extent that evangelicals want to work together to shape public life, there is an urgent need for a wider evangelical consensus on a basic political philosophy that combines the best of several Christian traditions in a way that is systematically shaped by biblical thought.[33]

Speaking to a Pluralistic Society

There is another huge problem. Even if a broad range of evangelicals could agree on major aspects of a biblically informed political philosophy, they would still face the tough reality that modern society is highly pluralistic. Muslims, Jews, Buddhists, Hindus, agnostics, and especially the secular intellectuals who dominate our great universities have little or no interest in political ideas offered by Christians as "biblical truths" for shaping politics. Radically divergent, mutually contradictory views about almost any topic relevant to politics pervade contemporary society.

Many thinkers have argued that any successful, lasting society requires some basic common values that most or all citizens share. More than a century and a half ago, Alexis de Tocqueville, the famous French commentator on American life, put it bluntly:

> For without ideas in common, no common action would be possible, and without common action, men might exist but there could be no body social. So for society to exist, and even more, for society to prosper, it is essential that all minds of the citizens should always be rallied and held together by some leading ideas.[34]

Many thinkers before and since have agreed. Princeton ethicist Max Stackhouse says every civilization needs at its core a "metaphysical moral vision, a spiritual and ethical guidance system."[35] In *The Naked Public Square*, Richard John Neuhaus argues that unless law is grounded in moral values rooted in transcendent religious belief chaos results.

> When in our public life no legal prohibition can be articulated with the force of transcendent authority, then there are no rules rooted in ultimacies that can protect the poor, the powerless and the marginalized, as indeed there are now no rules protecting the unborn and only fragile institutions surrounding the aged or defective.[36]

These thinkers may be right to argue that it is highly desirable to have some basic common values about the good and true to sustain a good society. Like it or not, however, no such consensus exists in our world today. Sweeping pluralism and radical relativism prevail. Secular thinkers like Princeton philosopher Peter Singer totally reject the historic Judeo-Christian affirmation of the inestimable value and dignity of every person grounded in the belief that each individual is made in the divine image. Instead, viewing persons merely as complex machines emerging by chance from a blind evolutionary process, Singer declares that human beings are no more valuable than monkeys or moles and advocates both infanticide (for the first month at least) and euthanasia.[37] For every concept important to political life—justice, freedom, equality, and human dignity—there are many competing, contradictory definitions.

The claim that every idea and value is relative is the only remaining absolute. Widely influential thinkers of the past two centuries, such as Marx, Darwin, and Freud, have argued that our most lofty beliefs and moral convictions are simply the result of economics, evolution, or early childhood. More recently, postmodernists insist that every claim about the true and good is simply a subjective power play to assert our self-interest.[38]

In two widely influential books, *After Virtue* (1985) and *Whose Justice?* (1988), Alasdair MacIntyre has concluded that it is impossible to develop a set of common values that all can endorse as the foundation of social order by starting with some allegedly neutral, objective philosophical starting point. No such place exists. We are simply left with competing values rooted in competing religious and philosophical traditions. At the end of a brilliant book wrestling with the problem of contemporary pluralism and the need for common values, Oxford professor Raymond Plant concludes, "There seems to be a clear impasse . . . and I do not have the intellectual resources to suggest in any detail how such an impasse could be resolved."[39]

Before we accept this conclusion, we need to review two of the most significant twentieth-century attempts to find a neutral, objective starting point for discovering common values that all citizens can embrace: natural law, and the political philosophy of John Rawls.

As we saw earlier, the natural law tradition articulated so clearly by Thomas Aquinas in the thirteenth century, developed by Catholics over many centuries, and promoted brilliantly by twentieth-century Catholics like John Courtney Murray claim that, simply on the basis of reason (which all persons share), it is possible to discern universal moral values adequate for building a good society. This approach is highly attractive.[40] If it were true and workable, it would offer a way out of our impasse. It would provide both shared values and a common language for public life.

Many objections, however, have been raised to natural law theory. Natural law theorists have defended both monarchy and democracy, both state enforcement of religious orthodoxy and the separation of church and state. Prominent philosophers including David Hume and Immanuel Kant have mounted powerful objections.[41] Many Protestants have argued that, since the fall, sin has distorted not just the will but human reason to such an extent that it is impossible for sinful persons to discern moral truth with unaided human reason. We need special divine revelation that we have in the Bible.[42] Liberation theologian José Miguez Bonino argued that, historically, a natural law approach has tended to water down the radical biblical call for change to bring justice for the oppressed and instead has supported the status quo.[43] Karl Barth insisted that when Christians build their political framework on natural law, they neglect Christ as the center of their politics.[44]

Biblical Christians, however, cannot totally dismiss the idea of natural law, because the New Testament clearly affirms it. It is certainly true that sin has distorted our minds as well as our wills. Because of the fall, our "thinking became futile" and we developed a "depraved mind" (Rom. 1:21, 28). But Paul insists that even gentile sinners who do not know of God's special revelation through Israel nevertheless have some moral insight. "When Gentiles, who do not have the law, do by nature things required by the law, they are a law for themselves, even though they do not have the law. They show that the requirements of the law are written on their hearts, their consciences also bearing witness, and their thoughts now accusing, now even defending them" (Rom. 2:14–15). This limited moral insight is not sufficient for salvation, but Paul does clearly insist that some fundamental awareness of right and wrong is embedded in every human being.

Unfortunately, human sin is so powerful that, to a great extent, it obscures and conceals this moral insight. That means that our only certain guide to ethics is God's special revelation in the Bible. Only the gospel has the power to overcome sinful humanity's perverse desire to deny the ethical truth that at some level it still partially understands. But the fact that no living person, however sinful, can fully obscure this moral insight written on the heart is enormously important when we try to appeal to non-Christians and urge them to accept moral claims that Christians understand clearly only on the basis of biblical revelation.[45]

What does this mean for a Christian political philosophy? It means that we should turn primarily to the Bible, not to unaided human reason, for a clear understanding of morality, the nature of persons, justice, and family. Our normative framework, our fundamental normative principles for politics, properly comes largely from the Bible, not mere philosophical reflection. It also means that careful systematic reflection on politics within the Christian community must be where we begin. We need structures and processes among Christians to think through both a uniquely Christian framework for politics and also the concrete implications of that framework. But when we seek to make a case in the larger, pluralistic society for political proposals (e.g., that abortion is the taking of innocent human life, that marriage is only between a man and a woman, or that justice demands a special concern for the poor), we know that at some deep level even secular thinkers who reject these claims actually have these truths written on their hearts, even though they deny it. And it also means that we may be able, at times, to develop common language that most, if not all, citizens will embrace. That means that although natural law will not work to overcome the impasse we noted earlier, it is, nonetheless, very important.

What about John Rawls? Does his political philosophy offer access to the basic principles needed for a fair, democratic society without any prior acceptance of the specific moral judgments that are so much disputed in our pluralistic society? In his famous book *A Theory of Justice* (1971)—probably the single most influential secular book on political philosophy in the last three decades of the twentieth century—Rawls claims that his approach offers a perfectly neutral starting point free of any specific definition of disputed claims about the good. Rawls's famous proposal is to imagine ourselves behind a veil of ignorance where we know nothing about the roles (president or worker, male or female, rich or poor, etc.) we will have in society. Rawls argues first that we would all opt for social and economic equality except where inequality would benefit the least advantaged, and second that we would choose to maximize individual freedom except when that infringed on a similar liberty for others.[46]

Many critics, including Michael Sandel, however, have rejected Rawls's claim to a neutral, objective starting point.[47] Sandel argues that Rawls's approach assumes a particular (and wrong) view of persons as isolated, abstract individuals unattached to any community.[48] In later writings (e.g., *Political Liberation*, 1993), Rawls himself admits that every person operates with some view of the good grounded in a religious or philosophical system, and he abandoned the search for a purely objective starting point. Instead, he seeks to listen to the major comprehensive viewpoints in society and then develop his theory of justice from the "overlapping consensus"—i.e., from the common ground shared by all the "reasonable" philosophical and religious worldviews in democratic societies. The very fact that he excludes "unreasonable" views (which include pro-life views on abortion!) shows that his approach is just one of many competing approaches, not some privileged, neutral, and objective starting point.[49] Thus the work of and debate about John Rawls confirms the fact that contemporary society is so fundamentally pluralistic that it is impossible to find a neutral, objective starting point for political thought.[50]

How then should biblical Christians proceed? We must start by accepting the fact of pluralism. This does not mean embracing relativism and abandoning Christian truth claims. John Courtney Murray once noted that he did not like pluralism (he wished everyone would accept the truth), but he accepted it as a reality. Christians can and should believe and claim that Jesus Christ and biblical revelation represent the truth, which all people should embrace, even as we respect the vast variety of people in our pluralistic society who disagree with us.

That means that Christians should start with biblical revelation and work within the Christian community to develop a framework for political engagement that is thoroughly grounded both in a biblical worldview and in systematic analysis of society. Applying this framework, we then encourage individual Christians as well as groups and associations of Christians to decide how to apply that framework to specific proposed laws and actual candidates for office.

At that point, a crucial question of language and translation emerges. "The Bible says" is not the most effective way to persuade non-Christians— whether Jews, Muslims, or "secular humanists"—to adopt our specific proposals. We must be ready to search for language and arguments that others can understand. As we do that, we remember that there is a basic natural law that is still written on the hearts of all our neighbors. Therefore we will not despair of the possibility of frequently persuading a majority of our neighbors that our proposals (grounded in a biblical worldview about persons, justice, etc.) offer a wise way forward. At the same time, knowing the depth of human sin, we will also expect our fellow citizens frequently to reject good proposals.

Precisely because of our own principles, however, especially our respect for human freedom and our recognition of the reality of widespread pluralism, we will distinguish between what biblical norms should be legislated and what should not. We will also refuse to seek to impose our good legislative proposals on society until a majority in our democratic society freely embraces our proposals. Because we respect the freedom and dignity of every person, we will nurture not a naked public square free of all religious reasons for political proposals, but rather an open, pluralistic, and civil public square open to all the different religiously and philosophically grounded arguments and proposals that every citizen and every particular community wish to advance.[51] Thus, "the separation of church and state" will not mean the exclusion of religious language and arguments from public, political debate. We will listen carefully to every view even as we argue that proposals shaped by unbiblical worldviews are wrong and destructive.

In *America Against Itself*, Richard John Neuhaus rejects the call for some neutral, public language. Instead, we must accept the fact that society is made up of diverse communities grounded in different religious and philosophical worldviews and expressing themselves in different languages. A civil and democratic public square welcomes all these voices to debate publicly about what society and politics should be like. The primary language of the Christian (coming from "Scripture, creed, and gospel teaching," Neuhaus argues) "can be spoken freely also in the public square, where it engages and challenges, and is engaged and challenged by, other languages."[52] Obviously any community that seeks to persuade other communities to endorse its views will frequently, when entering the public square, use whatever common language is available, but that is not a requirement for entering the public debate.

This approach to pluralism will produce not calm agreement but intense debate. There is not even any guarantee that it will avoid chaos and civil war. But diverse communities in every society have a lot in common. In the United States and in other Western democracies, commonalities include: a history rooted in both the Greco-Roman world and Judeo-Christian civilization; centuries of tested constitutional order and democratic practice; overlapping languages and beliefs about the shape of a good society; and human nature with its capacity for reason.[53] Radical postmodernists deny any common humanity, but Christians know that even those who deny it are made in the image of God and have the moral law written on their hearts and minds.

Four Components of Every Political Decision

Thus far, I have argued that if Christians are to think wisely and faithfully about politics, we need both a normative framework largely shaped by biblical revelation, and also careful analysis of society. Now I want to flesh out this claim and show that every careful political decision requires four different yet interrelated components: (1) a normative framework, (2) a broad study of society and the world, (3) a political philosophy, and (4) detailed social analysis on specific issues.[54]

Normative Framework

Virtually every political decision of any significance is grounded in fundamental beliefs about morality and the nature of persons. Many people do not think consciously about this normative framework. Some pretend that it does not exist. But in fact, it is simply impossible to make political decisions without some religiously or philosophically grounded normative framework about what is good and just.

Earlier I argued that Christians should derive their normative vision from biblical revelation. Discovering relevant biblical norms for politics is not, however, a matter of simple proof texting. The Bible is full of commands, stories, and proverbs—a wide variety of materials written over many centuries.

We dare not arbitrarily select one text or one theme. Some want to focus only on God's ordination of the state in Romans 13 or the state as the beasts of Revelation 13. Similarly, some one-sidedly emphasize the theme of exodus, others jubilee, still others Nehemiah's nation building. Instead of an arbitrary emphasis on this or that text or theme, we must submit to the full biblical canon with Christ at its center.[55]

To develop a fully biblical perspective on political issues, we need two things: (1) a biblical view of the world and persons (this comes especially from what I will call the biblical story), and (2) comprehensive summaries of biblical teaching related to many concrete issues—such as the family, economic justice, the poor, work, justice, or the dignity of persons (I call these biblical paradigms). To develop a normative biblical framework, we must in principle examine all relevant biblical passages, understand each text according to proper principles of exegesis, and then formulate a comprehensive summary of all relevant canonical material. The most sweepingly comprehensive summary would articulate a biblical view of the world and persons that flows from the biblical story.

Some may argue that the Old Testament, at least, is irrelevant for society today since it was God's special revelation for the people of Israel living in a theocratic society. But this is to ignore the fact that God promised Abraham that "all peoples on earth will be blessed through you" (Gen. 12:3) and that God called Israel to be a priest to the nations (Exod. 19:6). Israel was to be God's instrument of revelation to share with all people how the Creator wants people to live together in community. Repeatedly, the prophets applied the same standards they used to judge the Israelites to surrounding nations (Dan. 4:27; Amos 1–2). Again and again, the prophet Isaiah looked ahead to a messianic time when all nations would stream to Jerusalem to learn God's law (Isa. 2:2–4; 25:7–8; 66:18; cf. also Jer. 3:17).

That does not mean, however, that we should try to legislate today the specific details of Old Testament civil law.[56] Modern society is vastly different from either ancient Israel's agricultural society in the time of the judges or kings or first-century Roman society. It is the biblical *paradigms* that we apply. "A paradigm is a particular case used to illustrate a general principle. It functions as a pattern for other cases where details and contexts vary but a basic principle remains unchanged."[57] Thus the Bible does not offer a detailed blueprint for political life today,[58] but it does offer an important normative framework.

Broad Study of Society and the World

By itself, however, the biblical framework is insufficient. Nothing in the Bible talks explicitly about the pros and cons of a market economy or multinational corporations or the impact of over seven billion people on the natural environment.

In addition to a normative framework, we need a broad, comprehensive study of our world. That study takes many forms. It includes reflections on the historical development of society, the economy, and political systems. (As finite, historical beings, we come to see some things more clearly as history unfolds.) It also includes, in principle, detailed, comprehensive socioeconomic and political analysis of everything relevant to any particular political question.[59]

One's analysis of the history of economics or politics helps to shape one's political philosophy (see next section). For example, as the Marxist experiment worked itself out in the course of the twentieth century, it became more and more clear not only that Marxist philosophy contradicted the biblical view of persons but also that in practice Marxism led to economic inefficiency and political totalitarianism. Similarly, it is becoming increasingly clear that both good and evil accompany the functioning of today's market economies. Detailed social analysis of everything relevant to a particular politician or piece of legislation is also crucial (see below).

Political Philosophy

In addition to a normative framework and a broad study of society and the world, Christians engaged in politics also need a political philosophy. It is simply impossible, every time one wants to make a political decision, to spend days (actually years) reviewing mountains of relevant biblical material and complex studies of society. We need a framework, a road map, a handy guide—in short, a political philosophy. Furthermore, a political philosophy is much more than a handy road map. If developed carefully, it provides a coherent, systematic framework that reveals the many interconnections of different parts of one's political philosophy. But we dare not adopt our political philosophy uncritically from some non-Christian source. It must emerge from our normative biblical framework and our painstaking, extensive socioeconomic and political analysis.

Detailed Social Analysis on Specific Issues

Even after a Christian has a political philosophy shaped by both a normative biblical framework and careful study of society and the world, he or she still needs to do detailed social analysis on everything relevant to a particular legislative proposal or a specific election. Two people could have identical normative frameworks, identical historical analyses of modern society, and identical political philosophies, and still disagree about whether or not to raise the minimum wage. Why? Because they rely on different economic analyses of the actual effects of raising the minimum wage. The only way to make progress on settling such a disagreement is to go back together and do further detailed economic analysis. Careful social analysis of all the available information relevant to a specific political judgment is the fourth essential ingredient of responsible Christian political engagement.

In the next chapter, I will spell out the way the biblical story provides an overarching normative framework for political engagement. Then, in each of chapters 4 through 11, I will outline a biblical paradigm (on justice, government, etc.), show how a study of society adds insight, and articulate the aspects of a political philosophy that emerge from this combination of the biblical paradigm and a broad study of society. The final step of applying the political philosophy through the integration of still more detailed and relevant socioeconomic data to reach specific, concrete political conclusions is beyond the scope of this book. Occasionally, I will very briefly outline the final step in order to illustrate the methodology, but readers will have to look at other publications for detailed application of this fourth step.[60]

The method just described is complex—in fact, far more complex than I have been able to suggest here. Every one of the four steps intersects with all the others. Our reading of history, as well as our life today, shapes the questions we put to the Bible as we seek to develop a normative framework. That framework, in turn, shapes everything else.

In real life, we cannot wait to make political decisions until we have completed all the study that is desirable. We must make decisions based on our current understanding and then remain open to further insight and information.

The kind of study required for faithful Christian political engagement is far too complex for any one individual. We need communal activity, teams of scholars and activists, and organizations and networks working together to develop a common vision and agenda. For successful Christian political engagement, we need groups of Christians who can integrate a normative biblical framework, the study of society and the world, a political philosophy (derived from the former two ingredients), and a detailed social analysis as they approach every major issue of contemporary political life. That means working out concrete public policy proposals on everything from welfare to family policy to peacemaking.

Knowing the complexity of such political judgments and the possibility of mistakes at every step, we must always hold our specific political conclusions with humility and tentativeness. But we should dare to advocate boldly for specific policies, because we have sought to ground our specific conclusions in a biblical framework and responsible social analysis—even as we honestly invite friend and foe alike to help us improve our analysis of both Scripture and society at every point.

It would help immensely to reduce political disagreements among Christians (and others) if we would be more precise about exactly where we disagree. It is unhelpful to confuse a disagreement over the proper interpretation of Matthew 25 with lack of compassion for the poor, or disagreement over the relative merits of more or less government intervention in market economies, with whether a person cares about justice for poor people. To the extent that we can be precise about exactly where we disagree, we can make more progress in overcoming our differences.[61]

It is absolutely crucial, however, that Christians first articulate and develop their political agenda and concrete proposals within the Christian community on the basis of biblical norms. If we do not, we will end up adopting secular norms and values and their corresponding political ideologies. The result will be a compromised, often fundamentally unchristian political engagement.

A Few Definitions

Society, state, and *government.* It is crucial to distinguish the meaning of these three words.

The word *society* refers to the vast array of persons and institutions that exist in a particular geographical area. It includes churches, schools, businesses, unions, a wide variety of private volunteer organizations, communications organizations, and finally the state. Only in a totalitarian society (such as Nazi Germany or the Communist Soviet Union) does the state seek to dominate and control all these other institutions. Understanding and insisting upon the fact that the state is vastly less than society is crucial for a free social order.[62]

The *state* is that organization in society that has a monopoly on the use of coercion to help it achieve its purpose of overseeing just relationships among all the individuals and institutions in the society. The central functions of the state are promoting laws through legislative bodies, administering the law through executive structures, and enforcing the law through the courts and police. Politics includes all the activity focused on shaping the actions of the state.

People often use the word *government* as if it meant the same thing as the state. But it is probably better to speak of "the government" or "the current government" as the specific political officials (usually representing a particular political party) who currently control the structures of the state. Voters may throw out the current government at the next election and choose a new set of governing officials, but the structures of the state continue from government to government.

Public and *political.* The meaning of these two words parallels the meaning of society and state.

The term *public,* Lawrence Adams argues, "refers to all that occurs outside of the household."[63] "Of or pertaining to the people as a whole" is one definition of public in the *Oxford English Dictionary.*[64] It is clear how businesses, the media, unions, and artistic organizations, although usually not established and controlled by the state, are public in the sense that they shape and are shaped by the whole society. The Latin root of the word *republic* (*res publica*—i.e., "matters of the people") helps one understand the term *public*. So does "commonwealth," the English translation of *republic*, which refers to the common well-being of the whole community.[65]

Political refers only to those things related to the state. Political activity, focused on effecting what the state does, is a much narrower range of activity than the public activity that shapes the total life of the society.

Culture and politics. "*Culture* designates that complex, interlocking network of symbols, practices, and beliefs at the heart of society's life."[66] Philosophy, theology, art, popular and classical music, TV and the movies—all these and much more are part of culture. Politics, as we have seen, pertains only to the much more limited area of the state.

Culture and politics affect each other. Those elections that helped determine Supreme Court nominees whose decisions outlawed "separate but equal" public schools and legalized widespread abortion have obviously had a profound impact on the ideas and values of Americans. Political decisions do shape culture. But the reverse is at least equally true. Legislators simply dare not pass laws that fundamentally contradict prevailing cultural values, or they will be thrown out at the next election. On the other hand, if cultural values (e.g., about race, divorce, or homosexual practice) change, the laws will also soon change.

Power to change the political process comes from many sources. As Reinhold Niebuhr pointed out, there have always been intellectual, religious, military, and economic sources of power in every society, but their relative influence has varied greatly. Whatever group possessed the most powerful source of nonpolitical power at a given time enjoyed preeminent political power.[67] At times, that was the religious sector, at other times, the military. Today it is economic power that largely shapes politics, although the decentralized nature of modern democratic society means that many other sources of political power also exist.

In recent years, some conservatives have concluded that conservative political activity has largely failed (even when successful at elections) because conservatives have not succeeded in shaping the larger culture of the universities, the media, and law. A few have simply despaired of changing society and dropped out. But more have decided to undertake the tougher, more long-term project of reshaping the underlying cultural values that finally demand or prevent specific political changes.

Thus far, I have argued that evangelical Christians in recent decades have often either neglected politics or failed badly as they entered the political arena. At the same time, we have seen that politics is far too important to leave it to those who do not embrace a biblical perspective. We will never genuinely succeed in reshaping our societies for the good, however, unless we think far more carefully about the political task. We must develop a political philosophy that is firmly rooted in both the biblical worldview and careful, persistent analysis of our complex, glorious, and broken world.

The next chapter, on the biblical story, seeks to flesh out the key elements, relevant for politics, of a biblical worldview.

3

Politics and the Biblical Story

At the heart of biblical faith is an awesome story.

An infinite, eternally existing, all-powerful God chose in love to create a finite but gorgeously beautiful world full of astounding complexity and stunning splendor. At the center of everything, God placed man and woman, fashioned in God's very image, to exercise servant-like stewardship over the rest of his handiwork. God designed them to find great delight in each other, in the material world enfolding them, and in the complex cultures God invited them to craft from the materials he entrusted to their care. But the Creator shaped their very being in such a way that their deepest joy and lasting happiness could come only from right relationship with, and willing worship of, their Maker.

Tragically, they rebelled. They chose to worship themselves and the rest of creation rather than the Creator. They chose to write their own rules rather than follow God's design. The results were selfish persons, twisted social relationships and institutions, and even a groaning, disordered creation.

But God loved this world far too much to abandon it to a descending spiral of chaotic evil. So the Creator began a long history of saving action to restore right relationships among God, persons, and creation. He called Abram to be the father of the people of Israel through whom God planned to share wisdom and salvation with all people. Again and again, however, they defied God's law, and eventually God destroyed Israel and sent them into captivity.

God inspired their prophets, however, to promise a future day, on the other side of their punishment, when the Messiah would come to usher in the kingdom of God. In that day, the nations would stream to Jerusalem to experience

God's salvation, peace, and justice. The devastation wrought by human sin would end.

After many centuries, an obscure Nazarene carpenter became a wandering preacher, declaring that the long-expected kingdom of God was actually breaking into history in his own person and work. By example and teaching, he showed how people should live together in wholeness and peace. He died on a cross for the sins of the world and then rose on the third day to demonstrate that he was indeed Messiah and Lord and that the reign of God was truly invading history. Worshiping him as true God, his disciples insisted that this Galilean carpenter, not Caesar the mighty emperor, was Lord.

In spite of sweeping transformation and astounding social change in the new community of Jesus's disciples, it was clear that sin had not disappeared even though the kingdom of God had begun. Jesus's followers remembered that he had promised to return some day to complete his victory over sin, injustice, and even death itself. So they looked to that future day when all things would be made new, believers would be resurrected to live forever with their Lord, and God would dwell with his people on a transformed earth purged of every vestige of sin's devastation.

Over the centuries, many Christians have emphasized the political implications of one or another aspect of this story. Those who focused on creation tended to be optimistic about improving society through politics. Those who emphasized the fall were more pessimistic. Liberation theologians found hope for revolutionary socioeconomic change in the story of the exodus.[1] African Americans concerned to rebuild blighted urban neighborhoods often looked to Nehemiah's rebuilding broken walls. It is not wrong to find special insight for one's particular historical setting in specific biblical passages and themes, but we must be careful to allow the full biblical story, centered on Jesus Christ, to provide the overarching framework. Oxford theologian Oliver O'Donovan is right that we need to "connect political themes with the history of salvation *as a whole*."[2]

The full biblical story—creation, fall, salvation history centered on Christ, and the final restoration of all things—is chock-full of significance for Christian political engagement today.[3] The story provides the foundation for understanding the nature and grandness of creation, the dignity and destiny of persons, the depth of sinful brokenness, the importance of history, and the glorious destiny to which God invites us all.

Creation's Goodness and Splendor

Enormous political consequences flow from how we view the material world. Not everyone thinks the material world is real or good. Much of Eastern religious thought considers the material world to be an illusion that spiritual wisdom will teach us to ignore. Eastern religious thought teaches that we should focus instead on the divine spark within and eventually merge with the All, disappearing forever like a drop of water in the ocean. The Manicheans—a powerful movement that threatened Christian faith in the early centuries—taught that the material world was the creation of an evil god. If such views about the physical world are right, Philip Wogaman points out, then hunger, starvation, economic exploitation, slavery, and physical torture "are not moral problems for us."[4] We can live on a "spiritual" level, ignoring the illusions of the insignificant or evil material world.

Other views see the world as divine. Animists believe that the trees and the rivers are divinities to be worshiped—and left as unchanged as possible. How dare we then cut down trees and dam rivers to create human civilization?

The biblical story tells us something radically different. Repeatedly in the story of creation, after God calls a crucial part of the material world into existence, the text declares, "God saw that it was good." Indeed, at the end of the story, we hear that "God saw all that he had made, and it was very good" (Gen. 1:31).

But that is only the beginning. Later in the story, the Creator of the universe becomes a man with a material body, works as a carpenter shaping blocks of wood into things of usefulness and beauty, and delights in the glorious food of the earth. The authorities try to squelch his message by crucifying him on the cross, but he rises bodily from the tomb on the third day and promises at his return to give resurrected bodies to all who believe in him. Indeed, at that time even the nonhuman world, the "groaning creation," will be "liberated from its bondage to decay and brought into the glorious freedom of the children of God" (Rom. 8:21 NIV). That is how good the material world is.

Rather than an evil to escape, or an illusion to ignore, or a deity to worship, the world is a wondrously good, albeit finite, reality that God designed both to sing his praises and to provide a home for humanity.

At the same time, the biblical story denies that the world is divine. It is created out of nothing (*ex nihilo*) and is therefore finite. Because biblical faith rejects animism and thus desacralizes the world, humans rightly use the material world for wise human purposes.

The Nature of Persons

The biblical text declares that God created men and women in the very image of God. "Then God said, 'Let us make humankind in our image . . .' male and female he created them" (Gen. 1:26–27 NRSV). Only about human beings does the Bible make this amazing declaration. Human beings are fundamentally different from every other part of God's creation because they alone are declared to be made in the very image of the Creator.

As a consequence, human beings enjoy a dignity and value that no other creatures possess. Too often we have arrogantly distorted this uniqueness into an unbridled license to trample and destroy the rest of creation. Actually, the biblical text explicitly commands people to "work it and take care of" the rest of creation (Gen. 2:15). But the truth remains—and it is fundamental to the whole project of civilization—that human beings possess a unique dignity and worth.[5]

But what exactly does it mean to be created in the image of God? There have been two major ways that Christians through the ages have understood the *imago Dei*: a substantial, and a relational understanding.[6] Those in the substantial tradition (e.g., Thomas Aquinas) identify some essential capacity or faculty (e.g., our reason that makes rational thought possible, or our will that enables us to choose freely) that distinguishes persons sharply from the rest of creation. People in this tradition tend to put less emphasis on the way that the fall has damaged the *imago Dei* in sinful persons.

Those in the relational tradition (e.g., Luther, Calvin, Karl Barth) understand the *imago Dei* by analogy with a mirror that reflects some object. The *imago Dei*, then, is not something inherent in persons, but rather the *imago Dei* is the relationship with God, which exists when one obeys God. Through one's right relationship with God, one truly reflects God's will and thus bears God's image. In this view, sin largely or completely destroys the *imago Dei* in fallen people. In the section on sin, we will need to explore these two approaches somewhat further.

For the present, it is important to note that the text in Genesis explicitly points to two things. Verse 26 connects the *imago Dei* with our stewardship responsibility: "Let [human beings] rule over the fish of the sea and the birds of the air, over the livestock, over all the earth, and over all the creatures that move along the ground" (NIV 1984; cf. Ps. 8:6–8). We are placed as God's assistants to exercise a loving, watchful stewardship over the rest of the earth. Hence, an essential aspect of the *imago Dei* is that human beings are uniquely designated to be God's stewards, wisely ruling over the rest of creation in the way that God wills. That does not mean that God authorizes us to trample and destroy the nonhuman creation, but it does mean that we rightly use trees and rivers, birds and animals to create complex civilizations.

Verse 27 connects the *imago Dei* with our communal nature: "So God created humankind in his image, in the image of God he created them" (NRSV). An isolated individual cannot adequately image the God who is triune, a loving community of three persons in the one God. Only as we live in community in loving, mutual inter-dependence as male and female can we reflect the nature of God as he intended.

That is not to deny the importance of the individual. Whereas ancient Eastern and African civilizations as well as modern totalitarian societies have tended to emphasize the community (family and society) in a way that failed to affirm the value and freedom of each individual, biblical faith makes powerful claims about the value of each person. Although it is true and very important that the mutual love of man and woman image the triune God in a special way, it is not true that only the man, only the woman, or only the two together are made in the image of God. Each individual person is made in the image of God.

God also summons each individual to repent personally in free obedience to the divine call. Both Adam and Eve had to choose whether to obey their Creator. Throughout the Old Testament, we see individual men and women (Abraham, Moses, Hannah, Ruth) called to personal response. In the Old Testament, that faithful response was often, although not exclusively, communal.[7] In later parts of the Old Testament, there are very clear statements that every person is responsible for his or her own response to God—e.g., the parable of a person eating sour grapes (Jer. 31:29–30; Ezek. 18:1–4). Jesus explicitly taught that each individual must be ready to forsake father, mother, son, and daughter to follow him (Matt. 10:34–39). Son or daughter can and should choose to follow Jesus even if mother or father refuses. Jesus died on the cross to atone for the sins of every person who repents in personal faith. And God the Holy Spirit comes to dwell in the heart and life of every person who makes that personal choice. Every single person is invited to live forever with the Lord of the universe. Since every single person is summoned by the living God to make a personal response of faith and obedience, society must provide the freedom for each person to do so. Because each individual is directly responsible to God, no community (whether state, church, or family) dare seek to unconditionally control individuals.[8]

What an incredible affirmation of the dignity and worth of each individual person! It is not surprising that the affirmation and protection of individual freedoms (to choose one's own religious beliefs, to speak and write freely, to vote one's preference in a secret ballot) arose first in societies rooted in this powerful biblical affirmation about the freedom, dignity, and worth of each person.[9]

Biblical faith, however, balances this affirmation of the dignity of the individual person with an equal emphasis on the communal nature of persons. Until Eve arrived, Adam was restless. Mutual fulfillment resulted when the two became "one flesh" (Gen. 2:24). God severely punished Cain for violating community by killing his brother Abel, but God also allowed Cain to continue to enjoy the human community of family and city (Gen. 4). God commands children to honor father and mother (Exod. 20:12). Israel's leaders so identified with the sin of their community that they confessed those sins as their own (Dan. 9:4–11; Neh. 1:5–6). Throughout the Scriptures, God commanded economic sharing with other members of the community.[10] When the kingdom of God became powerfully visible in the Spirit-filled early church, we see the kind of redeemed community intended by the Creator: believers shared economically in such sweeping ways that "there were no needy persons among them" (Acts 4:34). Indeed, the mutual love and interdependence were so strong that when one person suffered, they all suffered, and when one rejoiced, they all rejoiced (1 Cor. 12:26).

Theologian Emil Brunner is right that this biblical emphasis on community rests in part on the fact that God created persons who are different.[11] Men and women have equal dignity, but they are certainly different—and need each other. Some thinkers (e.g., the ancient Stoics) supposed that the difference between persons is irrelevant. But if that were correct, then we could only have unity, not community. A community of mutual interdependence is possible only when persons are different. Only then can we lovingly serve each other, meeting each other's needs with our different abilities and creating a community of mutual interdependence.

God designed us for community. We simply cannot be the whole persons God intended without embracing the importance of communal joys and obligations. And the deepest foundation of this truth is that human beings are created in the image of the triune God, a loving community of three equal but distinct divine persons who together are one God.

The biblical story's affirmation of both the personal and the communal aspects of who we are is absolutely essential for political thought. Western liberalism in the tradition of John Locke overemphasizes the individual and ends up with the radical individualism of contemporary Western societies. The free, isolated individual is all-important, and communal obligations are largely abandoned. (We can see this individualism in divorce laws that ignore the needs of children, in abortion laws that place sole authority for choosing an abortion with the mother rather than the family, and in economic laws that ignore our mutual obligations to care for each other's material needs.)[12]

The other extreme is equally disastrous. A one-sided emphasis on our communal nature ends up in stifling traditional societies with little freedom for individual choice or in modern totalitarian societies (whether Nazi or communist) that crush all individual freedom.

"The significance of seeing people not first and foremost as separate individuals or constituent parts of a large collective, *but persons in mutual relationship* cannot be overstated."[13] We must hold together both the importance and freedom of each person and the interdependence of all upon one another. An understanding of people grounded in the biblical view of persons created in the image of the triune God will insist that people find fulfillment not in self-assertive individualism or totalitarian communalism but in a community of freedom, love, and mutuality that treasures both individual freedom and the common good. In his famous lectures titled *Christianity and the State* (1928), William Temple (the future archbishop of Canterbury) hardly overstated this point when he declared that "the whole problem of politics, the whole art of statesmanship" is to do full justice to each of these two principles without sacrificing one for the other.[14]

Another pair of affirmations that the biblical story demands that we hold together is the fact that human beings are a unity of "body and soul." We do not need to discuss the complicated and ferocious theological and philosophical debates that have raged around the question of the soul. What is important for our purposes is that persons have both a material and a spiritual side.[15]

We are material beings. Contrary to Plato and a good deal of Platonic thought throughout Christian history, that is not unfortunate. It is good that we are material beings. "Dust you are and to dust you will return," God says in Genesis 3:19. We are material beings, shaped like the rest of the material world by the natural causes that scientists increasingly understand. Like the plants and animals, our very existence depends on the material world of sun, water, air, and dirt. Nothing declares more vividly that this material existence is a good to be affirmed rather than a tragedy to be escaped than the incarnation. God became flesh! Plato was fundamentally wrong to think that the human dilemma results from human beings having a good soul trapped in an evil body. The body is very good.

Our material bodily existence, however, brings profound limitations. We are finite, limited. We simply cannot change the fact that much of our life is determined by material forces and "laws of nature" beyond our control.

There is, however, another profoundly important truth. We are also spiritual beings. The Creator not only formed us from the dust of the earth; God also breathed into us "the breath of life" (Gen. 2:7). We can transcend the material world in choice and thought. We are not entirely determined by the material world of which we are a part. We are self-conscious. We can reflect on the way things are and make rational and moral decisions about how to change them. We are free to choose in a way that no other material creature can.

At the heart of this spiritual aspect is the fact that we are placed in relationship with a personal God, invited to choose to live in obedient relationship with God, and—most astoundingly!—called to live forever in the presence of almighty God. During our life now, God gives us the freedom to transcend the bonds of the material world with its determined sequence of natural cause and effect and choose to obey him and treat our neighbors with unselfish, even sacrificial love. Even more amazing, death does not mark the end for us as it does for plants and animals. For those who respond in faith to the divine summons, our brief life here is just the beginning that leads to life eternal in the presence of the living God.

This spiritual, transcendent aspect of human beings has profound implications for political life. The fact that we can transcend any specific historical context through rational thought and moral judgment means that we can choose (within limits to be sure) to change history. Our choices determine the future of human society. Fatalistic acceptance of things as they are is unnecessary, indeed wrong. We need not simply accept the world as it is; we can change it.

The fact that we are called to life eternal dramatically reduces the importance of politics and powerfully limits the rights of the state. Life here is important. We rightly devote time to creating wealth and shaping politics, because God made us material beings dependent for our earthly wholeness on the right ordering of economic and political life in this world. But nothing in economic and political life, not even the whole material world, is as important as our relationship with the living God.

Therefore we courageously choose to defy governments that call us to disobey the will of God because material well-being given by the state for a decade or century wanes in comparison with the treasure of life eternal. Furthermore, since the invitation to life eternal is the truth about all persons, governments have no right to make laws that contradict or undermine this reality. When they do, their legitimacy disappears. Thus, the Christian belief in eternal life contributes significantly to placing limits on the state.

A one-sided emphasis on either our material or our spiritual side has disastrous political consequences. If one believes, as do philosophical materialists, that persons are just complex machines that evolved in a blind materialistic, evolutionary process, one will encourage society to place exaggerated emphasis on material well-being. One will also find it difficult, if not impossible, to develop moral norms that can check the totalitarian tendencies of the state. Whatever the state decrees is "right." There is no appeal to some "higher, divine law."

On the other hand, many Christians have so emphasized the spiritual side of human beings that they have belittled the importance of history, politics, and material well-being. For decades, many evangelicals taught that "saving souls" was all-important; therefore good Christians should ignore politics and focus largely or exclusively on evangelism.[16]

Because our bodies are a fundamental part of our created goodness, a generous sufficiency of material things is essential to human goodness. Any political or economic system that prevents persons from producing and enjoying material well-being violates our God-given dignity. Because our spiritual nature and destiny are so important that it is better to lose even the entire material world than lose one's relationship with God, any political or economic system that tries to explain persons only as economic actors, or that offers material abundance as the exclusive or primary way to human fulfillment, contradicts the essence of human nature. For persons invited to live forever with the living God, no material abundance, however splendid, can satisfy the human heart.

What we need is biblical balance. We are created to find joy and delight in a material world that wise politics can help shape for our blessing. The results, however, are always limited. They are never important enough to abandon our relationship with God. But the Creator wants us to spend substantial time, during our life in this material world, enjoying and shaping it so that everyone can share its bounty. In fact, this material world is so good that some day the risen Christ will return to finish his task of removing all evil from this earth. Then all who believe in him will receive resurrected bodies to live on this transformed earth and enjoy life eternal in the presence of the Lord.

Finally, the biblical view of persons means that political and economic injustice is a family problem. Since we are all "God's offspring" (Acts 17:29; cf. all of vv. 24–29), we all have the same Father. Therefore all human beings are sisters and brothers. "Exploitation is a brother or sister treating another brother or sister as a mere object."[17] That is not to overlook differentiation in human society;[18] we do not have exactly the same obligations to all children everywhere that we have to those in our immediate biological family. But a mutual obligation for the common good of all people follows from the fact that all persons are sisters and brothers created in the image of our one heavenly Father.

Sin

The biblical story shows that sin has devastated the created order. No part remains uncorrupted. The fall has wreaked havoc on our minds, our wills, our families, and our social structures.

At the fall, we refused to accept God as Lord, choosing instead to place ourselves at the center of reality and make our own moral rules. That set of decisions was also a refusal to accept our finitude. Had we embraced the truth about ourselves—that we are finite, limited beings who need the moral norms of the infinite Creator in order to live wisely—we would not have tried to replace God's moral laws with our own preferences. We proudly chose to go our own way.

The result has been devastation in all our relationships—with God, neighbor, self, and the earth.

Our relationship with God is radically broken. To the extent that we properly understand the *imago Dei* in terms of relationship to God, rebellious sinners have lost much of the divine image. Their disobedience means that they no longer rightly reflect who God is. The *imago Dei*, however, is not entirely lost, because God maintains a relationship with us even when we choose to break the relationship through rebellious disobedience. God continues to love even defiant children, providing a plan of salvation and continuing to call us to repent and return to him.

Moltmann calls this aspect of the *imago Dei* our "objective relationship" to God. Nothing we can do ends this relationship. Only God can do that. Here lies the foundation of the dignity of every single person. "God has a relationship to every embryo, every severely handicapped person, and every person suffering from one of the diseases of old age, and he is honored and glorified in them when their dignity is respected."[19]

To the extent that we understand the *imago Dei* and the loving community of the triune God which we are to reflect in our caring, mutual interdependence of family and society, we see again how deformed the *imago Dei* is in our fallen world. In our self-centered, individualistic actions we violate communal obligations and trample upon the common good of our neighbors. But we cannot abolish our communal nature, no matter how selfish we become. Since we are irrevocably social beings, our accumulating set of selfish personal choices eventually shape whole social systems that are radically flawed. Vast numbers of personal sinful choices that are racist or sexist or economically unjust eventually produce complex social and legal systems that are racist, sexist, and unjust.

That is why the Bible condemns both personal sin and evil social systems. The prophets condemned not just individual acts of lying, stealing, and adultery, but also unjust social systems, such as legal structures that failed to offer equal justice to the poor and economic systems that failed to provide everyone the opportunity to earn a decent living (e.g., Isa. 5:8–9, 11, 22–23; Amos 2:6–7; 5:10–15). Choosing to participate in evil social systems while failing to do what God wants us to do in correcting those systems is just as sinful as lying or adultery.[20] At the same time, it is essential to remember that the ultimate source of evil structures is the self-centeredness at the core of every individual. As Pope John Paul II has said, evil social structures are "rooted in personal sin."[21]

Earlier we saw that central to the meaning of the *imago Dei* is God's call to us to act as stewards of the rest of creation. That truth helps us understand how our sin has devastated even the nonhuman world. Genesis talks about the way the sin of Adam and Eve has led to a curse upon the ground (3:17). Paul notes that "the creation was subjected to frustration." Thankfully, when Christ returns and gives us resurrected bodies, then "the creation itself will be liberated from its bondage to decay" (Rom. 8:20–21). What all that means in detail remains a mystery, but it certainly means that human sin has also produced terrible disruption in the nonhuman world.

Finally, the fall has devastated not just our relationship with God, neighbor, and earth but also our very being. Every part of our being is affected. Not just our bodies, but also our reason and will are corrupted. Our rational minds no longer see truth clearly. The more brilliant we are, the more sophisticated are the subtle rationalizations we develop to defend selfish interests and wrong ideas. One only needs to read some of the subtle justifications written to defend slavery, racism, unjust treatment of women, or unfair economic arrangements to see how deeply our minds are corrupted.

We have largely lost the ability to understand the moral law originally written on our hearts by the Creator. Because we turned away from God, our thinking has become "futile" and our "foolish hearts [are] darkened." Our "depraved" minds are filled with "every kind of wickedness" (Rom. 1:21, 28–29). That does not mean that sinners have lost all sense of the moral law written on all our hearts (Rom. 3:12–15). But it does mean that we see it so imperfectly that we now require God's special revelation to properly understand morality. Our fallen wills seldom have the ability to choose the good even when we understand it. Central to what the Reformers meant by the words "total depravity" was that all parts of the human being, including the reason and the will, have been corrupted by the fall.

The biblical teaching on sin has vast implications for our understanding of politics. I mention several. First, every politician is a frail, finite, sinful person who will certainly make a mixture of good and bad decisions, and every political platform is a smorgasbord of good and evil, wise summons to justice and subtle rationalization of self-interest. Therefore Christians should never trust any politician completely and dare never embrace any party or platform uncritically.

Second, a central task of faithful political action is to design political systems built on this understanding of persons as being a complex mix of good and bad moral insight and self-centered distortion. As Lord Acton said long ago, "In a fallen world, power tends to corrupt and absolute power tends to corrupt absolutely." Therefore we need checks and balances on all power so that even though everyone acts selfishly, the competing acts of self-interest tend to balance each other and prevent great evil. The state must be limited. At the same time, precisely because sin has not destroyed all good in persons, we can also create social systems that appeal to and encourage the best in human beings.

Since sin became embedded in self-perpetuating social systems, we must seek to change unjust structures even though we know that no amount of wise structural change can create perfect persons or flawless systems. Since sin does have a social character, it is essential that we seek to change not just individual persons through personal spiritual transformation but also societal structures via political change. In the face of laws and legal structures that prevented African Americans from voting, we needed more than evangelism and a call to individual white Americans to treat African Americans fairly. We needed better laws and judicial systems that enforced everyone's right to vote.

It would, however, be fundamentally naïve to suppose (with thinkers like Rousseau and Marx) that we can create new, basically good persons if we only correct unjust social systems. We can make things better through wise structural change. We have been able to end slavery, promote democracy, and encourage economic justice through wise political changes. But the human problem lies far deeper than merely unjust social systems, however evil. At root, the human problem is grounded in fallen, selfish persons who continue to seek and find ways to manipulate even the best social systems. For that reason, Christians reject every utopian illusion that imagines, as did Marxists and some kinds of humanist educators, that we can eradicate evil in society if we will only make the right structural or educational changes.

The Importance of History

Many ancient thinkers believed that history is a meaningless cycle in which, eventually, everything is repeated. The biblical story shows that history is a purposeful process moving toward a final, glorious destiny. History begins with the Creator shaping a good world out of nothing. God then gave humanity the task of imitating the Creator by developing complex civilizations, thus shaping the course of history. When humanity chose to defy God and thereby injected devastating evil into God's good world, the Creator initiated a long historical process of salvation. It was in history that God called Abraham, led the chosen people out of Egypt, and gave them a home in Canaan. It was in history that God responded to Israel's choices, rewarding obedience and punishing disobedience. Finally, God sent Israel into captivity but also pointed toward the coming of the Messiah at a future historical moment. When Christ finally arrived, he waged a successful battle against evil and promised to return at some time in the future to complete the victory. Now, as history moves toward this final victory, God invites persons and societies to find their own meaning by embracing God's grand historical plan and becoming willing coworkers, as God shepherds the historical process to its ultimate goal. Every human decision and activity can find meaning in this linear movement of history.

Unfortunately, modern secular thinkers absolutize the historical process even while they say it is meaningless; even if life is absurd, our time here is all we have. Medieval thinkers, on the other hand, sometimes belittled history, viewing earthly existence merely as a preparation for eternity. The biblical story affirms the importance of history while insisting that persons are also made for life eternal. It is in history that the Redeemer chooses to turn back the invading powers of evil by launching the messianic kingdom. It is in history that persons not only respond to God's call to eternal life but also join the Lord's long march toward justice and righteousness. It is in history that kings of Israel corrected (or created!) unfair legal and economic systems that trampled the rights of the poor. And it is because we know where history is going, and are assured that the Redeemer will return to complete the victory over every evil and injustice, that we do not despair even when evil achieves sweeping, temporary triumphs. So we work for better political and economic systems, knowing that sin precludes any earthly utopia now, but rejoicing in the assurance that the kingdom of *shalom* that the Messiah has already begun will one day prevail, and the kingdoms of this world will become the kingdom of our Lord.

The Glory of Work

God works (Gen. 2:1–2). Jesus was a carpenter. The apostle Paul mended tents. Even before the fall, God summoned Adam to cultivate the earth and name the animals (Gen. 2:15–20).

Work is the way we meet our basic needs. Work is also the way we express our basic nature as persons made in the image of God who is Creator. We cannot create out of nothing as God does, but we are made to trace the finger of God's intricate design in the material world and then use our creative abilities to reshape what the Creator has given us in order to produce cultures of glorious beauty and intricate complexity.

The Creator could have directly created poetry, plays, sonatas, cities, and computers. Instead, God assigned that task to us, expecting us to cultivate the earth (Gen. 2:15), create new things, and expand human possibilities and wealth. Adam and Eve surely enjoyed a generous sufficiency. Just as surely, the Creator intended their descendants to probe and use the astoundingly intricate earth placed in their care to acquire the knowledge, power, and wealth necessary, for example, to build vast telescopes that scan the billions of galaxies about which Adam and Eve knew nothing. In a real sense, God purposely created human beings with very little so that we could imitate and glorify our Creator by working and thereby producing vast knowledge and wealth. Indeed, Jesus's parable of the talents sharply rebukes those who fail to use their skills to multiply their resources.

Finally, work is a crucial way in which we love our neighbors. Since we are finite beings, we need the work of others to enjoy the abundance God wills for us. As we love our neighbors by creating the things they need through our productive work, we embrace the fact that the Creator designed us for community.

Meaningful work, by which persons meet their needs, express their God-like creativity, and love their neighbor, is essential for human dignity. Any able person who fails to work disgraces and corrodes his very being. Any system that could but does not offer every person the opportunity for meaningful work violates and crushes human dignity.

Christ, the Kingdom of God, and Politics

There is almost universal agreement among New Testament scholars today that the core of Jesus's proclamation was the "gospel of the kingdom." At the beginning of Mark's Gospel, we find the summary of Jesus's message: "Jesus went into Galilee, proclaiming the good news of God. 'The time has come,' he said. 'The kingdom of God has come near. Repent and believe the good news'"

(Mark 1:14–15). Elsewhere, it is clear that Jesus believed that the kingdom of God was actually breaking into the present in his own work and person.[22]

What did Jesus mean when he talked about the gospel of the kingdom of God?

The first thing to note is that this is political language. Again and again in the Old Testament, Israel declared that Yahweh was king—king of Israel in particular, but also king of the nations. Israel was called to submit to the righteous rule of Yahweh.

Tragically, both the northern and southern kingdoms rebelled so repeatedly against Yahweh's righteous ways that eventually God destroyed both nations, sending them into captivity to the Assyrians (Israel in 734 BC) and Babylonians (Judah in 587 BC). Captivity and exile were God's punishment for their sinful rebellion against Yahweh's just rule.

The prophets, however, looked beyond the time of exile to a new day when God would send a Messiah, a mighty ruler from the seed of David who would lead the people in a glorious military victory over Israel's national enemies. The Israelites would return from exile, Yahweh's holy presence would return to Jerusalem, the temple would be restored, and God's peace and justice would spread through the whole earth.

It is important to understand that many of the biblical statements about the messianic hope for a future arrival of the kingdom of God include the expectation that at that time the nations would embrace the truth that God had earlier revealed to Israel. As early as the call of Abraham, we read in the Bible that God chose Abraham and his descendants, not for themselves, but so that "all peoples on earth will be blessed through [him]" (Gen. 12:3). Israel was to be a priest who would teach the nations God's way (Exod. 19:6).[23]

Isaiah is especially clear about the way Israel will be a light to the nations when they return from exile. Of Israel, Yahweh declares, "Here is my servant . . . and he will bring justice to the nations" (Isa. 42:1). "I will keep you and will make you to be a covenant for the people and a light for the Gentiles" (v. 6).

God promises not only to bring the tribes of Jacob back from exile but also, "I will make you a light for the Gentiles, that you may bring my salvation to the ends of the earth" (Isa. 49:6 NIV 1984; also 51:4). And Zechariah 9, the messianic passage on which Jesus explicitly modeled his understanding of the peaceful Messiah, promised that the Messiah's rule would extend "to the ends of the earth" (v. 10). The famous passage about the messianic future, often referred to as "the last days," in Micah 4 and Isaiah 2 contains the same promise.

> In the last days
> the mountain of the LORD's temple will be established
>   as chief among the mountains;
> it will be raised above the hills,
>   and peoples will stream to it.

Many nations will come and say,
"Come, let us go up to the mountain of the LORD,
    to the house of the God of Jacob.
He will teach us his ways,
    so that we may walk in his paths."
The law will go out from Zion,
    the word of the LORD from Jerusalem.
He will judge between many peoples
    and will settle disputes for strong nations far and wide.
They will beat their swords into plowshares
    and their spears into pruning hooks.
Nation will not take up sword against nation,
    nor will they train for war anymore.

                                    Micah 4:1–3; cf. Isaiah 2:2–4

In the time of Ezra and Nehemiah (the middle of the fifth century BC), a small number of Jews returned from exile. They rebuilt the walls of Jerusalem and erected a new temple, but it was so unimpressive that those who had a sense of Solomon's glorious building simply wept. First-century Jews still looked to a future time of messianic fulfillment. The majority expected a conquering military Messiah who would lead the nation in a decisive victory over the Roman imperialists. Then the kingdom of God would become powerfully visible as the exiled Jews returned, Yahweh became powerfully present in Zion, and the nations embraced God's law. This Jewish expectation was not about a "private existentialist or Gnostic experience, but about public events."[24]

That was the conceptual framework and the language that Jesus chose to define his mission and explain his work.[25] Indirectly at first, and then more openly, he claimed to be the long-promised Messiah. Calling twelve disciples (a clear allusion to the twelve tribes of Israel) Jesus gathered together a renewed people of God. His dramatic healings and ministry to poor and needy persons began to fulfill the messianic promises of renewal and justice. Jesus declared God's sweeping forgiveness that was to precede the exiles' return. (Since the captivity was God's punishment for their sins, the return from exile would mean that God had granted forgiveness.) All these actions radically challenged the centers of political power, but they made sense within the framework of first-century Jewish messianic hope for the arrival of the kingdom of God.

At crucial points, however, Jesus fundamentally redefined the popular understanding of what the Messiah would do. Jesus totally rejected the notion of a military Messiah doing violent battle with the hated Romans. He taught love, even for enemies, and urged his followers to turn the other cheek even to oppressive conquerors. At the triumphal entry, when he unmistakably made messianic claims, he chose to pattern himself after Zechariah's peaceful Messiah, riding on a donkey rather than entering Jerusalem on a warhorse (Matt. 21:5; cf. Zech. 9:9–10). Jesus's contemporaries, expecting a conquering military

Messiah, believed that any messianic claimant who died at the hands of his enemies was thereby decisively proven to be a fraud. Jesus, on the other hand, announced that he would challenge all the powers of evil (Satan, unfaithful Jewish leaders, and corrupt Roman officials) in a dramatic confrontation in Jerusalem, but that it would lead to his death, not military victory! Somehow, nonetheless, his death would bring the kingdom in a dramatic new way.

This radical redefinition of messianic expectation puzzled his contemporaries, even his disciples. After his death, they drew the proper conclusion. Jesus was finished. His messianic claims were no longer believable. That was the only possible conclusion for a first-century Jew—until Easter morning. The resurrection, of course, changed everything. The empty tomb and meetings with the risen Jesus convinced the discouraged disciples that Jesus had been right all along. He was the long-promised Messiah. The messianic kingdom had truly broken into history. Jesus's growing circle of followers were God's renewed people called to live the glorious truth that the kingdom of God had broken into history.

The resurrection also led to the claim that Jesus was not only Messiah but also Son of God. When Thomas met the risen Jesus, he uttered the awesome words, "My Lord and my God" (John 20:28). The rabbinically trained, rigidly monotheistic Jew, Saul of Tarsus, came to apply to Jesus words that the Old Testament used only for Yahweh (Phil. 2:9–11; cf. Isa. 45:23). Jesus was not only Messiah, he was God in the flesh. Even now he possesses "all authority in heaven and earth" (Matt. 28:18), reigning as "ruler of the kings of the earth" (Rev. 1:5).

It took some further prodding (e.g., Peter's vision at Joppa), but very soon the early Christians realized the implications of the fact that the Messiah had come and his messianic kingdom was now truly present in history. That meant, as the prophets had predicted, that the people of God were now to be light to the gentiles. God's salvation was now to be announced to the whole world. So they called all nations to embrace the gospel of the kingdom and live now according to the ethics of this dawning kingdom.

Far too often we miss the profound political implications of Jesus's proclamation of the kingdom of God and the resurrection's confirmation that Jesus was indeed the Messiah who had ushered in that long-expected kingdom. Pietists miss it by reducing Jesus's message to a promise of forgiveness of sins and life eternal for individuals who believe in Jesus. Emil Brunner does it by arguing that the kingdom of God "lies beyond the bounds of earthly history." It has nothing to do, Brunner argues, with marriage, family, law, justice, and the state.[26] But that is to fundamentally misunderstand Jesus's whole message. Jesus came claiming to be the Messiah for the whole Jewish nation. He declared, in his person and work, that he was actually inaugurating the climactic moment in history when God would fulfill his promises to Israel, restore his chosen people, and use them to transform the nations so that God's will would be done on earth as it is in heaven in dramatic new ways. We can argue that Jesus was naïve or wrong, but we cannot pretend that he did not make this astonishing claim.

One of the reasons we have misunderstood Jesus is that we have misunderstood the apocalyptic language he used. As evangelical New Testament scholar N. T. Wright points out, many—both conservative Christians and liberal scholars—have supposed that apocalyptic language (e.g., Mark 13) about momentous changes in heaven and earth mean that Jesus and his contemporaries expected the coming of the Messiah would mean the literal end of the world, the end of space-time history. To suppose this, Wright argues, is simply to misunderstand Jesus.[27] He shows that there is *virtually no evidence that* [first-century] *Jews were expecting the end of the space-time universe.* " Rather, they used vivid cosmic imagery to point to the "full theological significance of cataclysmic socio-political events" they expected to happen in the near future.[28]

We can see this clearly in Isaiah 65:17 (used directly in Rev. 21). Yahweh declares, "See, I will create new heavens and a new earth. The former things will not be remembered." But the passage does not go on to talk about the end of our space-time world; it talks about God restoring the actual historical city of Jerusalem so that infants no longer die prematurely, everyone plants and enjoys their own vineyards, and justice is restored. Cosmic language about new heavens and a new earth is dramatic cosmic imagery to underline the radical socioeconomic and political changes that Yahweh promises to bring when the people of Israel return from exile.

That is the language Jesus uses to describe his message. There will be a cataclysmic conflict, but the result will be the kingdom breaking into our space-time history in a dramatic new fashion, and the nations will embrace God's ways.

Elsewhere in the New Testament, it is clear that the early Christians grasped much of the radical political implications of the dawning of the kingdom. When the apostle Paul spoke about the "principalities and powers," he was referring to the socioeconomic and cultural structures of the world, including government, and the spiritual beings that lie behind these structures. Paul believed that these structures and the spiritual powers behind them had been created as part of the good creation (Col. 1:15–16). Tragically, they rebelled against God and were now in active resistance to him. At the cross, however, something dramatic happened to the principalities and powers: "And having disarmed the powers and authorities, he made a public spectacle of them, triumphing over them by the cross" (Col. 2:15). What does this text mean?[29]

By "powers and authorities" (*tas archas kai tas exousias*), Paul refers both to the structures and social mores of society as well as to supernatural, fallen beings who lie behind and work through these structures.[30] Exactly what happens to these powers and authorities at the cross? The language comes from

Roman military history. A successful Roman general forced the rulers of a conquered nation to march barefoot behind the Roman general's chariot in his triumphal victory march.[31]

Paul, therefore, means that at the cross, Christ won a decisive victory over the powers and authorities. He broke their power and humiliated them. Their ability to hinder Christ's purposes has been significantly weakened.

Paul, of course, does not mean that their evil power is totally broken. Frequently he talks about the way that Christians continue to do battle with these same powers (e.g., Eph. 6:12). Probably Jesus's conflict with Satan and his evil forces is instructive. Jesus said explicitly that he saw Satan fall like lightning (Luke 10:18). He saw himself as binding the evil strongman (Matt. 12:24–29). But he never supposed that those evil powers were totally defeated.

It is important to understand that Christ's victory on the cross was a decisive victory over the unjust socioeconomic and political structures of our world. Their evil power is weakened. Christians certainly need not and should not embrace or submit to their evil ways. The church should and can be the church no matter what the world does, and the gates of hell will not prevail. The long-expected kingdom has truly broken into history, and Christians worship the risen Lord. Let Caesar beware! His power is very limited. "Early Christianity was a counter-empire movement. When Paul said 'Jesus is Lord,' it is clear that he meant Caesar was not. This is not Gnostic escapism but Jewish-style no-king-but-God theology with Jesus in the middle of it."[32]

The absolute power of Caesar and every other political ruler is undermined. Absolute power claims, Oliver O'Donovan says, have "been in trouble ever since Christ rose from the dead."[33] God's people are a light to the nations, and they are now in full advance. Dramatic change, not just in the church but in the structures of the world outside, is possible because these fallen structures have been conquered at the cross and empty tomb. This side of the cross and resurrection, it is possible to accomplish more to correct unjust structures than before Christ "disarmed" the powers at the cross and resurrection.

Here again, however, it is essential to remember the already / not yet of Jesus's proclamation of the kingdom. He certainly taught that the kingdom was already present, breaking into history in powerful ways in his work and person, but he also said the kingdom was like a mustard seed that grows slowly (Matt. 13:31–32). The kingdom is not yet here in its fullness. It will come fully at that future day when the risen Lord returns to complete his victory over evil.

This "two-stage" understanding of the coming of the kingdom of God is very clear in 1 Corinthians 15 (the earliest written discussion of the early Christians' understanding of the kingdom of God).[34] Christ's resurrection is dramatic evidence that the kingdom of God has begun. But it is only the "firstfruits" (1 Cor. 15:20)—only the earliest fruit of the harvest. The fact that the resurrection has already happened is powerful evidence that the kingdom has begun. But it is only the firstfruit of the complete harvest that will surely come at Christ's return when the kingdom will reach its completion (vv. 23–28).

This means that a Christian political philosophy dare not be either naïvely utopian or socially pessimistic. A perfect society will always be beyond reach until Christ returns. Therefore Christians will be realists, expecting sin to persist in all human structures. On the other hand, we dare not be social pessimists, expecting nothing to change and therefore existing comfortably with societal injustice. Christ has won the decisive battle over the evil social structures. It is possible to produce dramatic improvements in history—we can end slavery, promote freedom and democracy, create wealth, and reduce poverty and injustice. We live "between the times"—between the time of Christ's first coming when he powerfully inaugurated the kingdom and the time of his second coming when he will bring the kingdom in its fullness. In this already / not yet period, perfection is not possible, but vastly greater levels of improvement than we usually dare to hope for are possible if we boldly embrace the full implications of the fact that Christ's kingdom has truly begun and Christians can now, in the power of the Holy Spirit, already live according to the kingdom's norms and standards. Certainly we should expect the most visible, most dramatic signs of the dawning kingdom in the church. Yet we can also anticipate less visible, less dramatic, but still significant signs of Christ's victory even in the political structures of our world.

To say, then, that the crucified and risen Christ is now King of the universe means several things. It means that the one who created the universe now continues to sustain it (Col. 1:15–16). It means that he holds sin in check so that society does not degenerate into total chaos and evil. It means that he rules the universe in a way that provides space and freedom for the gospel to be preached and the church to grow ("God placed all things under his feet and appointed him to be head over everything for the church" [Eph. 1:22]). And it means that, because he has already powerfully and decisively broken the power of the rebellious political structures of our world and intends to finish mopping up at his return, now, in this between-the-times period of history, it is possible for Christians and others of goodwill to move society substantially in the direction of justice and peace.

The Final Victory

Many evangelicals have an understanding of Christ's return and life eternal in "heaven" that is simply heretical. It comes from Plato, not the Bible. Many evangelicals talk about "saving souls" who are destined to live forever in a spiritual heaven. As the King James translation interprets 2 Peter 3:10–12, at Christ's return "the heavens shall pass away and . . . the earth also and the works that are therein shall be burned up." We will live forever in a "disembodied existence in an ethereal realm" that has virtually nothing to do with history, culture, and politics in the world as we know it.[35]

There is just one problem with this widespread view: it is not what the Bible says. We have already seen that the first-century Jewish view that Jesus embraced expected the coming of the Messiah to herald not the end of the physical earth but a sweeping radical defeat of evil and the transformation of this good earth. Since Jesus said that was what he was accomplishing, the natural conclusion from Jesus's teaching (that he had begun the victory at his first coming and would complete it at his second coming) would be that when Christ returns, he will restore this good, albeit broken, creation to wholeness.

That is exactly what we find the early Christians expecting and believing. Right at the center of their hope was the bodily resurrection of all believers who would live forever with the Lord. One does not need resurrected bodies to live in a Platonic heaven of immaterial souls. In fact, resurrected bodies simply contradict the entire idea of heaven as a spiritual, immaterial world. And when the New Testament gets around to talking about what things will be like after Christ returns, we hear words about a transformed earth purged of evil.

In Romans 8, the apostle Paul talks about what will happen to the nonhuman creation: "The creation waits in eager expectation for the children of God to be revealed" (v. 19). Verse 23 makes it clear that Paul is referring to the time, at Christ's return, when we receive resurrected bodies. What will happen to the nonhuman creation at that point? "The creation itself will be liberated from its bondage to decay and brought into the freedom and glory of the children of God" (v. 21).[36] At that point, God will purge the nonhuman creation of the evil caused by our sin so that this earth once again fully reflects the Creator's intention.

Revelation 21 and 22 record the glory of the new Jerusalem. It is true that Revelation 21:1 says that John saw "'a new heaven and a new earth,' for the first heaven and the first earth had passed away." But John is using almost the same language as Isaiah 65:17–25 ("See, I will create new heavens and a new earth"), and it is perfectly clear in Isaiah that the "new heavens and a new earth" is symbolic language to talk about the fact that this earth will be radically purged of evil. Isaiah goes on to show how on this "new earth" the people of Israel will live in the historical city of Jerusalem purged of evil and injustice.

In a similar way, Revelation 21–22 goes on to talk about "the new Jerusalem, coming down out of heaven from God" (21:2). God now dwells here on earth with human beings (v. 3), wiping away tears, mourning, and death. All sin is gone (v. 8). John's picture of this future city includes the gates and walls of a transformed Jerusalem.

In a striking affirmation of the continuity between history and society today and the glory of the new Jerusalem, the last two chapters of the Bible explicitly teach that the glory of the political kingdoms of our history will be brought into the "heavenly" city: "The nations will walk by its light [the glory of God who dwells in the new Jerusalem] and the kings of the earth will bring their splendor into it" (Rev. 21:24). That surely means that the best of human history, culture, and civilization will be taken up into the coming kingdom.

To be sure, it will have to be purged of all sin. Nothing evil will enter this city (21:20–22). In fact, John describes a river of life that flows through the center of the city. Beside the river grow the trees of life. "And the leaves of the tree are for the healing of the *nations*" (22:2). God intends to heal the nations!

All of this language, of course, is powerful imagery. We should not use these texts to map the geography of the new Jerusalem or give precise scientific definition to the streets of gold. But the text is surely talking about a gloriously transformed earth purged of all evil, not some Platonic heaven. As one evangelical writer said, "Heaven is not the end of the world."[37] "God in Christ does not take souls to heaven; he redeems whole persons—body and all—for full human life in this world and for resurrected life in the new earth."[38] We have misunderstood the text in 2 Peter 3:10–12.[39] Sometime in the kingdom, I expect to go sailing with my great-great-grandchildren in an unpolluted Nicatous Lake in northern Maine.

The future we await is life eternal in the presence of the living God in a transformed world that again fully reflects the goodness and beauty intended by the Creator. It will be a city, not a garden. We have failed miserably at faithfully fulfilling the creation mandate given to us in the Garden of Eden. We have created civilizations of great beauty and considerable justice, but they are pervasively marked with tears and injustice. Mercifully, the Creator who is the Redeemer intends, at his second coming, to remove the pervasive evil in our mixed efforts at building civilizations. God plans to take the glory of the nations into the new city. The story that starts in a garden ends in a city with God reweaving the tangled strands that we have wrought in vain, transforming our feeble efforts into glorious cultures that sing the Creator's praise.

That understanding of the future shapes faithful Christian political life now in numerous ways. First, that understanding of the future, just like the biblical understanding of creation, persons, and history, underlines the importance of the material world. It is so good that the Creator intends to restore it to wholeness. Christians do not want to escape the material world and fly away as souls to "heaven." We long for resurrected bodies to revel in the goodness of the material world just as the Creator intended.

Second, there is clear continuity between history, the present, and the coming kingdom. To be sure, the sin that will persist until Christ's return is certainly evidence of the discontinuity that exists as well. We cannot create perfect societies now. But if God plans to purge the glory of the nations of all evil and take it up into the new Jerusalem, then there is a connection between our imperfect work now, as we create somewhat more just, beautiful civilizations, and the perfection we await.

Third, the knowledge that persons are designed for a future that far transcends socioeconomic goods that any human government can provide this side of the coming kingdom dramatically relativizes all politics. A good life now of material abundance, justice, and freedom is important. But we are made for far more—for more than even the best human politics can ever deliver. Therefore politicians must make humble claims. They should promise only limited goods. Christians will reject political claims to offer more as idolatrous. And when faithful Christians have political power, they will only claim to offer modest, albeit significant, results. Knowing that persons are made to live forever in the presence of the living God, they know that the state at its best can only offer a modest portion of what persons need to enjoy the good life.

Fourth, because we know the whole story line, including the final chapter, we know where history is going. We know that God wants more justice, peace, and societal wholeness now, because we know that wholeness will be complete at Christ's return. And the vision of that future justice provides a powerful norm with which to judge the broken societies in which we live.

Knowing where history is going and knowing the One who promises to write the final chapter, Christians have hope. Hope is often a scarce commodity in our world. In a recent book published by Professor Duncan Forrester, the author notes that "hope is in crisis in our day."[40] He rightly sees that the Christian hope of the coming kingdom of righteousness and peace has, again and again in Western history, motivated and sustained great movements of social change.[41] To the extent that we truly believe the promise of Christ's coming victory, the Christian story can again today inspire and energize powerful political movements for justice, peace, life, and freedom.

Sometimes, of course, we will fail. Sin remains alive and powerful. Sometimes, for a generation or more, injustice, war, totalitarianism, and social evil of all kinds may advance rather than retreat. Even then, the assurance of Christ's final victory provides hope that sustains our persistent, faithful struggle for justice even when the political tide is sweeping in the other direction.[42] Knowing the Resurrected One, knowing that he will return, we also know that crusading evil can succeed only for a time. The decisive victory has already been won. Even when faithfulness involves martyrdom, even then we know who holds the future. Because he lives, we can face even the most terrifying tomorrows. Because one day the kingdoms of this world will become the kingdom of our Lord who will reign forever and ever.

Building a Solid Framework

*From Biblical Paradigms
and Societal Analysis
to an Evangelical Political Philosophy*

I n chapter 2, we saw that every political decision has four components.

A normative framework (whether conscious or not) provides the basic principles and norms.

A broad analysis—whether explicit or implicit—of history (economics, politics, indeed the whole complex web of the past) also informs our political thought.

Since we cannot take the time to do a comprehensive review of these two areas every time we want to make a political decision, we also need a handy road map, a political philosophy. Frequently, we unthinkingly adopt a political philosophy from our parents or neighbors. We ought, however, to carefully develop an ever-improving political philosophy that grows out of our integration of our normative framework and our careful study of societal history.

Finally, to make specific political decisions, we must apply our political philosophy to concrete situations by gathering additional, specific socioeconomic and political information.

Part 3 of this book seeks to develop key components of an evangelical political philosophy. In each chapter, I will combine discussion of relevant biblical and theological truth with historical analysis that pertains to the topic. Hopefully, the result in each chapter will be the emergence of an important piece of a comprehensive evangelical political philosophy.

I do not claim this is *the* evangelical political philosophy. It represents the best, current insight of one evangelical thinker. If you think my conclusions are wrong, don't call me names. Rather, show me concretely and specifically how I have failed to develop my normative framework in a faithful biblically grounded fashion; or how I have neglected, misunderstood, or improperly assessed the past and present socioeconomic and political data; or how I have improperly integrated my normative framework and my study of history. Greater precision about exactly where we disagree as Christians in our political thought will help us slowly move to a more biblically grounded, sophisticated evangelical political philosophy. That in turn could guide hundreds of millions of evangelicals all around the world to love their neighbors more effectively through wise political engagement.

4

The State

Its Nature, Purpose, and Limits

What is the state?

We all recognize it when we see it. We know it is not the same thing as a family, a business corporation, a union, a church, or a block club. To be sure the state has a number of things in common with all of these other institutions in society: they all are social entities. They all are in some sense public—i.e., they are visible in, speak to, and shape the total society. And they all exercise considerable pressure (i.e., coercion of some type) on their members to act in certain ways.

So how is the state different? A couple definitions may help.

Philip Wogaman, a contemporary Christian ethicist, defines the state as "society acting as a whole, with the ultimate power to compel compliance within its own jurisdiction."[1] Two things are important here. First, when the state acts, the whole society acts, not just one part of it. The state's decisions affect every sector of society. Second, although all social groups rightly exercise some coercion (e.g., parents rightly discipline their children), the state alone has the authority and power to use coercion to enforce its laws in every area of society. We will leave until later in this chapter the question of whether that means the state must and should use lethal violence. But it is a historical fact that virtually every state has tried to exercise a monopoly on lethal force to compel obedience to its laws and protect its borders.

Evangelical political scientist James Skillen offers a definition of the state that emphasizes a third crucial point: the state is the "public-legal integrator of all socially differentiating reality."[2] Society is a highly differentiated reality—i.e., it consists of different institutions, not just individuals and the state. The central role of the state is to integrate—i.e., rightly relate—all these different institutions and persons through fair laws so that they all enjoy justice.

Society and the State

Skillen's point is absolutely crucial. "The one great heresy," according to William Temple, one of the great twentieth-century archbishops of Canterbury, is to equate society and the state.[3] The state is only one of many important institutions in society.[4]

The very first institutions to appear in the biblical story are marriage and family. The Creator made persons male and female, designed for the divinely ordained institutions of marriage and family. Only when Eve arrives is Adam's heart satisfied. The social institutions of marriage and family are embedded in the very order of creation—at the very beginning. Only later does the text discuss what we now call the state.

In the history of Israel, we see the slow emergence of different social institutions.[5] In Abraham, a leader of an extended family, we detect hardly any distinction between the roles of parent, priest, and king. In the course of Israel's history, however, the institutions of the priesthood and the prophets emerge as distinct from both family and state. With the early church, as Christianity breaks the narrow bonds of ethnic religion and becomes a universal faith embracing people of every tribe and nation, the church becomes a powerful institution clearly distinct from—and often in sharp conflict with—the state.

Increasing differentiation of societal institutions continues over the course of human history as more and more institutions emerge as distinct entities independent of the state. Independent economic institutions—both business corporations and unions—become powerful. A vast variety of educational, cultural, and civic institutions flourish with very little dependence on the state. "The great array of differentiated social cohesions, which represent in their totality the free society of modern civilization, and from which the authority and force embodied in the state have withdrawn themselves, furnish the individual with that great variety of choice which constitutes real freedom."[6]

Christians understand this progressive emergence over the course of human history of more and more complex and differentiated institutions as the natural result of the divine image and creation mandate given by God. The Creator made us in his own image, placed us as stewards in a wondrous material world capable of almost infinite adaptability and change, and gave us the glorious task of imitating the Creator by shaping complex civilizations and intricate institutions. Since we are made in the image of the Trinity, we are communal beings and therefore shape a variety of social structures where our longing for community finds satisfaction. Since we are creative beings in the image of the Creator, we naturally create new things in history.

The fall accounts for what is twisted in present institutions, but our being designed in the image of the trinitarian Creator explains why we can and do design more and more differentiated communal institutions over the course of human history.[7]

Since the task of the state is to foster just relationships between all the individuals and all the other institutions in society, our understanding of justice is absolutely essential for our understanding of the state. For that discussion, however, we will have to wait until the next chapter. For now, it is enough to understand the importance of the claim that the state is only one of many different institutions in society.

Surely one of the clearest lessons taught by the history of the last one hundred years is that human freedom and flourishing collapse when the state refuses to accept its role as just one of many important societal institutions and instead seeks to dominate and control all others. As both Nazi and communist totalitarian governments sought to obliterate every other independent societal institution, human freedom largely disappeared—thus devastating for a time the kind of free flourishing that the Creator intended for persons made in his image. Both because the centralization of power is dangerous in a fallen world and because totalitarianism prevents individuals from responding to their Creator's call to freedom and engagement in the creative process of shaping history, the vast variety of societal institutions independent of the state are an essential ingredient of a good society. The state is not society.

One of many institutions in a complex, differentiated society, the state has the unique responsibility of providing the right framework so that all persons and all institutions in society treat each other justly and have the freedom to be and do what they ought to be and do. To prevent disorder and promote the common good of the entire society, we need an institution that has the authority and power to provide a good, accepted framework in which all the other institutions as well as all persons can both enjoy their own freedom and work together effectively. Hence, the need is for legislators to write the laws, administrators to implement them, and judges to enforce them.

What is the source for the state's limited yet still pervasive authority? The answer of historic Christianity differs sharply from modern contract theory. Since the time of the seventeenth-century thinker John Locke, contract theorists have argued that sovereign individuals living in a state of nature freely choose to form a social compact with other free individuals, surrendering some of their freedom to create the state. The state, consequently, derives its authority from this original contract between free individuals. However, as William Temple notes, contract theory is "not even good myth."[8] As a matter of historical fact, the state emerged in a far more organic way. And in terms of the state's ultimate authority, it comes not from some choice of individual persons, but from God.

Jesus bluntly informed Pilate: "You would have no power over me unless it had been given you from above" (John 19:11 NRSV). And Paul boldly declared that "there is no authority except from God, and those authorities that exist have been instituted by God" (Rom. 13:1 NRSV). The Creator, who made us communal beings, is the ultimate source of all governmental authority.

That does not mean that, secondarily, human agreements to write and approve constitutions that provide for the democratic election of governmental officials are unimportant. Nor does it mean that the democratic claim that in some important sense the "people are sovereign" and that both the state and specific governments rightly derive their authority from the choices of people in free democratic elections is wrong. But it does mean that the vote of the majority does not make something right. God is the ultimate source of all governmental authority and God wills that "the people" and governments do justice. "The fact that political authority stems not from the people but from God shows that the government does not have the right to do what it wills, and neither do the people."[9]

Essential Tasks of the State

It does not take much historical observation to notice that there is plenty of evil to restrain. Sin, and the oppression and violence to which it leads, is universal. Throughout the Scriptures we see the state (the kings, the courts, etc.) called to restrain evil and punish evildoers. God sent the prophet Jeremiah with a message to the king of Judah: "Hear the word of the LORD, O king of Judah. . . . Rescue from the hand of the oppressor the one who has been robbed" (Jer. 22:2–3 NIV 1984). Paul summarizes a vast amount of biblical teaching with his simple statement that the state "is the servant of God to execute wrath on the wrongdoer" (Rom. 13:4 NRSV). Peter makes the same point, urging Christians to submit to kings and governors because they are sent by God "to punish those who do wrong and to commend those who do right" (1 Pet. 2:14).

Over the course of Christian history, many theologians have understood the role of the state as largely or exclusively negative. In the biblical story, the state arrives only after the fall. Many Christians have concluded that its essential purpose is to restrain evil.[10] Many others, however, including Thomas Aquinas and John Calvin, while accepting this purpose of the state, also endorse a positive purpose—the promotion of the common good. Calvin denounced those who regarded magistrates "only as a kind of necessary evil." Civil authority, Calvin believed, is "the most honorable of all callings in the whole of life"—the state's function among people being "no less than that of bread, water, sun and air."[11]

In fact, in Romans 13, Paul specifies a positive role for the state before he refers to its negative function. The state is "God's servant for your good" (v. 4).[12] God approved and blessed the kings of Israel for leading their societies in positive activities. David brought the ark of the covenant to Jerusalem, and Solomon organized the nation in a massive societal project to build the temple.

Does the absence of specific reference to the state before the fall mean that the state is necessary only because of sin? If God had created persons as the kind of isolated individuals imagined by contract theorists, then probably the answer would be yes. But the trinitarian God who exists in the mutual, loving fellowship of Father, Son, and Holy Spirit created us in the divine image. We are made for mutual interdependence, not individualistic isolation. Quite apart from the fall, we only reach our God-given destiny when we interact with others in cooperative tasks and loving fellowship. Even without the fall, a growing human population would have needed cooperative efforts, and leaders to organize that cooperation, in order to carry out God's mandate to exercise dominion and stewardship in creating human civilization. The state's positive purpose—promoting the common good—flows directly from the fact that we are created as communal beings in the image of God.

The fact that the state comes into the biblical story explicitly only after the fall does not prove that it is necessary only because of sin. Music is also first mentioned after the fall (Gen. 4:21), but that hardly means that it results from sin.[13] Furthermore, "the fact that the book of Revelation says that kings will bring their glory and the honor of the nations into the New Jerusalem suggests that the political enterprise has its own intrinsic merit apart from the effects of sin" (see Rev. 21:24–26).[14]

First Timothy 2:1–4 adds something to our discussion of the purpose of the state: "I urge that supplications, prayers, intercessions and thanksgivings be made for everyone, for kings and all who are in high positions, so that we may lead a quiet and peaceable life in all godliness and dignity. This is right and is acceptable in the sight of God our Savior who desires everyone to be saved" (NRSV). This passage dares to say that a central purpose of the great Roman Empire is to provide space for the proclamation of the gospel.[15] Theologian John Howard Yoder rightly points out that the text reverses what frequently happens. Very often people, even Christians, view religion as a support for the state. Instead, this text finds the mandate for the state within the mandate for the church. "The glorious Roman Empire, standing as something unique in world history, existed for one purpose only: that God could use a small despised bunch of fishermen and tax collectors to carry forth the name of an executed Galilean from Jerusalem into the whole world."[16]

How did the Roman Empire serve the spread of the gospel? Both by restraining evil so that all could live in peace, and also by providing positive benefits that served the common good—one thinks, for example, of the extensive system of Roman roads that made relatively easy travel and communication possible for the apostles. The text in 1 Timothy supports the view that the state has both a negative and positive function.

Other biblical material throws further light on these two aspects of the task of the state. Both the biblical paradigm on justice (see the next chapter) and the biblical teaching on the ideal monarch present positive and negative roles of the state.

Statements like the following are at the center of the biblical teaching about justice: "[The Lord] has made you king to maintain justice and righteousness" (1 Kings 10:9; cf. Jer. 22:15–16). And these two key words (*justice* and *righteousness*) as we will see in the next chapter, refer not only to fair legal systems but also to just economic structures. The king must promote both not only by restraining and punishing those who violate the rights of others but by nurturing and encouraging situations where just legal and economic structures flourish.

We also see both the positive and negative role of the state in the biblical materials that present the ideal monarch. Both the royal psalms and messianic prophesies develop the picture of this ideal ruler.

Psalm 72 (a royal psalm) gives the following purpose for the ruler: "May he defend the cause of the poor of the people, give deliverance to the needy, and crush the oppressor" (v. 4 NRSV). And this task is identified as the work of justice (vv. 1–3, 7). This passage calls on the state to use power to deliver the needy and oppressed.

According to Psalm 72, there are oppressors of the poor (separate from the state) who need to be crushed. State power, despite its dangers, is necessary for society because of the evil power of such exploiting groups. "On the side of their oppressors there was power," Ecclesiastes 4:1 declares (NRSV). Without the state's force to counter such oppressive power there is "no one to comfort" (Eccles. 4:1 NRSV). Whether it is the monarch or the village elders (Amos 5:12, 15), state power should deliver the economically weak and guarantee the "cause of the poor" (Jer. 22:16; also Pss. 45:4–5; 101:8; Jer. 21:12).

Prophecies about the coming messianic ruler also develop the picture of the ideal ruler. "With righteousness he shall judge the poor, and decide with equity for the meek of the earth; he shall strike the earth with the rod of his mouth, and with the breath of his lips he shall kill the wicked" (Isa. 11:4 NRSV).

The ideal ruler will take responsibility for the needs of the people as a shepherd: "He shall feed them and be their shepherd" (Ezek. 34:23 NRSV). Ezekiel 34:4 denounces the failure of the shepherds (i.e., the rulers) of Israel to "feed" the people. Then in verses 15–16, the same phrases are repeated to describe God's promise of justice:

> "And I will make them lie down," says the LORD God. "I will seek the lost, and I will bring back the strayed, and I will bind up the injured, and I will strengthen

the weak, but the fat and the strong I will destroy. I will feed them with justice" (NRSV).

This promise is to be fulfilled by the coming Davidic ruler (vv. 23–24). Similarly, in Isaiah 32:1–8, the promised just and wise monarch is contrasted with the fool who leaves the hungry unsatisfied (v. 6).

These texts clearly see the ideal state as both restraining evil and promoting good. It both crushes oppressors and feeds the people like a shepherd. It both destroys unjust power and strengthens the weak.

This teaching on the role of the state applies not just to Israel but to the state everywhere. The ideal monarch was to be a channel of God's justice (Ps. 72:1), and God's justice extends to the whole world (e.g., Ps. 9:7–9). All legitimate rulers are instituted by God and are God's servants for human good (Rom. 13:1, 4). Romans 13 is similar to Psalm 72:1 in viewing the ruler as a channel of God's authority. All people everywhere can pray with the Israelites, "Give the king your justice, O God" (Ps. 72:1 NRSV).

Daniel 4:27 shows that the ideal of the monarch as the protector of the weak has universal application. God summons the Babylonian monarch no less than the Israelite king to bring justice and mercy to the oppressed. Similarly, in Proverbs 31:9, King Lemuel (generally considered to be a northern Arabian monarch) is to "defend the rights of the poor and needy." The general obligation of the Israelite king to guarantee that the weak enjoy fair courts and the daily necessities of life is, in the biblical perspective, a duty of all rulers.

The teaching on the ideal, just monarch of Israel, whether in royal psalms or messianic prophecies, cannot be restricted to some future messianic reign. God demanded that the kings of Israel provide in their own time what the messianic ruler would eventually bring more completely: namely, justice that delivers from oppression and strengthens the weak. God's concern, in the present and in the future, within Israel and outside of Israel, is that states promote the common good by restraining evil and promoting good.

Does Jesus's gospel of the kingdom add anything to our understanding of the state? We need to ask if our understanding of the role of the state now (between the time of Christ's first and second comings) and our discussion in chapter 3 about the fact that the kingdom of God has broken decisively into history in the work of Jesus carry any implications. In the preceding chapter, we saw that Jesus and the early Christians announced that the messianic hope for a future reign of God when all nations would embrace God's will began to become a reality in Jesus and the early church. At the cross and in the resurrection, Christ decisively conquered the fallen principalities and powers that now find expression in states and governments. At his return, Christ will complete this victory. What does this mean for our understanding of the present role of the state?

Yoder has argued that the state is not part of the good creation, but rather part of the rebellious world that opposes Christ. God still wills the state to play the limited role of restraining violence, but it is destined for destruction.[17] In a partially parallel way, Oxford ethicist Oliver O'Donovan states that Jesus "announced the coming of God's kingdom to sweep away existing orders of government."[18] In the already / not yet time between the powerful inauguration of this kingdom and its completion at Christ's return, the rulers of this old age rightly play the limited role of restraining evil, O'Donovan argues, but they are destined for destruction.[19]

It is certainly the case that Paul understood the principalities and powers of his day to be arrayed in fundamental opposition to Christ, but these powers were originally created as part of the good creation, and they have already been taken captive by Christ at the cross and resurrection (Col. 2:15). Furthermore, John, in Revelation 21:24, says that "the kings of the earth will bring their splendor" into the new Jerusalem. That sounds like restoration to wholeness, not destruction, at Christ's second coming.[20]

During the already / not yet time in which we live, the principalities and powers are often in terrible rebellion against Christ, the King of kings. But their power has been broken, and therefore, presumably, they are capable of significant good. They are not innately evil, and they will be restored to wholeness. Therefore it seems appropriate to suppose that the state rightly restrains evil and promotes good—which is exactly what the New Testament texts say (Rom. 13:4; 1 Pet. 2:14). In fact, Paul uses the same word (*exousiai*) to describe the fallen rebellious powers (Col. 2:15) and the state that is now "God's servant to do you good" (Rom. 13:4 NIV 1984; see also vv. 1–3).

The State's Limited Role

There are many reasons why the state should have major limitations put on its reach and power.

Probably the most crucial limitation on the state flows from widespread recognition of the theological truth that all state authority flows from God. And God insists that all state action conform to the divine standard of justice. Thus, we can always condemn specific governmental decisions by appealing to the higher law of divine justice.

Jesus and the early church's attitude toward Roman imperial power underlines how the knowledge of God's ultimate sovereignty relativizes and challenges all earthly state power. At his trial, Jesus bluntly reminded Pilate that his (and Caesar's) authority and power came from God. At a time when Roman emperors were beginning to claim divinity, Paul insists they are *God's servants*! "Paul relativizes the Roman Imperial order. He refuses to accept the Emperor's ultimate authority and says that the Emperor is *under* God, a servant."[21] Throughout Christian history, Christians have limited the power of the state by giving their ultimate allegiance to God alone, thus relativizing the power of every earthly ruler.

God creates each person as a free, creative being called to trace the Creator's steps by freely molding the material world, shaping history, and creating things never seen before. For that to happen, the state must be limited. Individuals simply cannot carry out their creation mandate if an all-powerful state makes all the decisions.

The dreadful reality of omnipresent evil underlines the importance of a limited state. History has confirmed the truth of Lord Acton's comment that power tends to corrupt and absolute power corrupts absolutely. Sinful persons almost always use immense power for their selfish advantage. The Scriptures are full of stories about oppressive kings and powerful, evil governments (e.g., 1 Kings 2; Revelation 13). There are also warnings about what powerful rulers will do (1 Sam. 8:11–17; cf. also Deut. 17:14–20). Only if the power of the state is significantly limited is there any hope of avoiding gross evil on the part of the state.

Finally, the fact that God has divinely instituted other institutions in society (e.g., the family, the church) also demands a limited state. God, not the state, creates and establishes family and church and gives them freedom and authority to carry out their responsibilities independently of the state. Only if the state is appropriately limited can the other institutions in society flourish as God intended.

In practice, of course, the actual existence of other societal institutions that demand independence from the state works to limit the state's power. Nowhere is that clearer than in the history of the Christian church. From its beginning, the church insisted on obeying God rather than human authorities (Acts 5:29). In the early centuries, the church refused to obey many demands of the Roman state. And during the Middle Ages, in spite of the close cooperation of church and state, the church vigorously insisted on its independence. In his *History of Political Theory*, George Sabine comments that "the rise of the Christian Church, as a distinct institution entitled to govern the spiritual concerns of mankind in independence of the state, may not unreasonably be described as the most revolutionary event in the history of Western Europe, in respect both to politics and to political thought."[22]

Fortunately, democratic societies have discovered numerous ways to implement the vision of a limited state: the constitutional separation of powers (legislative, judicial, and executive); the several, substantially independent spheres of different levels of the state (federal, state, and local in the American system); regular, free democratic elections; recognition of the importance of a vast range of non-state institutions with freedom from the state; acknowledgment that government officials are under, not above, the law; and freedom of speech, assembly, and dissent. In these and other ways, we implement a limited state.

When we understand the importance of these limitations, we see why it is crucial not to immediately turn to the state to solve every social problem. Other institutions—family, church, school, business, union—all have obligations to solve societal problems. In every case, we need to ask what institution in society, and what level of that institution, can best solve a particular problem.

We can see this principle at work in the biblical text, in which it is clear that the family has the first obligation to help needy members. In the great text on the jubilee in Leviticus 25, the first responsibility to help the poor person forced by poverty to sell land belongs to the next of kin in the extended family (vv. 25, 35). But the poor person's help does not end with the family. Even if there are no family members to help, the poor person has the legal right to receive his land back at the next jubilee (v. 28). Similarly, 1 Timothy 5:16 insists that a Christian widow's relatives should be her first means of support. Only when the family cannot provide assistance should the church step in. Any policy or political philosophy that immediately seeks state solutions for problems that could be solved just as well (or better) at the level of family violates the biblical framework that stresses the central societal role of the family.

On the other hand, that does not mean that there is no role for the state to promote the common good. The state is an instrument of the community and is an expression of our created social nature.

Sin also makes state action necessary. When selfish, powerful people deprive others of their rightful access to productive resources, the state rightly steps in with intervening power to correct the injustice. When other individuals and institutions in the community do not or cannot provide basic necessities for the needy, the state rightly helps.

Frequently, of course, the state contributes to the common good by encouraging and enabling other institutions in the community—whether family, church, nongovernmental social agencies, guilds, or unions—to carry out their responsibilities to care for the economically dependent. Sometimes, however, the depth of social need exceeds the capacity of non-state institutions. When indirect approaches are not effective in restraining economic injustice or in providing care for those who cannot care for themselves, the state must act directly to demand patterns of justice and to provide vital services—always, of course, in a way that does not further weaken, but rather restores and strengthens, the other non-state institutions.

Emil Brunner is probably correct in suggesting that the healthier a society, the more non-state institutions will be able to handle problems without state intervention. On the other hand, the greater the moral decay, the more the state must act. One can see this in the way that today's moral decay and the resulting family breakdown have led to greatly expanded state activity to care for children abandoned by parents. As long as this state intervention is done in a way that effectively aims to restore the non-state institutions (e.g., the family) so they can again as quickly as possible play their proper role, the state's action is justified.

Some people wrongly conclude from the fact that the state's power must be limited that the state has no legitimate role in aiding and empowering poor people. They embrace the libertarian argument that caring for the poor is a task for individuals, religious groups, and private charities—not the state.[23] Many evangelicals embrace this libertarian view with regard to helping the poor. (Interestingly, however, evangelicals vigorously—and inconsistently!—reject a libertarian attitude on abortion and marriage, promoting strong state action against abortion on demand, and supporting heterosexual marriage.)

The libertarian view that the state has no responsibility to care for and empower the poor flies in the face of clear biblical teaching.

First Kings 10:9 says of King Solomon: The Lord "has made you king to maintain justice and righteousness." Psalm 72:1 is a prayer for the leader of the government: "Endow the king with your justice, O God, the royal son with your righteousness." And Jeremiah declares that good king Josiah knew God because he "did what was right and just . . . he defended the cause of the poor and needy" (Jer. 22:15–16).

Central to biblical teaching about the task of a king is the responsibility to do "righteousness and justice." Each of the three passages just cited use the key Hebrew words (or their derivatives): *mishpat* and *tsedaqah*. These words, as we will see in the next chapter, refer to both fair judicial procedures (procedural justice) and just economic outcomes (distributive justice). These two tasks of procedural and distributive justice correspond to a substantial degree to the explicit New Testament teaching that the state has the double task of restraining evil and promoting the good (Rom. 13:4; 1 Pet. 2:13–14). The state cares for the poor by both restraining powerful evil people and assisting and empowering the poor.

After praying that God will give the king God's justice, the psalmist continues: "May he defend the afflicted among the people and save the children of the needy; may he crush the oppressor" (Ps. 72:2–4; cf. also Eccles. 4:1). In a similar way, Jeremiah says that king Josiah "defended the cause of the poor and needy and so all went well" (Jer. 22:16). There are wicked, powerful people in society who oppress the poor. One role of the state is to protect the poor from these powerful (nongovernmental!) oppressors.

But the biblical material in no way restricts the role of the state to operating fair courts that defend the poor. Many texts talk about the way the rulers assist the poor and promote economic justice.

Central to the Old Testament vision of economic justice and the avoidance of poverty, as we shall see in the next chapter, is the understanding that the land (the basic capital in an agricultural society) was divided up so that every family had their own portion of it. And it was the political leader Joshua who led the people in this decentralized division of the land (Josh. 18:1–10).

Furthermore, in order to avoid the emergence of persistent poverty among the people of Israel, God commanded that debts should be forgiven every seven years (Deut. 15:1–11), and that every family should return to their ancestral land every fifty years regardless of the reason they had lost it (Lev. 25). In neither case is there any suggestion that forgiveness of debts or the jubilee was a voluntary act that individuals were free to practice or ignore. It was God's law—and presumably the rulers were supposed to lead in its implementation.

The prophet also predicted a messianic time when justice would prevail and everyone would again enjoy their own land (Mic. 4:4; Zech. 3:10). In his vivid depiction of this messianic restoration of ancestral land, Ezekiel denounces the rulers for wrongly seizing people's land and predicts that the rulers will finally play their proper role in helping everyone enjoy their productive capital (Ezek. 45, especially vv. 8–9).

Nehemiah 5 contains a striking account of the governor (the top official of the state in Judah) denouncing powerful Jews who were oppressing their own people. Judah was a province of Persia at the time, but the Persian ruler had appointed Nehemiah as governor of Judah and allowed him to rebuild Jerusalem. After some time, Nehemiah discovered that powerful Jews were oppressing their fellow Jews. Because of famine, poor Jews had mortgaged and then lost their fields in order to buy food. Others had sold their children into slavery. Rich, powerful Jews were profiting from the desperate situation of the poor.

Furious, Nehemiah called a public assembly and denounced the powerful Jewish oppressors. "Give back to them immediately their fields, vineyards, olive groves and houses, and also the interest you are charging them," Nehemiah demanded (v. 11). The rich oppressors agreed, and Nehemiah made them take an oath to keep their promise. Nehemiah did not wait for the next jubilee to demand that the rich return the land of the poor so that they could again earn their own way. As the ruler, he insisted that the poor immediately recover their productive capital.

In a careful article on the various Old Testament provisions to care for the very poor (e.g., no interest loans, the third-year tithe for the poor), Christian economist John Mason asks whether these provisions were only suggestions for voluntary charity or laws to be enforced by the political leadership of the community. He concludes that these provisions were just as much part of the Mosaic legislation as the laws regarding murder and theft. They were laws that the state was to enforce.[24]

There is another major consideration that supports the claim that the state has a significant role in empowering the poor. Poverty results both from wrong personal choices and unfair systems. The prophets denounced unfair legal and economic systems that produced poverty (Amos 5:10–15; 2:6–7; Isa. 5:8–9). Isaiah 10 very explicitly says that sometimes rulers oppress the poor: "Woe to those who make unjust laws . . . to deprive the poor of their rights and withhold justice from the oppressed of my people" (10:1–2). Equally bluntly, Psalm 94 denounces "a throne that brings on misery by its decrees" (v. 20).

Legislation sometimes produces and/or nurtures unjust, oppressive structures that destroy the poor (e.g. legalized slavery). Just as clearly, good legislation (e.g., the abolition of slavery) can encourage more just structures that truly empower the poor and oppressed. The return of ancestral land every fifty years was a structural policy for empowering the poor, not a voluntary act of charity.

"For the Health of the Nation," the unanimously approved official public policy document of the National Association of Evangelicals (which represents 30 million evangelicals in the United States), clearly affirms the importance of wise state action to promote structures that empower the needy:

> From the Bible, experience, and social analysis, we learn that social problems arise and can be substantially corrected by both personal decisions and structural changes. On the one hand, personal sinful choices contribute significantly to destructive social problems (Prov. 6:9–11), and personal conversion through faith in Christ can transform broken persons into wholesome, productive citizens. On the other hand, unjust systems also help create social problems (Amos 5:10–15; Isa. 10:1–2) and wise structural change (for example legislation to strengthen marriage or increase economic opportunity for all) can improve society. Thus Christian civic engagement must seek to transform both individuals and institutions. While individuals transformed by the gospel change surrounding society, social institutions also shape individuals. While good laws encourage good behavior, bad laws and systems foster destructive action. Lasting social change requires both personal conversion and institutional renewal and reform.[25]

One basic statistic underlines the importance of state action to care for the poor. In the United States today, tens of millions of poor people need food assistance each month. There are thousands of voluntary organizations lovingly providing important food aid. But of all the food assistance provided each month in the United States, 94 percent comes from the state. A mere 6 percent comes from private sources.[26]

There is no basis in biblical thought to argue that the state should have no role in caring for and empowering poor people. We must hold two truths in balance: the state has a proper role in caring for and empowering poor people; and the state must be limited, not all-powerful.

No general principles about the proper role of a limited state in solving societal problems can replace the necessity of wisdom at every specific moment. We can agree (in parallel with the Roman Catholic principle of subsidiarity)[27] that social problems should be dealt with at as local a level as is effective; that state action should strengthen, not undermine, the vitality of non-state institutions; that sometimes social problems are so sweeping that the state must play a significant role; and that some things by their very nature are done better not just by the state but by higher levels of state institutions. (For example, minimum-wage laws and laws requiring companies to prevent or pay for the costs of pollution are necessary, because without them, companies that freely choose to pay fair wages or not pollute will find themselves at a comparative disadvantage with companies that do not.) But there is no mathematical calculus for determining how such a mix of principles applies to any given proposal for expanded action by the state. Always, we must make finite human judgments about how things are currently unbalanced and what correction of what magnitude is needed. Since our best judgments may be wrong, we must maintain a fundamental humility and tentativeness about all our concrete political conclusions.

Christians should respect and treasure the state as a good gift ordained by God to promote the good and restrain evil. But if it is to be helpful rather than harmful, it must be limited. We must recognize that society is much larger than the state and contains many crucial non-state institutions that have their own independence and worth.

What Should We Legislate?

About what things should the state pass laws that the police and courts enforce? Should there be public laws against murder and theft but not against adultery and gossip? If so, why? In chapter 1, we saw that one evangelical politician in Brazil recently proposed that the state should pass laws providing legal penalties for everything the Bible condemns. Secular libertarians argue that the state should legislate almost nothing but the minimal laws required to promote fair courts and police, and to offer internal security and an army to care for national self-defense. Who is right? And what are the principles for deciding what is appropriate legislation by the state and what is not?

One crucial way to begin thinking about these questions, as James Skillen rightfully points out, is to ask: What is the state supposed to do that other institutions in society are not called to do?[28] The state should not pass laws that interfere with the unique responsibilities of other institutions, such as family and church. The right of families and churches to govern their own lives without state interference comes directly from God, who has established them as important societal institutions with their own authority and sphere of responsibility. Very seldom should public laws infringe on the freedom of parents to raise their children in the way they deem best, although carefully written laws rightly protect children from sexual and physical abuse. Very seldom should public laws touch the internal activity and decisions of religious organizations except to criminalize things like theft and sexual abuse. Only within narrow limits should the state's laws dictate the activities of unions and corporations. All these and many other institutions should be free to conduct their affairs in ways that flow from their own vision and goals. That is not to say that the state's law should never make legal demands on these other institutions, but this should happen only under carefully defined circumstances.

Religious freedom for individuals and religious institutions is the most significant illustration of this principle. In chapter 9 we will explore the foundations of religious freedom. Here it is only essential to see that it is simply not a proper function of the state to pass laws that impose religious beliefs upon, or hinder the free expression of the religious beliefs of, individuals, churches, and religious organizations of all kinds.

Earlier we saw that the task of seeing that other institutions and individuals in society relate justly to each other is central to the purpose of the state. Providing fair procedures (e.g., fair courts, property laws, society-wide weights and measures) that enable other institutions to relate easily and settle disagreements between them is an appropriate state action. Normally, such laws apply to all institutions and all persons, whereas the accepted rules of a family or church apply only to that particular institution.

Since restraining evil is a central part of the state's proper function, state laws against such things as theft, murder, inappropriately harming others, and so on, are proper.

Since the state also rightly promotes the common good, a wide variety of laws for this purpose are also legitimate: to build transportation systems that everyone can use, to guarantee that all children have access to quality education, and to ensure that all citizens enjoy an appropriate level of health care.

State action to promote the common good, however, requires great care. Communist societies claimed to be promoting the common good with laws that enabled the state to dominate all other institutions and destroy personal freedom. When the state considers legislation to promote the common good by solving some social problem, it must always ask: What institution or institutions and what level of society can best deal with this problem? Bad social behavior on the part of children, for example, is primarily the responsibility of families and churches, not the state, although the state may be able to provide resources to encourage other institutions to play their proper role. When the state does intervene in the life of other institutions, because those institutions are weak and unable to play their normal role, the state must be especially careful to act in ways that restore those institutions to wholeness rather than permanently replace them. (For example, desperate single-parent families may need temporary state assistance, but it is terribly destructive if that assistance has the effect of encouraging rather than reducing single parenthood).

Laws must respect individual freedom. God has given persons the freedom to choose behaviors which he knows to be harmful, and of which he disapproves. The state should respect that God-given freedom and allow persons to choose destructive behavior as long as that behavior does not seriously harm others. That is why it would be a mistake to pass a law against getting drunk at home, but it is appropriate to have laws that criminalize drunk driving.

Implementing this principle is not easy. Since we are social beings, virtually all behavior by any individual has some impact on at least a small circle of other people—one's children, parents, or neighbors. Constantly quarreling parents harm their children, but the state should not regularly interfere in the separate institution of the family since it is an inevitable aspect of social institutions that the other members of that institution share its advantages and disadvantages. Only in the case of serious harm to children (e.g., sexual abuse or withholding of health care that could save a child's life) should the state intervene.

Another standard modifies this principle that individuals should be free to harm themselves if they do not harm others: laws have a teaching function. It is silly to think that whatever the law permits is morally right and whatever it condemns is morally wrong, but many people think that way—at least to a degree. Therefore, sometimes public laws rightly forbid private behavior that would largely affect just the person (or a small circle of family members) who chooses the behavior. Laws against the use of heroin and cocaine are examples. If one only applied the previous principle, one would argue that individuals should be free to destroy themselves with heroin as long as they do not seriously harm others while on a high, but legalizing those drugs would convey the message to many that using these drugs is morally acceptable. The result would probably be more drug addicts.

One might argue that the same argument should lead to prohibiting the production or sale of alcohol, since so many people abuse alcohol. But we tried that earlier in American history, and it did not work. Large numbers of people produced and sold alcohol illegally, and the result was widespread corruption of law enforcement and politics.

This historical experience points to another principle: it is unwise to legislate what is essentially unenforceable. If large numbers of people disobey a law, the result is loss of respect for law in general. To a significant degree, laws must be grounded in fairly widespread cultural agreement or they cannot be enforced.

Finally, as German theologian Helmut Thielicke has pointed out, laws properly deal with external behavior, not internal thoughts and feelings. "No one can be hanged for thinking."[29] Jesus condemned both murdering and being angry at one's neighbor (Matt. 5:21–22), but the state should have laws against and punish only the external act, not the inner emotion.[30] Religious leaders rightly deal with inner thoughts of the heart but the laws of the state should not. Over time, however, laws do frequently change the heart. Laws requiring integrated public education have probably, over time, reduced racial prejudice.

Applying these principles is not easy. They are not unambiguous. They have overlapping implications that pull in different directions. But we will be able to make wise decisions about what kinds of laws we should pass if we remember these principles:

- The state should only pass laws that deal with areas that are the proper domain of the state rather than that of other societal institutions.
- The state should adopt laws that restrain evil behavior that harms others.
- The state should pass laws that promote the common good.
- The state's laws should strengthen rather than weaken other important societal institutions.
- Normally, the state's laws should allow great personal freedom, even permitting destructive behavior that harms only the person, or a small circle that by definition rightly shares the advantages and disadvantages of that circle (e.g., his or her family).
- We must remember that the state's laws have an important teaching function.
- We should only adopt public laws that are substantially enforceable.
- Laws should deal with external behavior, not internal thoughts and feelings.

These principles may be helpful, but they cannot replace wise discernment and thoughtful prudence. Every historical situation is unique. There is no mathematical formula for weighing the competing implications of different principles. Wisdom and prayer—and then humility about one's conclusions—are essential.

Violence, the State, and Pacifist Political Engagement

The majority of Christians today stand within the just-war tradition. For them, the fact that the state uses lethal violence poses no problems for their political engagement. But a substantial minority of Christians believe that Jesus taught his followers never to kill. We need to ask whether political engagement is even a legitimate activity for this minority.

Must the state use lethal violence? Is it appropriate for pacifists who believe that killing persons is always wrong to engage in politics, or does their rejection of all killing remove all rational foundation for political engagement by pacifists? This chapter and book is not the place for a detailed discussion of all the crucial questions related to these questions, but it is appropriate to sketch briefly the kind of response a pacifist could make to these questions.

The first step, of course, would be to argue that Jesus taught that his disciples should never kill persons. Elsewhere, I and many others have marshaled the evidence for that much-contested conclusion.[31]

The next step would be to ask whether, since Jesus calls his disciples never to kill, God nevertheless wants the state to use lethal violence. Some pacifists say yes, concluding that Christians are not to participate in the state's lethal violence.[32] But such a position leads to the strange conclusion that, since God wants the state to kill but says Christians should not, God does not want everyone in a state to become Christians, because then there would be no one to do the killing God wants the state to do.

The alternative is to argue first, on exegetical grounds, that although God clearly *uses* lethal violence to restrain evil, God does not *will* that anyone should use it. Second, one would also need to argue that it would be possible for the state to use nonlethal coercion to restrain evil.

Many Christians think Romans 13 indicates that God wants the state to use lethal violence. In Romans 13:4, Paul says government uses the sword as a servant of God to "execute wrath on the wrongdoer" (NRSV). Obviously God uses lethal actions by government to punish evil and protect good, but not even this passage requires the interpretation that God *wants* government to punish evil and protect good through killing. In the Old Testament, God clearly used pagan empires to punish Israel and Judah for their sin. Isaiah describes the way God used pagan Assyria as "the rod of my anger" to punish godless Israel (Isa. 10:5), but that does not mean God approved of the vicious ways that Assyria wreaked havoc. In fact, the very text that describes Assyria as God's rod to punish unfaithful Israel sharply condemns Assyria's proud arrogance and destruction of many nations (Isa. 10:5–19). Isaiah 45:1 calls Cyrus (a pagan) God's "anointed one," because God used Cyrus to accomplish a divine purpose. But again, that does not mean God approved all of Cyrus's methods.[33] God did use Cyrus to accomplish his will for his chosen people, but that does not mean God wanted Cyrus's armies to rampage through other nations, killing and destroying. God used both Assyria and Cyrus but did not command or will their evil actions.

It is a historical fact that, almost without exception, no state has tried to govern without lethal violence. Many conclude that it is impossible. On the other hand, modern history demonstrates that a willingness to defy governmental power nonviolently and endure suffering for an alternative vision can have enormous political impact. Not just Gandhi and King, but also the vast crowds defying Marcos's dictatorship in the Philippines and communist totalitarianism in Poland and East Germany have won stunning victories. As Yoder says, "That suffering is powerful and that weakness wins is true not only in heaven but on earth."[34]

Many pacifists would argue that it is always God's will that human beings use nonviolent rather than lethally violent methods to restrain evil. No society has ever tried it consistently over a long period of time, so it is impossible to point to historical evidence, but pacifists would argue that if whole societies would abandon the sword, the result would be less killing than we now experience. Algeria used lethal violence in its ten-year campaign for independence, and one of every ten Algerians died. Gandhi's India used nonviolence in its own struggle for independence, and only one in four hundred thousand Indians died in the struggle.[35] Sin and murder would not disappear. Selfishness would persist. But human sinfulness does not need to take the form of dueling and slavery; maybe it need not take the form of killing by the state.

Obviously, if any society truly chose nonviolence, it would suffer. Outsiders would take advantage. The nonviolent society would have to share its goods, respond to evil with love, and forgive attackers. Many thousands, perhaps millions, would die. But just-war theorists consider World War II a great success even though tens of millions died. Not until whole societies dare to live out Jesus's call to love even enemies will we have substantial empirical evidence for or against the claim that the way of nonviolence would actually result in less killing than the way of war.

Could nonlethal tactics and weapons (e.g., stun guns that shoot an electric charge that temporarily disables an attacker) replace police revolvers as the courts have replaced lethal duels? This is not the place to try to develop a detailed answer, but there are serious thinkers today who advance this view.[36]

The third step is to ask, since all contemporary states do use lethal violence, whether pacifists in such states have any rational basis for political engagement. Is it theoretically and morally consistent for a pacifist to work to establish "good" laws when he or she knows that the power of lethal violence stands in the background as the ultimate enforcer of obedience to these laws? I think the answer is clearly yes.

First, a vast amount of political activity and debate does not deal directly with the issue of lethal violence.[37] A great deal of what contemporary states do consists of coordinating and organizing nonviolent communal activity to promote the common good.[38] The state provides health insurance, education, roads, Social Security, and assistance to the poor and needy. Pacifists can participate fully in political debates about the wisdom of such policies, and even partner with state agencies funding private organizations to carry out social programs approved by legislatures, without in any way violating their opposition to all killing.

It is true that behind every law and collection of taxes to fund social programs stands an implicit threat to use lethal violence, but pacifists can argue that the state should not and need not *use* lethal violence. In fact, in day-to-day practice, these types of state programs involve no use of lethal violence. Furthermore, pacifists do not give moral approval to the implicit threat of lethal violence merely by endorsing and participating in good social programs that operate day to day in completely nonviolent ways.

Second, pacifists can and do use a wide variety of nonviolent forms of power to shape the political process. It is empirically false to claim that the gun is the only source of power.[39] In our complex world, there are many sources of power that shape politics: truth; ideas; well-argued viewpoints; persuasive dialogue; education; economic decisions (including boycotts); and local, national, and global nongovernmental advocacy groups. Political scientist Karl Deutsch underlines the importance of people power; simply by accepting or refusing to cooperate with government, the masses wield enormous nonviolent power. "The voluntary or habitual compliance of the mass of the population is the invisible but very real basis of the power of every government," Deutsch argues.[40]

Third, it is entirely consistent for a pacifist who rejects all killing to conduct political debate within the framework of a traditional just-war framework, challenging non-pacifists to live up to their own just-war norms, including criteria like "last resort." For example, running a detailed argument that a proposed military invasion of a dangerous neighboring country is unwarranted, because the just-war tradition demands that war must be a last resort and all viable nonviolent alternatives have not yet been tried, is entirely consistent with opposing all war. The same is true of arguing that less expenditure on arms and more on economic development would be in the long-term interest of one's nation. Seeking to shape public opinion on such issues and lobbying elected officials, using arguments that fit within a just-war framework, are quite consistent actions for people who believe Jesus taught his followers not to kill.

The same is true of voting for the lesser evil among two or more candidates for office. Voting for, and otherwise promoting the election of, a specific politician in no way means accepting or endorsing all of that person's ideas and actions. It only means that one thinks that politician's platform and likely activities will be a little less destructive than those of other candidates.

Virtually all governments and political leaders claim to do good and act for the well-being of their people and the world. Without accepting every part of their vision of justice, or their means of achieving it, pacifists can challenge governments and politicians to live up to the good within the ideals they themselves claim to embrace.

It is true that a pacifist would probably not be elected to any major office, since honesty would demand that such a person tell voters that he or she opposes all use of lethal violence. But the fact that a person running on such a platform would hardly ever be elected does not mean that pacifists cannot be consistently engaged in political activity and debate using arguments grounded in premises that the majority share—even when one does not embrace those premises. Pacifists—who think that although states regularly do use lethal violence, they should not—nonetheless have a perfectly consistent framework for political engagement in our present context. They can work to persuade public opinion and elected politicians to try more nonviolent alternatives, both by arguing that the just-war framework demands nonviolence whenever possible, and also by articulating the much more radical claim that killing is always wrong. And, as we have seen already, in the majority of political discussions the explicit issue of lethal violence is not even on the agenda.

Conclusion

The state is a gift from God, not an invention of Satan. It is not the only (or even the most important) institution in society, but it is a crucial element of a good society. Since persons are communal beings created in the image of the Trinity, we naturally create a variety of different structural institutions. Consequently, we need an institution that organizes right relationships among persons and all the other institutions in society. The state rightly promotes the common good, especially for the poor and marginalized. Unfortunately, because of the fall, the state must also devote great effort to restraining evil.

Even as Christians embrace the state as a good gift from God, we must also insist on its limited role. The state dare not usurp the tasks of other institutions in society. Knowing that unchecked power regularly produces abuse, we must erect and maintain careful limits to the power of the state.

Christians must also develop clear guidelines for what the state should legislate and what it should not. Not all that the Bible condemns should become a criminal offense punished by the state. Nor dare we expect utopia from the state; it can only produce limited goods.

These limited goods are significant, however, and God has given the state authority to promote them. All Christians—whether in the pacifist or just-war tradition—should recognize their civic responsibilities to love their neighbor and promote the common good through wise political engagement that nurtures justice through the state.

5

Justice

Justice is easier to demand than to define.[1] Since the time of Aristotle, political thinkers have agreed that justice exists when persons receive what is due them. Persons, of course, live in groups and institutions, and something is also owed these different societal institutions. Therefore evangelical philosopher Nicholas Wolterstorff says, "Justice is present among persons, groups and institutions when their right, their legitimate claims, are honored."[2] That can happen only when persons and groups fulfill their responsibilities to give persons and institutions their due.[3]

What is the ultimate foundation of the obligation to give persons and institutions their due? For most of Western history, the nearly universal answer was: God and the order he embedded in nature. God, who is just, commands persons to be just. "Endow the king with *your* justice, O God. . . . May he judge your people in righteousness, your afflicted ones with justice" (Ps. 72:1–2, italics mine). Human laws, which spell out in detail what justice means, are just to the extent that they reflect divine law and justice.

In practice, of course, human laws are at best a very inadequate reflection of universal justice grounded in God. But the fact that human laws will never attain divine perfection in no way invalidates the claim that human attempts at just laws *ought* to be grounded in the divine standard of justice. An analogy of Brunner's is helpful here: No human being has ever actually drawn a perfectly straight line. But the concept of a straight line stands as a criterion measuring the inadequacy of all actual, somewhat imperfect, efforts to draw a straight line. It provides the ideal to nurture greater approximation of a perfectly straight line.[4] We know that human laws are ultimately grounded in divine justice and that we ought to seek constantly to make actual human laws and government actions a better reflection of divine justice. That knowledge provides a crucial foundation, a standard, and a motivation for our painfully slow groping toward justice. A striking passage about King Jehoshaphat's appointment of judges in Judah illustrates this point:

> He told them, "Consider carefully what you do, because you are not judging for mere mortals but for the LORD, who is with you whenever you give a verdict. Now let the fear of the LORD be on you. Judge carefully, for with the LORD our God there is no injustice or partiality or bribery."[5]

In the last two centuries, however, modern thinkers have rejected the notion of a divine standard of justice underlying actual laws. Instead, they have argued that human laws are merely human products designed by the powerful for their own self-interest. The result of this legal positivism, Emil Brunner has argued persuasively, is modern totalitarianism: "If there is no divine standard of justice, there is no criterion for the legal system set up by the state. If there is no justice transcending the state, then the state can declare anything it likes to be law. . . . The totalitarian state is the inevitable result."[6]

From the biblical perspective, God is clearly the ultimate foundation for justice. Numerous biblical texts say that God loves and does justice. "I, the LORD, love justice," God declares in Isaiah 61:8 (cf. also Pss. 37:28; 103:6). Persons made in God's image are called to reflect God's justice in their actions: "[God] executes justice for the fatherless and the widow, and loves the sojourner, giving him food and clothing. Love the sojourner therefore" (Deut. 10:18–19 ESV). Furthermore, because we must respect the image of God in other persons, we must give them what is their due.

But what is due to persons and institutions? The most basic theological answer is: the order of creation established by God. "The rights of man are rights which, so to speak, God gives men at their birth. The rights of communities are rights which go back to a definite relationship between men based on the order of creation—for instance that of man and woman in marriage. In the last resort all justice means these constants of creation as a basis on which every human being receives his due."[7]

But we need more specificity. We need more detailed guidance to spell out what is due persons and institutions. Political thinkers have often done this by talking about commutative justice, procedural justice, and distributive justice.

Commutative justice "requires fairness in agreements and exchanges between private parties."[8] Proverbs 16:11 declares: "Harvest scales and balances belong to the Lord; all the weights in the bag are of his making." Leviticus 19:35–36 is equally clear: "Do not use dishonest standards when measuring length, weight or quantity. Use honest scales and honest weights. . . . I am the Lord your God."[9] Weights and measures should be the same for everyone.

Procedural justice defines the procedures and processes that must be fair if justice is to prevail. Procedural justice requires such things as a transparent legal framework; unbiased courts; the rule of law; freedom of speech, assembly, and the vote; and honest elections. Some of these things are explicitly spelled out in the Bible. Others emerged over the centuries as believers applied basic biblical principles to the increasingly complex societies in which they lived.

Again and again, biblical texts demand fair courts. "Do not deny justice to your poor people in their lawsuits. . . . Do not accept a bribe" (Exod. 23:6, 8; cf. also Deut. 1:16–17; 16:18–20; Amos 5:10–15).

Slowly, the rule of law emerged as people applied the principle that since the law comes finally from God, not the king, even the rulers must submit to the law. Slowly, too, we realized that the basic dignity and freedom placed in every person by the Creator demands not just freedom of worship, but also freedom of speech, freedom to develop organizations independent of government, and freedom to vote for the government of one's choice. None of these were instantly clear or easily achievable. But over time, and at the price of costly struggle, we have come to see that these and other aspects of procedural justice flow from the application of biblical principles to the human task of organizing society with justice.

Distributive justice refers to how the numerous goods of society are divided. What is a just division of money, health care, educational opportunities—in short, all the goods and services in society? Who owes what of all these things to persons and institutions? What role if any does the state have in guaranteeing that there is a "fair distribution" of these goods? Is it enough for the state to ensure fair procedures (unbiased courts), or should the state seek to promote "fair outcomes"?

Obviously, if society (whether families, businesses, or the state) is to distribute goods and services fairly, we need criteria to define what is owed to each. Over the centuries, various criteria have been used: need, contribution, effort, ability, the market value of supply and demand, equality, and utilitarian judgment about what serves the public interest.[10] Merit, equality, and need have been the most common.[11] Distribution based on merit would allocate social goods on the basis of the person's merit (whether work effort, skillful productivity, or aristocratic worth). Distribution based on equality would allocate social goods on the basis of either equal outcomes (communism, at least in theory) or equal access (e.g., John Rawls). Distribution based on need would allocate goods largely on the basis of deficiency of basic things on the part of specific persons and groups and would pay special attention to correcting past injustice.

No one of these criteria is adequate by itself or applicable in every situation. We rightly distribute grades for an academic exam on the basis of the excellence or lack of excellence of each student's exam. (The principle is merit.) We properly distribute the right to vote (one person, one vote) on the basis of strict equality, not merit or need. And we should distribute access to adequate food on the basis of need, not the intellectual or even moral merit of the individuals involved, and certainly not on the basis of some principle of absolute equality that demands equal grams of food for each person regardless of size, age, and hunger.[12]

One of the most vigorous debates of the last century has been about whether justice exists if the procedures are fair, regardless of the resulting distribution of social goods or whether justice requires some "fair outcome." Political philosophers like Robert Nozick, particularly concerned with advocating a very limited state, argue for the former. According to Nozick, justice is whatever emerges from a just situation by just steps.[13] If the procedures are fair, the outcome is just. Some evangelicals have agreed with Nozick.[14]

Other evangelicals, however, have argued that justice requires at least some attention to "just outcomes" so that everyone enjoys, or at least has genuine access to, what is needed to experience a certain level of physical and social well-being. Mainline Protestants, Roman Catholics, and many evangelicals insist on this understanding of distributive justice.[15]

To search for answers to these questions about the nature of distributive justice, I want to examine the biblical material in several different ways: first, a discussion of aspects of the biblical story; second, a study of the key Hebrew words for justice and righteousness; third, the dynamic, restorative character of biblical justice; fourth, biblical teaching about God's concern for the poor; fifth, the emphasis on restoration to community; sixth, access to productive resources; and seventh, care for those who cannot care for themselves.

The Biblical Story

The biblical story tells us that the most important truth about human beings is that the Creator shaped us with the longing to find our ultimate fulfillment in right relationship with God. God also gave each person the freedom to embrace or refuse the divine invitation to fellowship. That means that the single most important thing that all human institutions, including the state, owe to persons is religious freedom, the space to respond freely to God's call.

The biblical story tells us that God gives every person the mandate to exercise faithful stewardship over the rest of the created order, using creation's abundant resources to shape art, music, culture, and civilization. Since this creation mandate falls on every person, society owes each person a share in the available resources and the space and freedom to exercise this divine mandate. Justice demands that every person have the opportunity to fulfill the creation mandate.

The biblical story also tells us that persons are body-soul unities. Made from "dust of the ground" (Gen. 2:7), we are solidly material, designed in our very essence as a part of the physical world and therefore unable to be what the Creator intended without a generous sufficiency of material things. Justice therefore demands that every person has the opportunity—within the limits of every particular historical setting—to enjoy a generous sufficiency of material necessities.

Furthermore, the biblical story also holds together the inestimable worth of each individual person and the communal nature of human beings. Both the radical individualism of contemporary Western liberal democracies and the totalitarian communalism of twentieth-century fascist and communist societies are one-sided perversions of a profound biblical balance. Justice, from a biblical perspective, must pay equal attention to the rights of individuals and the common good of all. Political and economic systems dare not either sacrifice individuals and personal freedom on the altar of some abstract common good or absolutize individual freedom of choice without regard to its impact on the well-being of everyone.

Even this very brief exploration of key aspects of the biblical story shows how it provides clues to a normative Christian understanding of justice. We can obtain further important help from a careful analysis of the Hebrew words for justice and righteousness.

The Hebrew Words for Justice and Righteousness

The two key Hebrew words for justice and righteousness are *mishpat* and *tsedaqah*, which very often appear together in Hebrew parallelism. Amos 5:24 is typical: "Let justice [*mishpat*] roll down like waters, and righteousness [*tsedaqah*] like an ever-flowing stream" (NRSV).

The noun *mishpat*[16] appears 422 times in the Old Testament, and it comes from the verb *shapat*, which means to govern and judge. Since Israelite society did not separate legislative, judicial, and executive aspects of governing, the noun *mishpat* can mean the act of deciding a case in court (Deut. 25:1), the actual judicial decision (1 Kings 20:40), or a legal ordinance and case law (the laws of Exodus 21–23 are simply called the *mishpatim*). If one wants to use just one English word, probably the best translation is "justice."

Tsedaqah (feminine) appears 157 times and *tsedeq* (masculine) appears 119 times in the Old Testament.[17] The basic connotation refers to that which is "straight" or matches the norm. *Tsedaqah* often means norm or standard—that is, the way things ought to be. There can be a bad law (*mishpat*) but not bad *tsedaqah*. *Tsedaqah* provides the standard for measuring specific laws because it defines the way things should be. The English word *righteousness* is a possible translation if one does not limit the word to personal relations and inner attitudes. *Tsedaqah* regularly appears with *mishpat* in Hebrew parallelism and includes the meaning of justice as the standard, or the way things should be. Thus, it is used to refer to accurate weights and measures (Lev. 19:36; Deut. 25:15) and straight paths (Ps. 23:3).

The first thing to underline about these two words is their theocentric foundation. The righteous and just God who commands his people to imitate his justice is the source and foundation of human justice. "God is a righteous judge" (Ps. 7:11) who gives divine justice to human rulers: "Give the king *your* justice [*mishpat*], O God, and *your* righteousness [*tsedaqah*] to a king's son" (Ps. 72:1 NRSV, emphasis added). Human justice must imitate God's justice (Deut. 10:17–19; also 1:17).

That procedural justice (e.g., fair courts) is central to the meaning of these key biblical words is clear in many texts. "You shall not render an unjust judgment; you shall not be partial to the poor or defer to the great: with justice [*mishpat*], you shall judge your neighbor" (Lev. 19:15 NRSV; Deut. 1:17; 10:17–19). In a long string of verses, Exodus 23 demands fair courts: "You shall not side with the majority so as to pervert justice" (v. 2 NRSV); you shall refuse bribes (v. 8); "You shall not pervert the justice [*mishpat*] due to your poor in their lawsuits" (v. 6 NRSV); "nor shall you be partial to the poor in a lawsuit" (v. 3 NRSV). Again and again the prophets pronounced divine judgment, exile and national destruction, on Israel and Judah because of their unfair courts (Amos 5:10–15). Since there is virtually universal agreement on the importance of procedural justice, we need not spend more time on it here.

These two words (*mishpat* and *tsedaqah*), however, refer to more than procedural justice in the courts. They are also the words the prophets use to call for economic justice—a point less widely understood by evangelicals and therefore needing much more attention. Immediately after denouncing Israel and Judah as an unfaithful vineyard where God sought in vain for *mishpat* and *tsedaqah* (Isa. 5:7), Isaiah goes on to denounce his society's economic injustice: "Ah, you who join house to house, who add field to field, until there is room for no one but you, and you are left to live alone in the midst of the land! The LORD of hosts has sworn in my hearing: Surely many houses shall be desolate, large and beautiful houses, without inhabitant" (vv. 8–9 NRSV; also Amos 5:11–12). Micah similarly condemned the rich and powerful who "covet fields and seize them; houses and take them away; they oppress householder and house, people and their inheritance" (Mic. 2:2 NRSV) instead of providing the justice (*mishpat*) God longs for (Mic. 6:8).

The eighth century BC prophets lived at the end of a time when the monarchies of Israel and Judah had, over the preceding two centuries, centralized land ownership in the hands of a small, powerful elite. The earlier arrangement of decentralized land ownership under the judges where every family enjoyed their own ancestral land had increasingly disappeared. Modern archaeologists have discovered that in the tenth century, houses seem to have been similar in size, but by the eighth century, there were large houses in one area and tiny houses in another.[18] This reflects the reality that the prophets denounced.

Many people had lost their land and become poor because of the oppression of the powerful.

Sometimes the oppression happened through raw royal power—witness Jezebel's seizure of Naboth's ancestral land (1 Kings 21). Sometimes it happened through unjust laws: "Ah, you who make iniquitous decrees, who write oppressive statutes, to turn aside the needy from justice [*mishpat*] and to rob the poor of my people of their right" (Isa. 10:1–2 NRSV). Sometimes it happened through disobedience to laws designed to protect the poor—Exodus 23:26–27 explicitly prohibited keeping a poor person's garment overnight as collateral, but the powerful of Amos's day did precisely that and then spread these garments out to kneel on when they went to worship (Amos 2:8)! And sometimes it happened as the powerful abused the judicial system (Amos 5:10).

According to the prophets, God became so angry at Israel's and Judah's corrupt courts and unfair economic practices (as well as their idolatry) that he destroyed first Israel and then Judah, allowing foreign invaders to devastate both nations. But the prophets' final word was not destruction and despair. They looked beyond the foreign captivity to a new day, a messianic time, when *mishpat* and *tsedaqah* would be restored (Isa. 1:26–27; 16:4b–5; 32:16–17). The messianic passages of Isaiah 9 and 11 promise that the Messiah will bring righteousness and justice for all (9:7). Concerning the shoot from the stump of Jesse, the prophet declared that "with righteousness [*tsedeq*] he shall judge [*shapat*] the poor" (11:4 NRSV). In that day, Micah declared, "they shall all sit under their own vines and under their own fig trees, and no one shall make them afraid" (Mic. 4:4 NRSV). Economic justice would be restored and each family would again have its own land.

In the glorious vision of messianic restoration in Ezekiel, the prophet paints a picture of an ideal, restored society with the temple at the center. The passage ends with a promise of the restoration of economic justice for the people: "My princes shall no longer oppress my people; but they shall let the house of Israel have the land according to their tribes. Thus says the LORD God: Enough, O princes of Israel! Put away violence and oppression, and do what is just [*mishpat*] and right [*tsedaqah*]. Cease your evictions of my people, says the LORD God" (Ezek. 45:8–9 NRSV). When the rulers did *mishpat*, the people who had lost their property through violence and oppression again enjoyed their own land. Active promotion of economic justice is clearly a central component of the prophets' understanding of *mishpat* and *tsedaqah*.

Clearly the Old Testament words for justice and righteousness indicate that, from a biblical perspective, justice is both procedural and distributive. Three other aspects of biblical teaching strengthen this argument.[19]

Justice's dynamic and restorative character. In the Bible, justice is not a mere *mitigation* of suffering in oppression; it is a *deliverance*. Justice demands that we correct the gross social inequities of the disadvantaged. The terms for *justice* are frequently associated with *yasha*, *yeshua*, the most important

Hebrew word for deliverance and salvation: "God arose to establish justice [*mishpat*] to save [*hoshia*] all the oppressed of the earth" (Ps. 76:9; cf. Isa. 63:1).[20] "Give justice to the weak" and "maintain the right of the lowly" are parallel to "rescue the weak and the needy; deliver them from the hand of the wicked" (Ps. 82:3–4 NRSV).[21]

Justice describes the deliverance of the people from political and economic oppressors (Judg. 5:11),[22] from slavery (1 Sam. 12:7–8; Mic. 6:4), and from captivity (Isa. 41:1–11 [cf. v. 2 for *tsedeq*]; Jer. 51:10). Providing for the needy means ending their oppression, setting them back on their feet, giving them a home, and leading them to prosperity and restoration (Ps. 10:15–18; 68:5–10).[23] Justice does not merely help victims cope with oppression; it removes it. Because of this dynamic, restorative emphasis, distributive justice requires not primarily that we maintain a stable society, but rather that we advance the well-being of the disadvantaged.

God's special concern for the poor. Hundreds of biblical verses show that God is especially attentive to the poor and needy.[24] God is not biased. Because of unequal needs, however, equal provision of basic rights requires justice to be partial in order to be impartial. (Good firefighters do not spend equal time at every house; they are "partial" to people with fires.) Partiality to the weak is the most striking characteristic of biblical justice.[25] In the raging social struggles in which the poor are perennially victims of injustice, God and God's people take up the cause of the weak.[26] Rulers and leaders have a special obligation to do justice for the weak and powerless.[27] This partiality to the poor provides strong evidence that in biblical thought, justice is concerned with more than fair procedure.

The Scriptures speak of God's special concern for the poor in at least four different ways.[28]

1. Repeatedly, the Bible says that God works to lift up the poor and oppressed. Consider the exodus. Again and again the texts say God intervened because he hated the oppression of the poor Israelites (Exod. 3:7–8; 6:5–7; Deut. 26:6–8). Or consider the psalm: "I know that the LORD maintains the cause of the needy, and executes justice for the poor" (140:12 NRSV; cf. 12:5). God acts in history to lift up the poor and oppressed.

2. Sometimes the Lord of history tears down rich and powerful people. Mary's song is shocking: "My soul glorifies the Lord. . . . He has filled the hungry with good things but has sent the rich away empty" (Luke 1:46, 53). James is even more blunt: "Now listen, you rich people, weep and wail because of the misery that is coming on you" (James 5:1).

Since God calls us to create wealth and is not biased against the rich, why do the Scriptures warn again and again that God sometimes works in history to destroy the rich? The Bible has a simple answer: because the rich sometimes get rich by oppressing the poor. Or because they often have plenty and neglect the needy. In either case, God is furious.

James warned the rich so harshly because they had hoarded wealth and refused to pay their workers (5:2–6). Repeatedly, the prophets said the same thing (Ps. 10; Isa. 3:14–25; Jer. 22:13–19). "Among my people are wicked men who lie in wait like men who snare birds and like those who set traps to catch men. Like cages full of birds, their houses are full of deceit; they have become rich and powerful and have grown fat and sleek. . . . They do not defend the rights of the poor. Should I not punish them for this?" (Jer. 5:26–29 NIV 1984).

Repeatedly, the prophets warned that God was so outraged that he would destroy the nations of Israel and Judah. Because of the way they "trample on the heads of the poor . . . and deny justice to the oppressed" (Amos 2:7), Amos predicted terrible captivity (5:11; 6:4, 7; 7:11, 17). So did Isaiah and Micah (Isa. 10:1–3; Mic. 2:2; 3:12), and it happened just as they foretold. According to both the Old and New Testaments, God destroys people and societies that get rich by oppressing the poor.

But what if we work hard and create wealth in just ways? That is good—as long as we do not forget to share. No matter how justly we have acquired our wealth, God demands that we act generously toward the poor. When we do not, God treats us in a similar way to those who oppress the poor. There is not a hint in Jesus's story of the rich man and Lazarus that the rich man exploited Lazarus to acquire wealth. He simply neglected to share. So God punished him (Luke 16:19–31).

Ezekiel's striking explanation for the destruction of Sodom reveals the same point: "Now this was the sin of your sister Sodom: She and her daughters were arrogant, overfed and unconcerned; they did not help the poor and needy. . . . Therefore I did away with them" (16:49–50). Again, the text does not charge them with gaining wealth by oppression. They simply refused to share.

The Bible is clear. If we get rich by oppressing the poor or if we have wealth and do not reach out generously to the needy, the Lord of history moves against us. God judges societies by what they do to the people at the bottom.

3. God identifies with the poor so strongly that caring for them is almost like helping God. "Those who are kind to the poor lend to the LORD" (Prov. 19:17). On the other hand, "whoever oppress the poor shows contempt for their Maker" (14:31).

Jesus's parable of the sheep and goats is the ultimate commentary on these two proverbs. Jesus surprises those on the right with his insistence that they had fed and clothed him when he was cold and hungry. When they protest that they cannot remember ever doing that, Jesus replies, "Whatever you did for one of the least of these brothers of mine, you did for me" (Matt. 25:40 NIV 1984). If we believe his words, we look on the poor and neglected with entirely new eyes.

4. Finally, God demands that his people share God's special concern for the poor. God commanded Israel not to treat widows, orphans, and foreigners the way the Egyptians had treated them (Exod. 22:21–24). Instead, they should

love the poor just as God cared for them at the exodus (Exod. 22:21–24; Deut. 15:13–15). When Jesus's disciples throw parties, they should especially invite the poor and disabled (Luke 14:12–14; Heb. 13:1–3). Paul held up Jesus's model of becoming poor to show how generously the Corinthians should contribute to the poor in Jerusalem (2 Cor. 8:9).

The Bible, however, goes one dramatic step further. God insists that if we do not imitate God's concern for the poor, we are not really God's people—no matter how frequent our worship or how orthodox our creeds. Because Israel failed to correct oppression and defend poor widows, Isaiah insisted that Israel was really the pagan people of Gomorrah (Isa. 1:10–17). God despised their fasting because they tried to worship God and oppress their workers at the same time (58:3–7). Through Amos, the Lord shouted in fury that the very religious festivals God had ordained made God angry and sick. Why? Because the rich and powerful were mixing worship and oppression of the poor (Amos 5:21–24). Jesus was even harsher. At the last judgment, some who expect to enter heaven will learn that their failure to feed the hungry condemns them to hell (Matt. 25:41–43). If we do not care for the needy brother or sister, God's love does not abide in us (1 John 3:17).

Jeremiah 22:13–19 describes good King Josiah and his wicked son Jehoiakim. When Jehoiakim became king, he built a fabulous palace by oppressing his workers. God sent the prophet Jeremiah to announce a terrible punishment. The most interesting part of the passage, however, is a short aside on this evil king's good father: "'He defended the cause of the poor and needy, and so all went well. *Is that not what it means to know me?*' declares the LORD" (v. 16, emphasis mine). Knowing God is *inseparable* from caring for the poor. Of course, we dare not reduce knowing God only to a concern for the needy, as some radical theologians do. We meet God in prayer, Bible study, worship—in many ways, but if we do not share God's passion to strengthen the poor, we simply do not know God in a biblical way.

All this biblical material clearly demonstrates that God and God's faithful people have a great concern for the poor. Earlier, I argued that God is partial to the poor, but not biased. God does not love the poor any more than the rich. God has an equal concern for the well-being of every single person. Most rich and powerful people, however, are genuinely biased; they care a lot more about themselves than about their poor neighbors. By contrast with the genuine bias of most people, God's lack of bias makes God appear biased. God cares equally for everyone.

How then is God "partial" to the poor? In concrete historical situations, equal concern for everyone requires special attention to specific people. In a family, loving parents do not provide equal tutorial time to a son struggling hard to scrape by with Ds and a daughter easily making As. Precisely in order to be "impartial" and love both equally, they devote extra time to helping the needier child. In historical situations (e.g., apartheid) when some people oppress others, God's lack of bias does not mean neutrality. Precisely because God loves all equally, God works against oppressors and actively sides with the oppressed—to liberate both!

We see this connection in the texts that declare God's lack of bias: "For the LORD your God is God of gods and Lord of lords, the great, the mighty, and the awesome God, who is not partial and takes no bribe. He executes justice for the fatherless and the widow, and loves the sojourner, giving him food and clothing" (Deut. 10:17–18 ESV). Justice and love are virtual synonyms in this passage. There is no suggestion that loving the sojourner is a benevolent, voluntary act different from a legal demand to do justice to the fatherless. Furthermore, there is no indication in the text that those needing food and clothing are poor because of some violation of due process such as fraud or robbery; the text simply says they are poor, and therefore God, who is not biased, pays special attention to them.

Leviticus 19 is similar. In verse 15, the text condemns partiality: "You shall not be partial to the poor or defer to the great" (ESV). The preceding verses refer to several of the Ten Commandments (stealing, lying, and blasphemy [v. 11]). But special references to the poor are in the same passage. When harvesting their crops, God's people must leave the grain at the edge of the field and not pick up the grapes that fall in the vineyard: "You shall leave them for the poor and the alien" (v. 10 NRSV). This is a divine command, not a suggestion for voluntary charity, and it is part of the same passage that declares God's lack of bias.[29]

Precisely because God is not biased, God pays special attention to the poor. Consequently, an understanding of justice that reflects this biblical teaching must be concerned with more than procedural justice. Distributive justice, which insists on special attention to the poor so they have the opportunity to enjoy material well-being, is also crucial.

Justice as restoration to community.[30] Restoration to community—and to the benefit rights necessary for dignified participation in community—is also an important part of what the Bible means by justice. Since persons are created for community, the Scriptures understand the good life as sharing in the essential aspects of social life. Justice includes helping people return to the kind of life in community that God intends for them. This is especially clear in Leviticus 25, which talks about how poor people who lose their land receive it back in the year of jubilee. Leviticus describes the poor as being on the verge of falling out of the community because of their economic distress. "If members of your community become poor in that their power slips *with you*, you shall make them strong . . . that they may live *with you*" (Lev. 25:35–36, emphasis added).[31] The word translated as *power* here is *hand* in the Hebrew. *Hand* (*yod*) metaphorically means "power." The solution is for those who are able to correct the situation, and thereby restore the poor to community, to do so. The poor, in fact, are their own flesh or kin (Isa. 58:7). Poverty is a family affair.

To restore the weak to participation in community, the community's responsibility to its diminished members is "to make them strong" again (Lev. 25:35). This translation is a literal rendering of the Hebrew, which is the word "to be strong" and is found here in the causative (*hiphil*) conjugation and therefore means "cause him to be strong." The purpose of this empowerment is "that they may live *with you*" (v. 35, emphasis added), that is, be restored to community. According to Psalm 107, God's steadfast love leads God to care for the hungry. Through his care they "establish a town to live in; they sow fields and plant vineyards. . . . By his blessing they multiply greatly" (vv. 36–38 NRSV). God acts to enable the poor to develop productive fields and establish a town. As a result, the hungry can again be active, participating members of a community. The concern is for the whole person in community and what it takes to maintain persons in that relationship.

Community membership means the ability to share fully within one's capacity and potential in each essential aspect of community.[32] Participation in community has multiple dimensions: it includes participation in decision making, social life, economic production, education, culture, and religion. Also essential are physical life and the material resources necessary for a decent life.

Providing the conditions for participation in community demands a focus on the basic needs for life in community. Since God created persons as bodily beings, achieving such justice includes guaranteeing proper access to the material essentials of life, such as food and shelter. It is God "who executes justice for the oppressed; who gives food to the hungry" (Ps. 146:7 NRSV); "who executes justice for the orphan and the widow, and who loves the strangers, providing them with food and clothing" (Deut. 10:18 NRSV). "Food and clothing" is a Hebraism for what is indispensable.[33]

Job 24, one of the most powerful pictures of poverty in the Bible, describes the economic benefits that injustice takes away. Injustice starts with assault on a person's land, the basis of economic power (v. 2). It moves then to secondary means of production, the donkey and the ox (v. 3). As a result, the victims experience powerlessness and indignity: "They thrust the needy off the road; the poor of the earth all hide themselves" (v. 4 NRSV). The poor are separated from the bonds of community, wandering like wild donkeys in the desert (v. 5). They are denied basic needs of food (vv. 6, 10), drink (v. 11), clothing, and shelter (vv. 7, 10). Elsewhere in Job, failure to provide food and clothing for the needy is condemned as injustice (22:7; 31:19).[34] Opportunity for everyone to have proper access to the material resources necessary for life in community is basic to the biblical concept of justice.

As we shall see at greater length in the following section, enjoying the socioeconomic benefits crucial to participation in community goes well beyond "welfare" or "charity." People in distress are to be empowered at the point where their participation in community has been undercut. That means restoring their productive capability. Therefore restoration of the land, the basic productive resource, is the way that Leviticus 25 commands the people to fulfill the call to "make them strong again" so "they may live with you" in the land (v. 35). As the poor return to their land, they receive a new power and dignity that restores their participation in the community.

Other provisions in the law also provide access to the means of economic well-being.[35] In the sabbatical years, the lands remain fallow and unharvested so that "the poor of your people may eat" (Exod. 23:11 NRSV). Similarly, the farmer was not to go back over the first run of harvesting or to harvest to the very corners of the field so that the poor could provide for themselves (Lev. 19:9–10; Deut. 24:19–22).

There are also restrictions on the processes that tear people down so that their "power slips" and they cannot support themselves. Interest on loans was prohibited; food to the poor was not to be provided at profit (Lev. 25:36ff.). A means of production, like a millstone for grinding grain, was not to be taken as collateral on a loan because that would be "taking a life in pledge" (Deut. 24:6 NRSV). If a poor person gave an essential item of clothing as a pledge, the creditor had to return it before night came (Exod. 22:26). All these provisions are restrictions on individual economic freedom that go well beyond merely preventing fraud, theft, and violence. The law did, of course, support the rights of owners to benefit from their property, but the law placed limits on the owners' control of property, and on the quest for profit. The common good of the community outweighed unrestricted economic freedom.

The fact that justice in the Scriptures includes socioeconomic benefits means that we must reject the notion that biblical justice is merely procedural, merely the protection of property, person, and equal access to the procedures of the community. That is by no means to deny that procedural justice is important. A person who is denied these protections is cut off from the political and civil community. Such a person is not only open to abuse but is diminished in his or her ability to affect the life of the community. Procedural justice is absolutely essential to protect people from fraud, theft, and violence.

Biblical justice, however, also includes socioeconomic benefits, which are the responsibility of the community to guarantee. (*Who* in the community has an obligation to guarantee these benefits is a separate question to be discussed in the chapter on human rights.) Biblical justice has both an economic and a legal focus. The goal of justice is not only the recovery of the integrity of the legal system; it is also the restoration of the community as a place where all live together in wholeness.

The wrong to which justice responds is not merely an illegitimate process (like stealing). What is wrong is also an end result in which people are deprived of basic needs. Leviticus 19:13 condemns both stealing *and* withholding a poor person's salary for a day. Isaiah 5:8–10 condemns those who buy up field after field until only the rich person is left dwelling alone in his big, beautiful house. Significantly, however, the prophet here does not denounce the acquisition of the land as illegal. Through legal foreclosing of mortgages or through debt bondage, powerful people could seize poor persons' property legally.[36] Isaiah nevertheless condemns the rulers for permitting this injustice to the weak. He appeals to social justice above the technicalities of current law. Restoration to community is central to justice.

From the biblical perspective, justice demands more than fair procedures: It demands both fair courts and fair economic structures. It includes both freedom rights and benefit rights. Precisely because of its equal concern for wholeness for everyone, it pays special attention to the needs of the weak and marginalized.

The Content of Distributive Justice

None of the above claims, however, offer a norm that describes the actual content of distributive justice. The next two sections seek to develop such a norm. I will argue that, from a biblical perspective, distributive justice demands adequate access to productive resources for those able to earn their own way and a generous sufficiency for those who are too old, too disabled, or otherwise unable to work to earn a living.

Justice as adequate access to productive resources. Equality has been one of the most powerful slogans of the twentieth century—and one of the most popular definitions of distributive justice. But what does it mean? Does it mean equality before the law? One person, one vote? Equality of opportunity in education? Identical income shares? Or absolute identity as described in the satirical novel *Facial Equality*—where the faces of both the especially beautiful and especially ugly are "corrected" by surgery so that all faces are "equal."[37]

History shows that full equality of economic results is not compatible with human freedom and responsibility. Free choices have consequences; therefore, when immoral decisions reduce someone's earning power, we should, other things being equal, consider the result just. Even absolute equality of opportunity is impossible unless we (wrongly) prevent parents from passing on any of their knowledge or other capital to their children. So what definition of equality—or better, equity—do the biblical materials suggest?

Capital in an agricultural society. The biblical material on Israel and the land offers important clues about what a biblical understanding of equity would look like. The contrast between early Israel and surrounding societies was striking.[38] In Egypt, most of the land belonged to the pharaoh or the temples. In most other Near Eastern contexts, a feudal system of landholding prevailed; the king granted large tracts of land, worked by landless laborers, to a small number of elite royal vassals. This feudal system did not exist in early Israel, except in their relationship to Yahweh. Yahweh the King owned all the land and made important demands on those to whom he gave use of it. Under Yahweh, however, each family had their own land. Israel's ideal was decentralized family "ownership" understood as stewardship under Yahweh's absolute ownership. In the period of the judges, the pattern in Israel was free peasants on small landholdings of approximately equal size.[39]

Land was the basic capital in early Israel's agricultural economy, and the Bible says the land was divided in such a way that each extended family had the resources to produce the things needed for a decent life.

Joshua 18 and Numbers 26 contain the two most important accounts of the division of the land,[40] and represent Israel's social ideal with regard to it. Originally, the land was divided among the clans of the tribes so that a relatively similar amount of land was available to all family units. The larger tribes got a larger portion and the smaller tribes a smaller portion (Num. 26:54). In Ezekiel's vision of a future time of justice, the land is said to be divided "equally" (this could be literally translated as "each according to his brother," Ezek. 47:14).

Several institutions served the purpose of preserving a just distribution of the land over the generations. The *law of levirate* helped to prevent the land from going out of the family line (Deut. 25:5). The provision for a *kinship redeemer* meant that when poverty forced someone to sell his land, a relative was to step in to purchase it for him (Lev. 25:25).

The picture of land ownership in the time of the judges suggests some approximation of equality of land ownership—at least up to the point where every family had enough to enjoy a decent, dignified life in the community if they acted responsibly. Decentralized land ownership by extended families was the economic base for a relatively egalitarian society of small landowners and vinedressers in the time of the judges.[41] Israel's ideal called for each family to have enough land so they had the opportunity to acquire life's necessities.

"Necessities" is not to be understood as the minimum necessary to keep from starving. In the nonhierarchical, relatively egalitarian society of small farmers depicted above, families possessed resources to earn a living that would have been considered reasonable and acceptable, not embarrassingly minimal. That is not to suggest that every family had exactly the same income. It does mean, however, that every family had an equality of economic opportunity up to the point that they had the resources to earn a living that would enable them not only to meet minimal needs of food, clothing, and housing but also to be respected participants in the community.[42] Possessing their own land enabled each extended family to acquire the necessities for a decent life through responsible work.

The year of jubilee. Two astonishing biblical texts—Leviticus 25 and Deuteronomy 15—show how important this basic equality of opportunity was to God. The jubilee text in Leviticus demands that the land return to the original owners every fifty years. And Deuteronomy 15 calls for the release of debts every seven years.

Leviticus 25 is one of the most astonishing texts in all of Scripture.[43] Every fifty years, God said, the land was to return to the original owners. Physical handicaps, death of a breadwinner, or lack of natural ability may have led some families to become poorer than others. But God did not want such disadvantages to lead to ever-increasing extremes of wealth and poverty with the result that the poor eventually lacked the basic resources to earn a decent livelihood. God therefore gave his people a law to guarantee that no family would permanently lose its land. Every fifty years, the land returned to the original owners so that every family had enough productive resources to function as dignified, participating members of the community (Lev. 25:10–24). Private property was not abolished. Regularly, however, the means of producing wealth was to be "equalized"—not fully, but up to the point of every family having the resources to earn a decent living.

What is the theological basis for this startling command? Yahweh owns the land! "The land shall not be sold in perpetuity, for the land is mine. For you are strangers and sojourners with me" (Lev. 25:23 ESV).

The assumption in this text that people must suffer the consequences of wrong choices is also striking. A whole generation or more could suffer the loss of ancestral land. Every fifty years, however, the basic source of wealth would be returned so that each family had the opportunity to provide for their basic needs.

This passage prescribes justice in a way that even the most well-intentioned private philanthropy can never deliver. The year of jubilee was intended to be an institutionalized structure that affected all Israelites automatically. It was to be the poor family's right to recover their inherited land at the jubilee. Returning the land was not a charitable courtesy that the wealthy might extend if they pleased.[44]

Interestingly, the principles of jubilee challenge modern extremes of the political Left and Right. Only God is an absolute owner; no one else has absolute property rights. The right of each family to have the means to earn a living takes priority over a purchaser's "property rights." At the same time, jubilee affirms not only the right but the importance of private property managed by families (normally extended families) who understand that they are stewards responsible to God. This text does not point us in the direction of the communist model where the state owns all the land. God wants each family to own the resources to produce their own livelihood. Why? To strengthen the family (this is a very important "pro-family" text!), to give people the freedom to participate in shaping history, and to prevent the centralization of power and the oppression and totalitarianism that almost always accompany centralized ownership of land or capital by either the state or small elites.

The teaching of the prophets we explored earlier in the section on *mishpat* and *tsedaqah* underlines the principles of Leviticus 25. In the tenth to the eighth centuries BC, major centralization of landholding occurred. Poorer farmers lost their land, becoming landless laborers or slaves. The prophets regularly denounced the bribery, political assassination, and economic oppression that destroyed the earlier decentralized economy described above.

The prophets also expressed a powerful eschatological hope for a future day of justice when "they shall all sit under their own vines and under their own fig trees" (Mic. 4:4 NRSV; cf. also Zech. 3:10) and the leaders will guarantee that all people again enjoy their ancestral land (Ezek. 45:1–9).

In the giving of the land, the denunciation of oppressors who seized the land of the poor, and the vision of a new day when all will once again delight in the fruits of their own land and labor, we see a social ideal in which families are to have the economic means to earn their own way. A basic equality of economic opportunity up to the point that all can at least provide for their own basic needs through responsible work is the norm. Failure to act responsibly has economic consequences, so there is no assumption of absolute equality of outcome. Central, however, is the demand that each family have the necessary capital (land in an agricultural society) so that responsible stewardship will result in an economically decent life.[45]

The sabbatical year. God's law also provided for liberation of soil, slaves, and debtors every seven years. Again the concern is justice for the poor and disadvantaged (as well as the well-being of the land). The central goals are to protect people against processes that would result in their losing their productive resources and to restore productive resources after a time of loss.

Hebrew slaves received their freedom in the sabbatical year (Deut. 15:12–18). When they left, their masters were commanded by God to give them cattle and other products from the farm (Deut. 15:13–14; see also Exod. 21:2–6). As a consequence, the freed slave would again have some productive resources so he could earn his own way.[46]

The sabbatical provision on loans is even more surprising if, as some scholars think, the text calls for cancellation of debts every seventh year (see Deut. 15:1–6).[47] If followed, this provision would have protected small landowners from the exorbitant interest of moneylenders and thereby helped prevent them from losing their productive resources.

As in the case of the year of jubilee, this passage involves structural justice rather than mere charity. The sabbatical release of debts was an institutionalized mechanism to prevent the kind of economic divisions where a few people would possess all the capital while others had no productive resources.

The sabbatical year, unfortunately, was practiced only sporadically. Some texts suggest that failure to obey this law was one reason for the Babylonian exile (Lev. 26:34–36; 2 Chron. 36:20–21).[48] Disobedience, however, does not negate God's demand. Institutionalized structures to prevent poverty are central to God's demand for justice among his people.

Does the biblical material offer a norm for distributive justice today? Some would argue that the biblical material on the land in Israel only applies to

God's covenant community. But that is to ignore both the fact that God chose Abraham and his descendants to be a witness to the nations and also that the biblical writers did not hesitate to apply revealed standards to persons and societies outside Israel. Israel was to be a priest to the nations (Exod. 19:6), disclosing the Creator's will for all people, and thus blessing all nations (Gen. 26:24). Amos announced divine punishment on the surrounding nations for their evil and injustice (Amos 1–2). Isaiah condemned Assyria for its pride and injustice (Isa. 10:12–19). The book of Daniel shows that God removed pagan kings like Nebuchadnezzar in the same way he destroyed Israel's rulers when they failed to show mercy to the oppressed (Dan. 4:27). God obliterated Sodom no less than Israel and Judah, because she neglected to aid the poor and feed the hungry (Ezek. 16:48–50). The Lord of history applies the same standards of justice to all nations.

That does not mean, however, that we should try to apply the specific mechanisms of the jubilee and the sabbatical release to twenty-first-century global market economies. It is the basic paradigm that is normative for us today. Appropriate application of these texts requires that we ask how their specific mechanisms functioned in Israelite culture, and then determine what specific measures would fulfill a similar function in our very different society. Since land in Israelite society represented productive power, we must identify the forms of productive power in modern societies. In an industrial society, a central area of productive power is the factory, and in an information society, it is knowledge. Faithful application of these biblical texts in such societies means finding mechanisms that offer everyone the opportunity to share in the ownership of these productive resources, guaranteeing in an information society, for example, that every child has genuine opportunity to receive quality education. If we start with the jubilee's call for everyone to enjoy access to productive power, we must criticize all socioeconomic arrangements where productive power is owned or controlled by only one class or group (whether bourgeois, aristocratic, or proletarian)—or by a state or party oligarchy. We must follow the example of the prophets who protested the development of an economic system in which landownership was shifted to a small group within society, and we must develop appropriate corrective processes in society to restore access to productive resources to everyone.

The central normative principle about distributive justice that emerges from the biblical material on the land and the sabbatical release of debts is this: *Justice demands that every person or family has access to the available productive resources (land, money, knowledge) so they have the opportunity to earn a generous sufficiency of material necessities and be dignified participating members of their community.*

It is important to note what this norm does and does not demand. It does not say that society should provide food, clothing, housing, etc. to everyone no matter what people do. Rather, it insists that everyone has access to the productive resources that will enable them to earn a living if they act responsibly.

Nor does this norm demand equality of wealth or income. There has been vigorous debate in the modern world about how much equality is desirable. Libertarians, who essentially limit justice to fair procedures, place virtually no limits on inequality. Marxists, on the other hand, have advocated for almost complete economic equality.

Some inequality is not only permissible, but desirable.[49] When laziness and other forms of disobedience result in less income, inequality is appropriate. When parents rightly pass on an inheritance to children and grandchildren, some inequality is appropriate. When the economic rewards of work create incentives for creativity and diligence, some inequality is desirable.

Biblical principles, however, suggest at least two important limits on economic inequality.

The first concern is the biblical principle just discussed that every person and family should have access to adequate productive resources. Whenever the extremes of wealth and income limit or prevent some people from having access to adequate productive capital, then that inequality is unjust and must be corrected. The prophets repeatedly denounced the rich and powerful who acquired more and more land in a way that forced many smaller landowners to lose their land and fall into poverty. One crucial measure for evaluating the economic inequality in a society is to determine whether everyone, especially the poorer members of society, have adequate access to productive resources.

Other things being equal, if a growth in economic inequality has the effect of improving the lot of the poorer members of society and increasing their access to productive capital, it is just. On the other hand, any increase in economic inequality that harms the poorer members of society and hinders their opportunity to obtain access to adequate productive capital is unjust.

A second key consideration about economic inequality is also important. Especially in a market economy, money is power. And as Lord Acton said long ago, power tends to corrupt and absolute power corrupts absolutely. The biblical teaching on sin helps explain Lord Acton's dictum. In a fallen world, sinful people will almost always use power for their own selfish advantage. They will use it to abuse others and acquire more power even at the expense of their neighbor.

That is why Christian political thinkers insist on limiting power of every kind. This principle applies to economics just as much as politics. One of the most basic principles of historic conservative political thought is that we must avoid unchecked, concentrated power if we want justice and freedom. In a sinful world, no one, absolutely no one, is to be trusted with unlimited power. Great economic inequality inevitably produces injustice in a fallen world; therefore Christians must oppose it.

Biblical principles demand equality at least up to the point where everyone has access to the productive resources, so that if they act responsibly they can work to acquire a decent living and be dignified members of society. This norm offers significant guidance for how to shape the economy so that people normally have the opportunity to earn their own way.

But what should be done for those—whether the able-bodied who experience an emergency or dependents such as orphans, widows, the elderly, or the disabled—who for shorter or longer periods simply cannot provide basic necessities through their own efforts alone?

Generous care for those who cannot care for themselves. Again the biblical material is very helpful. Both in the Old Testament and the New Testament, we discover explicit teaching on the community's obligation to support those who cannot support themselves.

The Pentateuch commands at least five important provisions designed to help those who could not help themselves:[50]

1. The third-year tithe goes to poor widows, orphans, and sojourners as well as the Levites (Deut. 14:28–29; 26:12).
2. Laws on gleaning stipulated that the corners of the grain fields and the sheaves and grapes that dropped were to be left for the poor, especially widows, orphans, and sojourners (Lev. 19:9–10; Deut. 24:19–21).
3. Every seventh year, fields must remain fallow and the poor may reap the natural growth (Exod. 23:10–11; Lev. 25:1–7).
4. A zero-interest loan must be available to the poor and if the balance is not repaid by the sabbatical year, it is forgiven (Exod. 22:25; Lev. 25:35–38; Deut. 15:1–11).
5. Israelites who become slaves to repay debts go free in the seventh year (Exod. 21:1–11; Lev. 25:47–53; Deut. 15:12–18), and when the freed slaves leave, their temporary "master" must provide liberally, giving the former slaves cattle, grain, and wine (Deut. 15:14) so they can again earn their own way.

In his masterful essay on this topic, John Mason argues that the primary assistance to the able-bodied person was probably the no-interest loan. This would maintain the family unit, avoid stigmatizing people unnecessarily, and require work so that long-term dependency did not result.

Dependent poor such as widows and orphans received direct "transfer payments" through the third-year tithe. But other provisions such as those on gleaning required the poor to work for the "free" produce they gleaned. The widow Ruth, for example, labored in the fields to feed herself and her mother-in-law (Ruth 2:1–23).

It is important to note the ways that the provisions for helping the needy include a major emphasis on the role of non-state actors. Not only did Ruth and other poor folk have to glean in the fields; wealthier landowners had responsibilities to leave the corners of the fields and the grapes that dropped. And in the story of Ruth, Boaz, as the next of kin, took responsibility for her well-being (chapters 3–4).

The texts seem to assume a level of assistance best described as "sufficiency for need"—"with a fairly liberal interpretation of need."[51] Deuteronomy 15:8 specifies that the poor brother receive a loan that is "enough to meet the need" (NRSV). Frequently, God commands those with resources to treat their poor fellow Israelites with the same liberality that God showed them at the exodus, in the wilderness, and in giving them their own land (Exod. 22:21; Lev. 25:38; Deut. 24:18, 22). God wanted those who could not care for themselves to receive a liberal sufficiency for need offered in a way that encouraged work and responsibility, strengthened the family, and helped the poor return to self-sufficiency.

Were those "welfare provisions" part of the law to be enforced by the community, or were they merely suggestions for voluntary charity?[52] The third-year tithe was gathered in a central location (Deut. 14:28) and then shared with the needy. Community leaders would have had to act together to carry out such a centralized operation. In the Talmud, there is evidence that the proper community leaders had the right to demand contributions.[53] Nehemiah 5 deals explicitly with violations of these provisions on loans to the poor. The political leader calls an assembly, brings "charges against the nobles," and commands that the situation be corrected (Neh. 5:7 NRSV; cf. all of vv. 1–13). Old Testament texts often speak of the "rights" or "cause" of the poor. Since these terms have clear legal significance,[54] they support the view that the provisions we have explored for assisting the poor would have been legally enforceable. "The clear fact is that the provisions for the impoverished were part of the Mosaic legislation, as much as other laws such as those dealing with murder and theft. Since nothing in the text allows us to consider them as different, they must be presumed to have been legally enforceable."[55]

The sociopolitical situation is dramatically different in the New Testament. The early church is a tiny religious minority with very few political rights in a vast pagan Roman Empire. But within the church, the standard is the same. Acts 2:43–47 and 4:32–37 record dramatic economic sharing in order to respond to those who could not care for themselves. The norm? "It was distributed to each as any had need" (4:35 NRSV—i.e., up to the point of an adequate sufficiency for a decent life). As a result, "there was not a needy person among them" (v. 34 NRSV).

The great evangelist Paul spent much of his time over several years collecting an international offering for the impoverished Christians in Jerusalem (2 Cor. 8–9). For his work, he found a norm (2 Cor. 8:13–15)—equality of basic necessities—articulated in the exodus story of the manna where every person ended up with "as much as each of them needed" (Exod. 16:18 NRSV).[56]

Throughout the Scriptures we see the same standard. When people cannot care for themselves, justice demands that their community provide a generous sufficiency so that their needs are met. As we saw in the last chapter on the state, there are many institutions (including family and church) that share the responsibility to implement this demand of justice that society care for those who cannot care for themselves.

Conclusion

How should we summarize the implications of this vast amount of biblical material for our understanding of justice?

Procedural justice is very important. So is commutative justice. God wants honest weights and measures and insists that persons keep their promises so that a fair exchange of goods and services is possible.

At the same time, fair distribution is also central to the biblical understanding of justice. This is clear from the meaning of the biblical words *mishpat* and *tsedaqah*, the restorative character of justice, the special concern to empower the weak and needy, and the emphasis on restoring people to community. The biblical material also provides significant content for our understanding of fair distribution. The able-bodied must have genuine access to the productive resources of their society so they can earn their own way and be dignified members of their community. And those unable to care for themselves must receive a generous sufficiency of life's necessities.

Over the course of our history, we have learned a great deal about how and how not to implement these biblical principles. Some attempts at land redistribution have been economically disastrous. Other attempts to enable each family to own their own land have been highly successful. One significant reason for both the flourishing of democracy and the growth of the economy in the United States is that when Europeans moved across the continent (tragically and unjustly seizing Indian land), the government decided to make it possible for each family to own their farm rather than divide the land into huge estates owned by a few aristocrats. Similarly, an important reason for the dramatic economic success of South Korea in the second half of the twentieth century is that after the Japanese were driven out, the land was divided into family-owned farms.

In some parts of our world, land redistribution would still be one significant way to implement the biblical teaching on justice. But today, knowledge is the primary source of wealth creation. Therefore one of the most important ways to implement the biblical teaching on justice is to offer quality education to all children regardless of race or family income.

Our attempts to care for those unable to care for themselves have also had mixed results. Certain kinds of state efforts have created devastating dependency. At other times, the right mix of societal support where families, churches, other parts of civil society, and the state all do what they do best have worked well to support the needy in ways that build dignity and proper self-sufficiency.

Applying biblical paradigms to the ever-changing societies in which we live is never easy; it requires wisdom and careful experimentation to discern what works and what does not. But having a framework of principles that define the nature of justice provides a clear sense of direction. We live in a world in which about a billion people try to survive on one dollar a day, and in which half of the world's people have very little capital (whether land, money, or knowledge). In that kind of world, the biblical understanding of justice demands clear, dramatic change. We must find wise ways to care for those who cannot care for themselves. And we must change our societies so that all able-bodied persons and families have access to the productive resources so that, if they act responsibly, they can care for their families, enjoy a generous sufficiency of material resources, and be dignified members of their community. The biblical understanding of distributive justice calls for dramatic transformation in every society on this planet.

6

Human Rights, Democracy,
and Capitalism

Huge battles raged in the twentieth century over human rights. Communists denounced civil and political freedoms as phony rights in the absence of economic rights. Some Westerners wanted to limit human rights to civil and political rights, denouncing social and economic rights as vague and secondary. Some Asians rejected the whole notion of universal human rights as an imperialist imposition of Western thought on Asian cultures. Totalitarians of many varieties trampled the human rights of hundreds of millions.

At the same time, and in spite of all the controversy, more and more people embraced the notion of universal human rights. The General Assembly of the United Nations adopted the Universal Declaration of Human Rights in 1948. President Jimmy Carter (a self-identified evangelical) made the promotion of human rights around the world more central to American foreign policy. Pope John Paul II's support of human rights contributed to the emergence of an independent trade union in communist Poland and eventually the collapse of the Soviet Union. At the end of the twentieth century, strong evangelical support for global human rights (especially religious freedom) led to what some have called a new evangelical "internationalism" and a stronger emphasis on human rights in US foreign policy.[1] The topic of human rights is current and controversial.

But what are human rights? What is their foundation? What all do they include? And how do they help us think about democracy and market economies?

Human rights spell out in some detail what is owed to persons, thus fleshing out what justice means. The discussion of civil and political rights, such as freedom of speech and assembly and the right to vote, leads naturally to a discussion of democracy. Similarly, the discussion of social and economic rights leads to the question of the best way to order economic life. Therefore, in this chapter, we start with human rights and then move to the questions of how to justly order political and economic life.

"Rights represent claims to those things which are due individuals."[2] But if something is owed to a person, someone else normally has an obligation to provide it. Therefore human rights involve relationships between persons.[3] My right to religious freedom demands that others treat me in a way that provides the space for me to make free choices about religion. "Your right to life is bought by my accepting my obligation not to kill you."[4] Rights and duties consequently are closely interrelated.

Human rights are also universal. The idea of a human right includes the claim that all persons everywhere have the right to be treated in a certain way. That does not mean that everyone actually believes or respects any particular human right, but "the phrase 'human rights' implies a universal ethic which claims that they *ought* to be believed and observed everywhere by everyone."[5]

What is the ultimate foundation of human rights? From a biblical perspective, the answer is God, who creates every person in the divine image and commands every person to respect the God-given dignity of all persons.[6] Human rights are not something that human beings possess on their own or earn by their conduct. Human rights flow directly from God, from the way God made us, and the commands God gives us about how we should treat our neighbors.

What biblical revelation says about the dignity of every man and woman is simply breathtaking. God makes every single human being in the very image of God. God calls every person to exercise dominion over the rest of creation as a faithful steward watching over and caring for creation. God calls each person to exercise his or her creation mandate by understanding more and more about the created world and using it to shape objects and institutions of usefulness and beauty. Most important, God summons each person to respond in freedom to the divine invitation to walk in obedience, friendship, indeed personal partnership, with the Creator of the entire universe.

The Bible goes even further in affirming the dignity of every single person. God longs so much to be in personal right relationship with each person that after human sin radically disrupts our relationship with God, God becomes flesh and suffers the agony of Roman crucifixion in order to offer to each and every person the opportunity to return to intimate fellowship and right relationship with God Almighty. And as the Incarnate One, God renews his command to us to love our neighbors as ourselves—even those neighbors who are enemies. Furthermore, at his resurrection, Jesus defeats the powers of evil in a decisive way and then calls his followers to continue the struggle against injustice in the power of the Holy Spirit who will strengthen us until Christ returns to complete the victory. Consequently, redemption in Christ motivates and strengthens the Christian's ability to work for the human rights bestowed on all people by the Creator.

God demands that within the limits of our finite, historical setting, we treat our neighbors in such a way that they can reach their full human dignity and flourish in the way the Creator intended. My obligation to treat my neighbors that way is the foundation of my neighbor's human rights. And their obligation to treat me that way is the foundation of mine.[7] Human rights have their deepest foundation in the dignity of each person, which is grounded in humanity's relationship to God.

Many modern Western thinkers, of course, have sought to ground human rights in autonomous humanity rather than God. In the seventeenth century, John Locke (one of the most influential shapers of modern political thought) argued that individual liberty is the most precious human value. Freedom to do whatever one desires is the essence of persons. In the state of nature, Locke argued, all persons have "perfect freedom to order their actions, dispose of their possessions and persons, as they see fit, within the bounds of the law of nature, without asking leave, or depending upon the will of any other man."[8] By contrast, earlier Christian thinkers had insisted that persons in their essence are communal beings with mutual obligations imposed by God to serve the common good and use their freedom to obey God. Locke, on the other hand, starts with an alleged state of nature where each individual enjoys an absolute freedom. Only as free individuals choose to enter social contracts, in order to acquire things like security via the state, is this radical freedom restricted. In this approach the primary focus of human rights becomes the assertion and protection of the freedom of individuals.

The result, as many have pointed out, is today's highly individualistic Western societies that have trouble affirming persons' responsibilities and obligations to promote the common good. Consequently, as Harvard law professor Mary Ann Glendon has lamented, American society has a near-total fixation on personal rights.[9] In such a setting, the only "coherent public moral language is that of subjective rights" and the only universally respected right is freedom "understood as the sovereignty of the subject [individual person] over his/her physical and moral world, that is, the subject's emancipation from all externally imposed material and spiritual constraints on his/her freedom of choice."[10]

One ironic result is that this understanding undermines another widespread value of modern society: the affirmation of equality. Most modern thinkers affirm that in some important sense all persons are equal. But if individual freedom is the ultimate value, including the right to define morality and truth for oneself, then it is hard to see how to develop a solid foundation for the affirmation of the equality of all persons.

There are significant numbers of people today who deny all notions of equality. There certainly is no empirical basis for the claim that all people are equal. People are unequal in virtually every visible way: size, color, physical ability, mental ability, knowledge, skill, wealth, social power—the list goes on and on. Historically, the affirmation of equality has been grounded in the religious conviction that all persons are created in the image of God.[11] In a widely used introductory political science text, Glenn Tinder raises the question of whether it will be possible to maintain a belief in the equality of persons without a return to a religious foundation for that claim.[12] Probably not.

It is important to reject radical Western individualism and its inadequate affirmation of obligation, duties, the common good, and our creation as communal beings without denying the profoundly important truth about the dignity, worth, and freedom of each individual. A biblical understanding of the person differs from both secular individualism as well as traditional and modern communalism. Over against radical individualism, Christians insist on the social nature of persons, the importance of community, and every person's obligation to contribute to the common good. On the other hand, Christians reject both traditional societies (that almost totally subordinate individuals to their family, clan, or tribe) and modern totalitarian societies (that completely subordinate the individual to the state).

It is not an accident that the modern, Western insistence on the freedom of the individual emerged in societies immersed for centuries in the biblical teaching about the dignity, importance, and freedom of each person. If each person is as free and important as the Bible claims, if the Creator of the universe invites every single person to respond freely to God's call no matter what other members of the family, tribe, or community may do, then individual freedom (properly understood) is important and right.[13] All modern declarations of human rights correctly find their basis in this dignity of the individual.[14]

Christians, as we have seen, ground their thinking about the human rights of persons in God, but the mere Christian belief in the dignity of each person described earlier does not by itself bring us to the detailed understanding of specific human rights that many contemporaries, including most Christians, embrace today. The articulation and acceptance of these detailed claims happened over a long historical process. We need to explore in more detail some of these specific human rights and see how biblical principles and historical experience contributed to their definition and acceptance.[15]

Civil and Political Rights[16]

The right to life. This is the most basic of all rights. Every other right is irrelevant if this right is violated. The God who creates every person in the divine image declares that each human life is immeasurably precious. That is the reason for the command: "You shall not murder" (Exod. 20:13). The right to life means that one person should never deprive another of the right to life (except, perhaps, in narrowly defined situations governed by due process).[17]

The right to life applies to every person, no matter how young, old, weak, or disabled, because every person has an objective relationship to God that nothing, not even human sin, can destroy. In the words of Jürgen Moltmann, "God has a relationship to every embryo, every severely handicapped person, and every person suffering from one of the diseases of old age, and he is honored and glorified in them when their dignity is respected. Without the fear of God, God's image will not be respected in every human being."[18]

The right to freedom of religion. We see development within the biblical canon on this issue. On the one hand, there are clear, explicit Old Testament texts that prescribe stoning for those who blaspheme God or worship false gods (Lev. 24:10–16; Deut. 17:2–5). On the other hand, both the Old and New Testaments reveal a God who invites but does not compel us to respond in faith and obedience. God gave Adam and Eve the freedom to disobey. Again and again we see God pleading with the people of Israel to embrace his commands. Just as often, we observe God giving the Israelites the space to reject God's way. When God becomes flesh, he invites but does not force anyone to accept the gospel.

In fact, Jesus's parable of the wheat and tares underlines the importance of religious freedom. In Jesus's parable, after a farmer sows wheat in his field, an enemy spreads weed seeds in the same land. When both wheat and weeds spring up, people urge the owner to pull up the weeds. But he refuses, saying both must be allowed to grow together until harvest.

Jesus's detailed interpretation is especially important:

> The one who sowed the good seed is the Son of Man. The field is the world, and the good seed stands for the people of the kingdom. The weeds are the people of the evil one, and the enemy who sows them is the devil. The harvest is the end of the age, and the harvesters are angels.[19]

The world, or society, is the place where evil persons may grow along with good people until the end of the age. In society at large, people must be free to accept or reject God without losing their place and rights as citizens. People's freedom to reject God and still enjoy God's gift of life in society continues until the end of the age.

Only slowly did Christians grasp the full implication of this biblical teaching for the issue of religious freedom. At great cost and with frequent martyrdom, the early Christians asserted their right to believe in and follow Christ no matter what Caesar said. But soon after Caesar announced faith in Christ in the early fourth century, Christians started using the power of the state to deny religious freedom to others. Persecution, inquisition, and execution of "heretics," Jews, and Muslims were the tragic result. More than a millennium later, the sixteenth-century Anabaptists outraged Catholics, Lutherans, and Calvinists with their demand that the church should enjoy full freedom from the state. Slowly, however, first in Holland and England in the seventeenth century[20] and then dramatically in the new United States in the late eighteenth century, genuine religious freedom emerged and the state was forbidden to interfere in the life of the church.

What prompted this dramatic change? Reflection on biblical principles undoubtedly played a significant part. But so did revulsion from the terribly bloody wars of religion that European Catholics and Protestants fought in the sixteenth and seventeenth centuries. The religious skepticism of the eighteenth-century Enlightenment also contributed. The result has been the rapid spread of religious freedom during the last two centuries. At the beginning of the twenty-first century, the vast majority of the nations of the world (many Muslim countries are the exception) embrace religious freedom at least in theory, and the majority also seek to practice and protect it.

Individuals and religious communities have the right to practice and share their faith without interference from the state. Individuals have the right to share or change their religious beliefs and practices even when family, friends, and neighbors disagree. Respecting and protecting the right to religious freedom of every person—including those we think are dangerously wrong—is one of the most basic ways Christians respect the dignity of every person.

The right to freedom of speech. Freedom of speech is certainly not an explicit demand in the Bible. In fact, the Old Testament specifies severe penalties for some kinds of speech (e.g., blasphemy; Lev. 24:10–16). All persons, however, even the most devout, are both finite and less than fully sanctified. For both reasons, we all make intellectual mistakes. Allowing everyone to speak and promote whatever ideas they believe to be true is an important way that we overcome error and move toward better understanding as a society. Furthermore, allowing each person to speak, write, and publish freely is a crucial way that we respect the dignity of each person and grant them the space to carry out their God-given mandate to study and understand God's created order.

The right to a fair trial. On this topic, the Bible is clear and explicit (see pp. 79 and 82). God demands that judges are fair to rich and poor. Witnesses must tell the truth. God denounces the use of bribes to affect judges or witnesses.

The right to vote. There is nothing in the Bible about the right to vote, although there are several instances where the people are called upon to ratify decisions made by others.[21] Christians have lived under all types of governments and at times defended monarchy, but the importance of allowing every person to vote slowly emerged, in part, as people experienced the self-serving activities of monarchs, dictators, and small aristocratic elites who held a monopoly on political power. To defend their own interests, those excluded from political decision making demanded a role.

One of the best arguments to support this change is a twofold reason for the decentralization of power. If the Creator calls each person to be a coworker with God in creating new things and shaping history, then everyone can fulfill this creation mandate only if they have a role in political discussions. That is the positive reason. The negative reason is that, in a sinful world, power tends to corrupt and unchecked power almost always leads to decisions that unfairly benefit the powerful. The solution is to decentralize power so that no one has enormous unbalanced power. One of the significant ways to decentralize political power is to guarantee that every citizen, no matter how rich or poor, educated or not, has the right to vote regularly to help determine who will govern.

The rights we have discussed (the right to life, religious freedom, freedom of speech, fair courts, universal suffrage) and others that could have been included (e.g., the right of assembly, the right not to be tortured, the right not to be imprisoned without due process) are often described as civil-political or procedural rights. Many of them define what the state dare not do. In our world, many governments frequently violate these human rights, but there is widespread agreement in many countries that these are universal human rights. Biblical principles and historical experience prompt Christians to agree.

Social and Economic Rights

A right to food. This right flows from the right to life. If people have a right to life, then they have a right to the food necessary to sustain life. It is obvious that every particular historical setting qualifies this right in some way. Occasionally, widespread famine makes it impossible for society to provide even enough food to prevent starvation. But these extreme situations do not undermine every person's right to food whenever it is possible to provide it.

An important biblical principle qualifies the right to food. Able-bodied people have a moral obligation to work and earn their own way. If people act irresponsibly, their neighbors have no moral obligation to feed and clothe them generously. Certainly, we should not let them starve. All people, even the morally irresponsible, retain their basic human dignity as persons created in God's image. But those who are able to feed themselves and irresponsibly choose not to, have only a right to "bread and water" from their neighbors. People unable to care for themselves, on the other hand, have a right to a generous sufficiency of food.

A right to productive assets. In the chapter on justice (chapter 5) we saw that God wants every person and family to have access to the productive assets that will enable them, if they act responsibly, to meet their own material needs and be dignified members of the community. That means land in an agricul-tural society and knowledge, via education, in an information society. This right flows from the fact that God creates all persons as coworkers with him, called to exercise their creation mandate to care for themselves and serve their neighbors by using the material world around them to create new things. They cannot do that without access to productive resources. Obviously, the nature and extent of the productive resources society can allocate varies in different historical circumstances. But within the limits imposed by particular historical settings, every person has the right of access to enough productive resources so that, if they act responsibly, they can care for themselves, be dignified members of their community, exercise their creative gifts, and serve the common good.

A right to private property.[22] Throughout the Scriptures—from the com-mandment not to steal to the early church's insistence that Ananias and Sap-phira had no obligation to donate the proceeds from the sale of their home (Acts 5:4)—we see the assumption that private property is good. When the Israelites enter Canaan, every family receives its own land. God, to be sure, is the only absolute owner (Lev. 25:23). But with that important qualification—that we are only stewards and the ultimate owner calls us to use our property to serve our neighbors—private property is good.

Emil Brunner is probably correct to argue that this right to private property flows, at least in part, from the Creator's gift of freedom. "Without property there is no free personal life. Without property there is no power to act."[23] Without some private property, we would have to have permission from oth-ers to do anything. We simply cannot be free without some property that we have the right to use largely as we choose.

A right to health care. Like the right to food, this right flows from the right to life. Every person created in the image of God has the right to the level of health care that the science, technology, and wealth of a given time can make available to all its members. That does not mean everyone has a right to iden-tical health care. But it does mean that, within the limits of every historical setting, every person has a right to a level of health care that protects life and helps the person flourish physically and emotionally.

A right to education. The Creator made persons as social beings, depen-dent on others to learn what we need to know to be free, dignified persons. Without a basic grasp of the knowledge available in our society, we cannot exercise our divine calling to be dignified participants in our community. The God who loves each unique person and demands that we help each other to flourish insists that every person has a right to education that enables them, within the limits of their ability, to learn enough to be a dignified, contributing participant in their community and to exercise their creative gifts. Again, the limits of a particular historical setting will shape the extent and character of that education. But every child has the right to education that enables that child's innate ability to flourish.

A right to work. The God who works made persons in his image to be coworkers, discerning the intricate design divinely embedded in the material world and using that knowledge to create new wonders. God made us so that it is through work that we express our unique identity as persons, care for our needs, and serve our neighbors. All persons have a right to work in a way that enables them to live out this divine intention. Obviously, the type of work varies enormously in different historical settings. But the right to work is a basic human right.[24]

Basic socioeconomic rights, I have argued, include a right to food, productive assets, private property, health care, education, and work. (Other related rights would include a right to shelter and clothing.)

But are socioeconomic rights really universal human rights in the way that civil-political rights are? For decades, a fierce debate has raged over this question. At least some of the civil-political rights guarantee things that only the state provides. Almost all socioeconomic rights, on the other hand, guarantee things that many institutions (family, church, business corporations, etc.) as well as the state can supply. Furthermore, some argue, civil-political rights are negative rights that only require the state to do nothing (e.g., not imprison persons without a fair trial or not restrict free speech) and therefore cost nothing. But socioeconomic rights have costs, and sometimes economic scarcity prevents them from being met. Political rights are limits, whereas economic rights are goals. Furthermore if we say both sets of rights are equal, then totalitarian governments will say that they accept the goal of implementing both civil-political and social-economic goals, but just as their poverty prevents them from fully implementing the social-economic human rights immediately, so too they must be excused for not granting their people full civil-political rights.[25]

There are good responses to each of these arguments.[26] The fact that families, churches, and other non-state institutions can satisfy persons' rights to food and education, does not negate or decrease their status as rights. Further, most civil-political rights do require the state to do things and therefore cost money. To uphold the right to life in a sinful world requires police. To uphold the right to freedom of religion and speech in a world where others seek to deny people these rights requires enforcement mechanisms. All this, not to mention funding fair courts and universal suffrage, costs money. The problem of scarce resources applies to both civil-political and social-economic rights.

In chapter 5 on justice, we saw that the same Hebrew words that are used to talk about things like fair courts are also employed to discuss fair economic arrangements such as access to food and productive resources. There is nothing in the biblical material to suggest that one is more important than the other. Certainly having enough food to avoid starvation and enough shelter and clothing to avoid freezing to death are just as essential to human dignity and well-being as freedom of speech or a fair trial. I agree with that large group of Christians who insist that both civil-political and social-economic rights are basic human rights.[27]

When Rights Collide

It would be most convenient if all the human rights we have discussed always meshed together harmoniously. Unfortunately, they often present conflicting demands. As we saw earlier, Marxists and Liberals[28] in the twentieth century often debated the relative importance of civil-political and social-economic rights. Marxists argued that they had to restrict political freedoms in order to meet the basic social-economic rights of the poor masses. Western liberals often argued that civil-political rights were more important than social-economic rights. One might be able to cite some historical evidence for both claims, but I believe the bulk of historical evidence suggests that the two sets of claims are mutually reinforcing. With some frequency, military dictators (e.g., in Brazil and the Philippines in the 1960s and 1970s) both severely restricted political freedom and also used their dictatorial political power to organize the economy in ways that failed to meet the basic economic needs of poor persons.[29] Nobel laureate Amartya Sen points out the positive correlation between political and economic rights. He shows that only countries run by dictators (countries without a democratic political structure) have experienced widespread famine. (The free press in democratic countries would expose the presence of widespread famine, and the government would do whatever was necessary to avoid it, knowing that their reelection depended upon avoiding famine.)[30] On balance, historical experience supports the view that we should refuse to give priority to either civil-political or social-economic rights. In real life, persons need basic economic rights met in order to participate fully in political life, and they need political freedom in order to demand and secure economic rights. That historical experience, furthermore, is just what we should expect from the basic biblical understanding of persons: we are both spiritual beings (for whom freedom is essential) and material beings (who cannot exist without material necessities).

Arguing that we must affirm and embrace both civil-political and social-economic rights, however, does not solve the problem of conflicting rights. The rights to freedom of action and private property often clash with the rights to enjoy basic social and economic necessities (e.g., food, shelter, health care). For example, taxing wealthy persons to provide the resources to supply basic necessities for poorer persons obviously somewhat restricts the economic freedom of richer persons in order to meet the social-economic rights of poorer persons.

Professor David Hollenbach has proposed three principles that help us decide between competing claims:

1. The needs of the poor take priority over the wants of the rich.
2. The freedom of the dominated takes priority over the liberty of the powerful.
3. The participation of marginalized groups takes priority over the preservation of an order that excludes them.[31]

These three principles flow from clear biblical principles. God and his faithful people have a special concern for the poor. Biblical justice has a corrective, restorative character that enables the weak and needy to return to a place of wholeness, dignity, and participation in community. God measures societies by what they do to the people at the bottom.

We have explored many specific human rights—both civil-political and social-economic. But simply defining and codifying these rights is not enough. We must apply them to the concrete task of shaping actual, detailed social systems. We must acknowledge and implement these rights in actual laws, policies, institutions, and systems.

Two of the most important ways we do that are the political and economic systems that we shape. We turn therefore to a discussion of whether and to what extent a democratic political order and a market economy are good ways to implement biblical principles and human rights.

There is no treatise in the Bible on democracy or a market economy. Christians can and have lived under many types of political and economic systems. No specific political or economic arrangement is "the" Christian system. To baptize democracy or capitalism in that way is idolatrous.

That does not mean, however, that biblical principles and the human rights we have discussed have nothing to say about how we should organize political and economic life. When we combine these principles and rights with an analysis of historical experience, we do, I believe, arrive at both a preferred political and a preferred economic structure.

Democracy

There is widespread agreement on the basic features of a democracy even though existing democracies differ in the details. A democracy has a limited state at many levels: every citizen has the right to vote in free, secret elections to select who will govern; there is a limited term of office after which there must be an election to select the next government; there are several different branches of the state (executive, judiciary, legislative) with independent powers that serve as checks and balances for each other; there is a clear distinction between the state and the total society, and the state recognizes the freedom and independence of many other societal institutions (e.g., family, church) and does not try to dominate those other institutions;[32] and the government must submit to the law (defined by a constitution or common law). There are constitutional protections of the rights of minorities. A democracy has an open, transparent judicial system and enjoys a regular, peaceful transfer of power from one government to another. A democracy also respects human freedoms—of religion, speech, and assembly. Citizens are not imprisoned without due process. A democracy embraces the truth that since human rights flow from the dignity of persons, the state dare not trample upon human rights.

It is clear that democratic governance fits well with our previous discussion of biblically grounded principles about justice, the state, and human rights.[33] Because God calls every person to be a coworker with him in shaping history, power must be decentralized so all can fulfill their God-given mandate. Negatively, because centralized, unchecked power in a fallen world almost inevitably leads to abuse and injustice, it is essential to limit the state's power in various ways.

Reinhold Niebuhr's famous line captures well how the biblical teaching on human nature (especially our sinful nature) fits well with democracy: "Man's capacity for justice makes democracy possible; but man's inclination to injustice makes democracy necessary."[34] If the fall had totally destroyed human ability to do anything good, democracy would be impossible. But the pervasive selfishness present in every person since the fall means that unchecked power will always lead to injustice. The many ways that democracy decentralizes power—especially by granting every citizen a vote to decide who governs—promotes a decisive protection against the abuses that flow from centralized, unchecked power.

Democracy also embraces the freedom and dignity of each person by acknowledging and implementing a wide variety of ways to protect personal freedom. Allowing every citizen, no matter how poor or uneducated, to vote underlines the worth of each person. The wide variety of personal freedoms that democracies respect and protect serves to affirm the dignity of each person, which biblical faith teaches so clearly.

Democracy also fits well with the fact that morally imperfect and intellectually finite persons see only through a glass darkly. Our understanding and insight are painfully limited. Therefore it is crucial for a good society to keep the future open, to always have the ability to correct mistakes. A society with a free press, free speech, and regular free elections has a better ability than totalitarian societies to overcome wrong ideas and chart a new course.

Historical experience confirms the importance of democracy. It was developing democracies that first embraced religious freedom, just as today thriving democracies most fully embrace religious freedom. Famines occur under dictatorial governments in a way they do not in democracies.

Democracies have obvious weaknesses. They often make decisions slowly. Too many people accept the silly notion that a majority vote determines not only who governs but what is morally right. In fact, democratic majorities frequently embrace immoral ideas and engage in evil activities. In practice, most self-identified democracies are far less democratic than they claim; small wealthy elites often have enormous power that overrides the self-interest and desire of the majority. Winston Churchill, the British prime minister during World War II, may have been right with his remark that "democracy is the worst form of government except all the others that have been tried."[35]

Christians today should never claim that democracy is the Christian form of government, but we can and should claim that biblical principles fit better with democratic government than with existing alternatives. In addition, Christian virtues—honesty, tolerance, love for neighbor—strengthen democratic life. Therefore Christians should actively nurture democracy in their own country and around the world.[36]

Market Economies

One of the greatest debates of the twentieth century was over whether a social-ist[37]/communist approach or a capitalist/free-market approach was a better way to organize economic life. In the communist economy, the state owned all the means of production and state planners set wages, prices, and production levels. (There used to be a central office in Moscow that set twenty-five million prices each year.)

In a market economy, on the other hand, the bulk of the wealth and means of production are privately owned, and supply and demand set most wages and prices.

Simply on the basis of the biblical principles we have explored, the communist model has problems. It does not grant or protect private property. In addition, by having the state own all productive assets, it combines political and economic power in a centralized way that is dangerous in a fallen world. Historical experience confirms what these principles suggest. The unchecked power of communist rulers led to the loss of freedom (religion, speech, assembly, etc.) and the control of every other sector of society by the state.

In addition, state ownership of the means of production did not work very well. We discovered in the course of the great Chinese and Soviet communist economic experiments of the twentieth century that communist economies are simply less efficient than market economies. No set of officials in Moscow knows enough to set wages, prices, and production levels wisely. Supply and demand works more efficiently. As a result, communist economies produced less wealth than market economies. When, in the late 1970s, China's communist rulers began to embrace substantial aspects of a free-market economy, their economy began a long period of stunningly rapid economic growth. In fact, economists attribute much of the substantial decline of the percentage of

Asians living in poverty from 1970 to the present to the widespread adoption of market economies throughout much of Asia.[38]

The twentieth century also taught us that there is a connection between communist economies and totalitarianism on the one hand and market economies and freedom on the other. A market economy's decentralized power (expressed especially in private property) means that it is harder for political authorities to restrain freedom of speech or religion. Each private owner has substantial power to do what he or she chooses. It is not surprising, therefore, that political and religious freedom has flourished better in market economies. On balance, a market economy respects human freedom better, creates wealth more efficiently, and tends to be better at reducing poverty.

That is not at all to say that present market economies have no problems from the perspective of biblical principles. In a moment, we will explore those. Rather, it is to say that both biblical principles and historical experience suggest that a market economy provides a better basic framework for economic life than existing alternatives.

This suggestion by no means implies that we should overlook glaring injustices in the way current market economies work. For starters, billions of people lack adequate capital to participate substantially in today's market economies. Market economies are simply failing to meet the biblical demand that everyone has access to productive resources. Second, in practice, market economies tend to produce a consumeristic materialism that promotes devastating cultural decay. Third, today's global capitalism is producing devastating environmental decay. And finally, many market economies (including the United States, the United Kingdom, and China) are becoming more and more unequal in distribution of wealth in a way that dangerously centralizes power and tends to neglect the poor.[39]

None of these problems are insurmountable. They do not mean we must abandon the fundamental framework of the market economy. But they do mean that substantial adjustments are necessary.

Both biblical principles and historical experience suggest that one important thing we need is the right kind of state intervention to correct the injustice in today's market economies. The Bible makes it clear that private property is good, but only God is an absolute owner. The common good and everyone's right of access to some productive resources qualifies the right of private property. Claiming that there dare be no government modification of supply and demand means we worship a laissez-faire economic system rather than the God who is Lord of economics.

The historical experience of countries like South Korea, Taiwan, Hong Kong, and Singapore demonstrates that it was a combination of a basic market framework plus wise government expenditures on things like education and health care for everyone that produced their economic "miracles."[40]

In fact, in all democratic, capitalist countries today, governments do intervene in economic life for the sake of justice and the common good. When we tax rich people to provide free education or health care for poor children, we are abandoning a purely laissez-faire economy. Done in the right way—for example, the way grants to poor university students create not dependence but opportunity and empowerment for a lifetime—government intervention can correct the injustices in a market economy without destroying the basic market framework. In fact, most economic debates today start with the double assumption that a basic market framework is the right place to start and that some kinds of government intervention are necessary and good. The real debates are over what kinds of government interventions are helpful (and which kinds are counterproductive) and when government intervention becomes excessive. Only slowly, through patient trial and error, do we learn better answers to those questions.

I conclude that Christians today ought to be ardent champions of human rights for everyone. And as they do so, they should endorse and promote democratic governance and market economies without claiming in any simplistic way that the Bible endorses either. Nor dare we overlook the weaknesses of both. In fact, precisely our commitment to a biblically grounded understanding of human rights will lead us to challenge and correct the glaring weaknesses and injustices in the way today's existing democracies and market economies function, even as we affirm their basic structure.

7

The Sanctity of Human Life

The sanctity of human life is under attack today in ways that we have not seen for millennia. Abortion destroys millions of unborn babies each year. Since the United States legalized abortion in 1973, more than 47 million babies have been aborted in the United States alone.[1] Increasingly euthanasia gains support and governments legalize doctor-assisted suicide. Breathtaking scientific advances make it possible, now or in the near future, to clone human beings and modify inheritable genes to produce more "intelligent," more "athletic," or more "beautiful" persons. Widely respected philosophers denounce as "speciesism" any claim that human beings have any special status different from monkeys. "We can no longer," Princeton philosopher Peter Singer says, "base our ethics on the idea that human beings are a special form of creation, singled out from all other animals, and alone possessing an immortal soul."[2] Not surprisingly, Singer concludes that not just abortion and euthanasia but also infanticide are all moral.

Historic Christian faith offers a radically different vision. Nothing affirms the special dignity and inestimable worth of each human being as strongly as the biblical teaching on creation and redemption.

Genesis makes the breathtaking claim that all human beings—and only human beings—bear the very image of the Creator of the universe.

> Then God said, "Let us make human beings in our image, in our likeness, so that they may rule over the fish in the sea and the birds in the sky, over the livestock and all the wild animals, and over all the creatures that move along the ground."

117

> So God created human beings in his own image,
>   in the image of God he created them;
>   male and female he created them.[3]

Our dignity and worth do not come from a government decision, a humanly defined quality of life, or a socially defined level of human usefulness. They come from the fact that the Creator selected human beings alone out of all the created order to bear the divine image and exercise a unique stewardship over the rest of creation. It is because every person bears the divine image that God forbids murder and considers it abominable (Gen. 9:6; Exod. 20:13).

The incarnation, cross, and resurrection clarify and deepen our understanding of the inestimable value of each person. The Creator of the universe becomes a human being—an embryo, a baby, a young man, a carpenter. God incarnate sanctified "human nature by his life as a Palestinian Jew."[4] The incarnation shows that the human person is "no mere accident of history but God's own image impressed into space and time."[5] Nor is that all. God loves every single person so much that God incarnate suffered crucifixion so that "whoever believes in him shall not perish but have eternal life" (John 3:16). God does not will that any should perish (2 Pet. 3:9). God is glad to die for every person, no matter how poor, how weak, how marginalized and neglected. God invites every person to an intimate personal relationship that continues forever in life eternal. That is how precious every person is.

Moltmann's statement is worth quoting again:

> God has a relationship to every embryo, every severely handicapped person, and every person suffering from one of the diseases of old age, and he is honoured and glorified in them when their dignity is respected. Without the fear of God, God's image will not be respected in every human being, and the reverence for life will be lost, pushed out by utilitarian criteria. But in the fear of God there is no life that is worthless and unfit to live.[6]

What does this biblical teaching about the sanctity of human life mean for Christian citizens wrestling with tough questions about what the law should say about abortion, euthanasia, genetic engineering, starvation, smoking, and capital punishment?

Abortion

What should Christians do about the fact that scores of nations have legalized abortion in a wide range of circumstances?

The starting point is clear: if the Creator endows every person with immeasurable worth and dignity, then the directly intended taking of innocent human life is simply wrong and unacceptable.[7]

This, however, does not settle the question, because many who defend abortion claim that the unborn fetus is not a human being. Only at "quickening," it is argued, or the point of viability outside the womb, or birth, does the developing fetus become a human being.

It would be very helpful if the Bible offered clear, explicit teaching about when the baby growing in the mother's womb becomes a human being. But, as a careful, very pro-life, study by the Orthodox Presbyterian Church has said, the Bible simply does not tell us whether or when the fetus is a person.[8]

However, nothing in the Bible suggests that the fetus is not a human being.[9] In fact, the Bible often uses words for the fetus that are normally used for persons who are already born (e.g., Gen. 25:22; 38:27–30).[10] Luke calls Elizabeth's unborn child a baby (Luke 1:41, 44). The psalmist declares that God knew him when God "knit me together in my mother's womb" (Ps. 139:13–16). Nowhere in the Bible is there a hint that the unborn child is less than a human person from the moment of conception.

The ever-clearer scientific evidence is indisputable. From the moment of conception, we have a genetically distinct being who grows, without any biological break, to become the baby whom at birth almost everyone accepts as a human being to be protected. This scientific fact about the uninterrupted biological development of human life from the moment of conception was acknowledged honestly in a *proabortion* editorial in the official journal of the California Medical Association:

> Since the old ethic [the traditional Christian viewpoint] has not been fully displaced, it has been necessary to separate the idea of abortion from the idea of killing, which continues to be socially abhorrent. The result has been a curious avoidance of the scientific fact, which everyone really knows, that human life begins at conception and is continuous whether intra- or extra-uterine until death. The very considerable semantic gymnastics which are required to rationalize abortion as anything but taking human life would be ludicrous if they were not often put forth under socially impeccable auspices.[11]

Both biblical teaching and scientific information suggest that we should start with the assumption that from conception the developing fetus is a human being.

To be sure, there is no explicit biblical teaching that unambiguously asserts such a view.[12] But not a word in the Scriptures suggests the contrary, and much in the Bible tends to point in this direction. If we remain agnostic, uncertain when the developing fetus becomes truly human, we have no choice but to adopt this working assumption. If there is any serious possibility that we are dealing with human beings, we must reject abortion. To do otherwise would be like shooting blindly into a darkened theater with the justification that we cannot know whether we will hit empty seats or murder innocent people.

Christians, then, should conclude that from the moment of conception, we must act on the assumption that we are dealing with persons created in God's image. Choosing to end the life of innocent persons is wrong. It is murder. Abortion, therefore, is wrong, except when the physical life of the mother is threatened (for instance, tubal pregnancy or cancer of the uterus).

That conclusion, however, does not settle the question of what public laws on abortion Christians should promote. Some Christians argue that since we live in a pluralistic society where some people think abortion is permissible (since they say the fetus is not yet a human being) and others reject abortion (since they consider the fetus a human being) public law should be neutral. It should allow abortion for those who believe that it is morally permissible while at the same time allowing "pro-life" citizens to reject abortion for themselves.

Unfortunately, the problem is not so easily solved.[13] In many kinds of situations, neutrality by the state in the face of competing perspectives is precisely the right course. But that is totally unacceptable and unworkable when the issue is life itself. Honest conviction and sincere belief are not adequate grounds for taking the life of another person. Adherents of early Canaanite religion truly and sincerely believed in child sacrifice. Today, occult worshipers honestly affirm the rightness of ritual sacrifice. Some contemporary thinkers truly believe that a baby should not be treated as a human being until it demonstrates certain minimal ability. Others believe that the severely handicapped should be starved to death.

Nor is it true that laws against abortion violate the separation of church and state. It is true, as we saw in chapter 2, that everyone's views about the nature of persons flow from their deepest religious or philosophical convictions. But proposing legislation that protects the sanctity of human life (affirmation of which, to be sure, flows from one's deepest beliefs about persons) is not the same as demanding laws that require everyone to affirm specific Christian doctrines.

I believe that all people should be free to believe and worship as they please. I also believe that people should be free to act in ways that I consider ethically wrong. But there is at least one important restriction on this freedom that every just society must maintain. My religious and ethical freedom does not include the right to kill other people.

Except in the case of abortion, nobody argues that one person should be free to take the life of another merely because the first person believes that the other person is not truly human. That would allow Nazis to kill Jews. If the earlier argument is valid, then we must act on the assumption that unborn babies and handicapped newborns are truly human. Therefore abortion and infanticide are murder. In a pluralistic society, people should be free to do many things that others consider stupid or sinful. But tolerance toward others does not extend to allowing them to kill other people.

What kind of legislation should we promote? One consideration must always be: What is possible? Sweeping proposals that have no hope of implementation are seldom helpful. For decades, public opinion polls have made it clear that a solid majority of the American people want abortion to be legal under some circumstances. Legislation that would totally abolish abortion is politically impossible.[14]

We can, however, do two things. We can press for laws that restrict abortion. And we can do things (both via legislation and civil society) that make abortion less attractive.

There are many laws that do or could restrict abortion. Laws can require notification of parents in the case of minors, forbid certain types of abortions (e.g., partial-birth abortion), or specify waiting periods. Electing presidents who will nominate Supreme Court justices who would reverse the 1973 decision (based on the highly questionable claim that the constitution includes a right to privacy that requires a right to abortion) offers another route. (If this actually succeeded, then the issue would return to the political process and all state legislatures would be able to pass laws that reflect the majority view in each state.)

Women—especially poor, single women—often feel they have no alternative to abortion. We can make abortion less attractive—both through legislation and through the activities of churches and other groups in civil society. We can improve adoption laws and get tougher on fathers who fail to support their children. Churches and Christian agencies can (and do) operate crisis pregnancy centers that provide information and offer support for single women who decide not to abort. We can prosecute sexual violence against women, expand services for disabled children, and improve opportunities in education, jobs, and housing for poor people so they no longer feel they have to choose between desperate poverty and abortion.

Both by changing public policy and by strengthening civil society, people who believe in the sanctity of human life should work to dramatically reduce the number of abortions.

Euthanasia

The word *euthanasia* means "good death." But is it good for society to decide to kill the very elderly or very disabled? Is it good for a person to decide to kill himself or herself to avoid a slow and painful death?

Over the centuries, some societies have killed the very old or left them alone, exposed to severe weather, to die. Today, more and more people argue that it is right and good for individuals who are very sick or frail to be able to commit suicide and have doctors assist them. Both the Netherlands and the state of Oregon have legislation that permits "doctor-assisted suicide."

If the patient so requests, a doctor may legally administer a lethal dosage of drugs.

The biblical tradition understands human life as a gift of God. Ending human life (except, some Christians argue, in the case of just war and capital punishment) is wrong. We are finite, weak human beings, and it is not our role to play God and decide when we should die. The core of human sinfulness is rebellious pride that refuses to accept the limits of our finitude; only the divine Author of life has the right to choose to end human life. We should humbly accept the gift of life as long as God grants it—even when it involves wrenching pain or slow, anguishing deterioration of body and mind. Even the most weak and frail still bear the image of the Creator. Until almighty God withdraws the breath of life, we must humbly respect that divinely bestowed dignity. We dare not take our own lives. Just societies dare not sanction anyone to take another person's life.

Modern technology, however, raises difficult problems. Today, it is possible to use new scientific advances and technological breakthroughs to keep people alive artificially—even when there is no hope of recovery. It is absolutely essential to distinguish between actively causing death on the one hand, and choosing not to use extraordinary measures (when there is no hope of recovery) on the other. The first is murder; the second is right. To be sure, precise definitions and exact dividing lines are hard to draw, but the basic distinction is clear and important. It is not wrong to choose (ahead of time, perhaps, in a living will) that one does not want to be treated with extraordinary measures when there is no hope of recovery,[15] but we dare not try to kill ourselves or our neighbors.

Christians should vigorously oppose laws that allow anyone (a doctor, a friend, a family member) to actively cause another person's death. That would be both immoral and dangerous. It would be dangerous because family members are sometimes tempted to get rid of the heavy burden of caring for very old, very sick relatives (especially if they stand to inherent their wealth). As the cost of caring for the elderly continues to escalate, society will find it increasingly attractive to cut health-care costs by helping the very sick to die. Nazi history shows how easy it is to slide down the slippery slope toward exterminating other despised or unwanted persons. Cultures that embrace the biblical understanding of the sanctity of human life will not start down that road.

Genetic Engineering

Breathtaking scientific breakthroughs pose a fundamentally new threat to the sanctity of human life. We have already cloned animals. We can or very soon will be able to clone human beings. We are quickly learning how to make genetic changes in human beings that will not only cure disease (which is good) but also "improve" human beings. By introducing genetic alterations, we will be able to add new traits that make people with "better" brains, "faster" legs, or "more beautiful" bodies. In the next few decades, many of the most complicated, most dangerous threats to the sanctity of human life will come from the field of genetic engineering, which is roaring ahead at a frantic pace.

The challenges are so new that answers are far from clear. But the solid foundation for all our thinking must be the inestimable worth of every person and the theological truth that God alone is Creator; God alone creates out of nothing. Our far more limited calling is to trace God's footsteps in nature and reshape the creation God has given us into things of beauty and complexity.

Tragically, we seem to want to play God. "The task of creator is personal to God, and his election of the interpersonal mystery of human sexuality as the context for procreation preserves his creator-hood absolutely."[16] Using genetic engineering to counter diseases that ultimately stem from the fall is one thing. Proudly using genetic engineering to make human beings better and wiser than the Creator made us is quite another.

We should not try to genetically alter our genes so our children are 50 percent—or 500 percent—more intelligent or more athletic than we or our neighbors. We should not proudly clone ourselves, trying to produce a human slave for replaceable body parts or a human thing arrogantly made in our own image. "The uniqueness of human nature is at stake."[17]

Christians should work for laws that outlaw all cloning of human beings. (Fortunately, on this issue, some pro-choice feminists and environmentalists are joining with pro-life Christians.)[18] In the whole area of genetic engineering, we should urge government and society as a whole to err on the side of caution—always measuring new innovations claiming to provide wonderful cures by asking the simple question: Does this activity affirm or undermine the God-given dignity of persons?

Starvation

Every day, twenty to thirty thousand children die of hunger and diseases we know how to prevent. That adds up to millions of childhood deaths per year.[19] Every year, millions of people die of infectious and parasitic diseases we know how to prevent.[20] In Africa, large numbers of people die every year of AIDS because they cannot afford the effective, relatively inexpensive drugs that could preserve their lives.[21] These deaths are directly related to the fact that about one billion people in the world are so poor that they must struggle to survive on one dollar a day.[22] Millions—at least eleven million and probably more than twenty million—die unnecessarily every year.

Are not these starving children in developing nations created in the image of God—just as much as aborted babies in the United States? Why do some

Christians seem to apply the principle of the sanctity of human life only, or primarily, to the unborn and the very old threatened by euthanasia? If we start with the biblical principle that every human being possesses inestimable worth and dignity, then Christians must also work vigorously to reduce and end death caused by starvation and diseases we know how to prevent. Both through effective private programs and wise government activities to reduce global starvation, malnutrition, and preventable disease, we can live out our respect for the sanctity of human life.[23]

Smoking

Smoking kills an estimated 438,000 Americans every year.[24] Around the world, the death toll from smoking rises to 5 million each year.[25]

The social costs are enormous. The US Department of Health and Human Services estimates that smoking costs the nation $75.5 billion each year in medical bills and $92 billion in low productivity.[26] Lung cancer snatches fathers and mothers away prematurely.

Given the devastation caused by smoking tobacco, it is especially ironic that Senator Jesse Helms, long heralded as one of the great pro-life supporters, strongly supported government funding to send American tobacco to developing countries under our "Food for Peace" program.[27]

Christians must insist that the sanctity of human life applies to everyone, including people seduced by clever cigarette advertising. Christians must work for effective laws that prevent tobacco advertisements, forbid smoking in most public buildings and facilities, and educate the public on the dangers of smoking. American experience over the last thirty years demonstrates that this kind of mix of government programs can reduce smoking and the deaths it causes.[28]

Capital Punishment

Is it really wise and moral to kill people to show that killing people is immoral?

Many Christians think the Bible has a clear answer. Genesis 9:6 says, "Whoever sheds human blood, by human beings shall their blood be shed; for in the image of God has God made humankind." A number of Old Testament laws demand death for certain evil acts (Deut. 17:2–7; 19:15–21). There is no question that the Old Testament prescribed capital punishment.

Before we quickly assume that Christians today should support capital punishment, however, we need to consider several things.

First, it is most intriguing that in the case of the first murderer, God himself punished the murderer—but did not execute him. In fact, God placed a special mark on Cain precisely so that other people would not kill Cain (Gen. 4:9–16). If God wants murderers executed to show how evil it is to kill someone made in the image of God, then why did God not kill Cain for killing Abel? Since this is the first and most dramatic instance in which God himself directly deals with a murder, God's failure to execute Cain is surely significant.

Second, the Old Testament clearly says that no one should be put to death on the basis of only one witness. There must be at least two witnesses (Num. 35:30; Deut. 17:6; 19:15). It is interesting that Charles Colson for many years concluded from these texts that since we almost never have two eyewitnesses to a murder we should oppose capital punishment.[29]

Third, we have a clear case in the New Testament where Jesus rejects capital punishment in a situation where the Old Testament explicitly called for it. John 8:3–11 tells the story of a woman caught in adultery. The religious leaders bring her to Jesus and remind him that the law of Moses ordered execution of an adulteress (Lev. 20:10; Deut. 22:22). "Now what do you say?" they ask Jesus. Instead of calling for her execution as the law prescribed, Jesus says, "Let any one of you who is without sin be the first to throw a stone at her." After the guilty accusers slink away one after another, Jesus tells her he does not condemn her and orders her to sin no more.

The fact that Jesus clearly sets aside an explicit Old Testament law is less surprising when we remember that a number of times Jesus quoted Old Testament commands and then set them aside, saying, "but I tell you." Jesus quoted the Mosaic law's provision allowing divorce (Matt. 5:31; cf. Deut. 24:1) but then on his own authority reversed the Old Testament law. He did the same on oaths (Matt. 5:33–37). Most strikingly, he did the same thing in the case of the central principle of Old Testament jurisprudence: "You have heard that it was said, 'Eye for eye, and tooth for tooth.' But I tell you, do not resist an evil person" (Matt. 5:38–39; cf. Deut. 19:21). In fact, he taught that his followers must love even their enemies (vv. 43–44). For the first three centuries, every Christian writer who discussed killing said that all killing was prohibited—whether in war, capital punishment, or abortion.[30] Whether or not the early church was correct in thinking that is what Jesus intended, it is perfectly clear that in the one case where Jesus was explicitly called upon to affirm the Old Testament's call for capital punishment, he refused.

If Jesus is God's final revelation of God's will for us, then how dare we do what he rejected? There are some people who have done evil things and pose such an ongoing danger to society that we rightly imprison them for the rest of their lives, but biblical faith tells us that God continues to love even the worst sinners. Even the worst murderers continue to bear the divine image as long as they live. Is it not more respectful of the image of God (even in very evil persons) to say that we will as a society pay the costs of imprisoning them for a lifetime rather than killing them?[31]

It is interesting that Pope John Paul II almost totally rejected capital punishment. "Today," he argues, the cases where capital punishment would be morally justified "are very rare, if not practically non-existent."[32] And the place where he made this argument was precisely his famous encyclical (1995) on the gospel of life where he argued so vigorously against abortion and euthanasia.

Human experience presents one further set of problems with capital punishment. The legal system has sometimes made mistakes and executed innocent people. Would it not be better to imprison people for life rather than execute them, so that we would be able to release people wrongly convicted of murder? Further, poor people and minorities who cannot afford good lawyers face the death penalty in far higher numbers than others.

A Completely Pro-Life Agenda

Decades ago, I published a book called *Completely Pro-Life*.[33] Increasingly, Christians are embracing this broader agenda. Even the Manhattan Declaration (2009), which some interpreted as a call for a narrow focus on just a few issues, insisted that "ours is, as it must be, a truly consistent ethic of love and life for all humans in all circumstances." It called Christians to implement this consistent ethic of life by combatting the abuse of children, the exploitation of vulnerable laborers, the sexual trafficking of women, and the spread of preventable diseases.[34]

Biblical teaching on the sanctity of human life, I believe, calls Christians to a consistently pro-life agenda. Abortion, euthanasia, starvation in a world of abundance, smoking, and capital punishment all destroy persons created in the image of God.

In his book *Abortion and the Early Church*, Michael J. Gorman shows that the early church lived out this completely pro-life vision:

> The earliest Christian ethic, from Jesus to Constantine, can be described as a consistent pro-life ethic. . . . It pleaded for the poor, the weak, women, children and the unborn. This pro-life ethic discarded hate in favor of love, war in favor of peace, oppression in favor of justice, bloodshed in favor of life. The Christian's response to abortion was one important aspect of this consistent pro-life ethic."[35]

The late cardinal Joseph Bernardin of Chicago made a very similar argument in several widely publicized speeches on what he called "The Seamless Garment":

> The principle [the sanctity of human life] . . . cannot be successfully sustained on one account and simultaneously eroded in a similar situation. . . . Asking questions along the spectrum of life from womb to tomb creates the need for a consistent ethic of life. For the spectrum of life cuts across the issue of genetics, abortion, capital punishment, modern warfare and the case of the terminally ill. . . . Success on any one of the issues threatening life requires concern for the broader attitude in society about respect for human life."[36]

Christians today have a precious treasure that our world desperately needs. John Paul II rightly spoke of a gospel of life. Contemporary society urgently needs to recover a deep respect for the full sanctity of human life, but our neighbors will hear our words much more clearly if we live out a completely pro-life vision in every area of life.

8

Marriage and Family

Marriage and family have almost collapsed in the Western world in the last fifty years. Escalating divorce and out-of-wedlock birthrates mean that vast numbers of our children do not live with both their biological parents. The resulting emotional agony and social destruction are devastating not just our homes but entire societies.

In the United States, about 50 percent of all first marriages end in divorce,[1] and over 40 percent of children are born to unmarried parents. The level of cohabitation (couples living together without marriage) has exploded so rapidly that some reports today indicate that two-thirds of young Americans cohabitate before marriage—and many never marry.[2]

Nor is it just in the United States. Similar patterns hold throughout the Western world. Out-of-wedlock birthrates are as high or even higher in many European cultures: in France, 40 percent; in the United Kingdom, 38 percent; in Denmark, 45 percent; in Sweden 54 percent.[3]

One sociological study after another now shows that the consequences of divorce and single parenthood are horrendously destructive for our children. Children in single-parent homes in the United States are at least five times more likely to live in poverty. They are far more likely to have academic trouble, drop out of high school, become pregnant as teenagers, abuse drugs, commit crimes, become mentally ill, and get into trouble with the law.[4] Fatherless boys are twice as likely to go to jail. In fact, for every year boys spend without their dads, the odds of going to prison jump 5 percent.[5] The last two generations of parents have done to their children what no previous generation has ever done. We have undermined their well-being on a colossal scale.

That, in brief, is the historical context in which contemporary Christians must seek a framework to guide our political activity in the area of marriage and family. How can a normative biblical vision and a careful analysis of human experience (especially the last fifty years) help us define wise principles for reshaping public policy in this area?

Normative Vision

At the heart of the Genesis story is the double truth that persons are communal beings who come in two distinct types: male and female. Persons reach fulfillment only when men and women live in right relationship. "God created human beings in his own image . . . male and female he created them. God blessed them and said to them, 'Be fruitful and increase in number; fill the earth and subdue it'" (Gen. 1:27–28).

Adam was restless until he encountered Eve (Gen. 2:15–25). Immediately after describing Adam's delight with Eve, the text underlines the importance of marriage and family: "For this reason a man will leave his father and his mother and be united to his wife, and they will become one flesh" (Gen. 2:24; Matt. 19:5–6).

The New Testament shows that singleness for the sake of the kingdom is a very high calling (1 Cor. 7:7–8, 25–40). The single person—enjoying wholesome male-female relationships in the biological family and also the family of Christ—is certainly fully human and genuinely fulfilled. But Genesis makes it clear that the Creator's intention for most men and women is marriage. David Gushee is right to underline the fact that marriage was the very first institution God created: "Before there was sin, before there was either Israel or the church; before there were laws or governments; before there were children; before there was any other institution, there was marriage."[6]

Marriage is not a human invention. Nor is it some uniquely Christian idea. Marriage is central to the order of creation. Marriage and the nuclear and extended families that flow from marriage are simply the way the Creator designed reality. Marriage and family are universal human institutions essential for the well-being of all people everywhere.[7]

Marriage is the most basic unit of every social order because it is the best context for producing many things essential to a decent society.

By structuring and stabilizing adult sexual relationships, marriage reduces social stress and frees up adult energies for constructive participation in work and community life. By clarifying paternity, marriage eliminates uncertainty about the status and identity of children. By harnessing what can become dangerous human desires for love and sex, marriage protects the social order from chaos and violence. By functioning as a context of shared labor, marriage contributes to family and community economic well-being. Marriage provides a context in which children are socialized, thus preparing them for later participation as responsible adults in society rather than as morally or psychologically ruined wards of the state.[8]

Marriage and the family that results are the best setting for learning how to love others in a sacrificial way. The kind of love that society needs but cannot create grows almost naturally in the family. A wholesome family is the first and best teacher of children.

God ordained marriage for several reasons: Companionship is clear in the story of Adam's restlessness, which disappears only when Eve appears. Again and again in the Bible it is clear that the delights of sexual intercourse are also part of the Creator's purpose for marriage (Gen. 2:25; Song of Songs). The purpose of procreation is explicit in God's command at the beginning to be fruitful and multiply (Gen. 1:28).

Finally, as we have already seen, marriage is for society. Society requires wholesome marriages anchoring wholesome families if it is to be a good, sustainable community.[9]

Reserving sex for one's marriage partner and remaining faithful to one's spouse for life are both essential supports for strong, wholesome marriage. The biblical witness is unanimous that God intends sexual intercourse to be reserved only for a man and woman united in life-long marriage. The Bible condemns sex before marriage (fornication), sex outside marriage (adultery), and homosexual sex.[10]

Equally clear is the canonical condemnation of divorce.[11] "I hate divorce," God says in Malachi 2:16. Because of divorce, God's altar is flooded with tears and God rejects the sacrifice offered there. Why? "Because the Lord is witness between you and the wife of your youth. You have been unfaithful to her, though she is your partner. The wife of your marriage covenant" (Mal. 2:13–14). It is true that Moses permitted men to divorce their wives (Deut. 24:1), but Jesus explicitly set Moses aside with his authoritative word, "But I tell you." Jesus reversed Moses's permissive law and returned to the Creator's original intention.

> "Haven't you read," he replied, "that at the beginning the Creator 'made them male and female,' and said, 'For this reason a man will leave his father and mother and be united to his wife, and the two will become one flesh'? So they are no longer two, but one. Therefore what God has joined together, let no one separate."
>
> "Why then," they asked, "did Moses command that a man give his wife a certificate of divorce and send her away?"
>
> Jesus replied, "Moses permitted you to divorce your wives because your hearts were hard. But it was not this way from the beginning. I tell you that anyone who divorces his wife, except for sexual immorality, and marries another woman commits adultery."[12]

Except within very narrowly delimited parameters, Jesus forbids divorce. Surely one of the reasons for this is the devastation divorce inflicts on children. "Wrong is done to the child if it loses father or mother by divorce. The parents thereby deprive the child of something which is due to it by right, and the law in virtue of which it has that right is no human law but the law of the order of creation."[13]

The normative biblical vision for marriage and family, then, is for a man and woman to live in covenant together and be faithful to each other for their entire lives, raising their children in the nuclear family, and nurturing and being nurtured by the larger extended family of grandparents, uncles, aunts, cousins, nephews, and nieces. Human history, I believe, supports the wisdom of this vision.

Historical Experience

For centuries, as Christianity grew and flourished in Europe, many biblical values about marriage and family became deeply embedded in culture and law.[14] By the twelfth century, marriage had become a sacrament, thus elevating the state of marriage—although celibacy enjoyed even loftier status. Divorce became totally unacceptable, and by the thirteenth century, the Roman Catholic Church was able to enforce the view that divorce is never allowed. A marriage could be annulled (if it could be shown never to have been validly consummated), but divorce was not possible. Across Europe, the state enforced the church's canon law on marriage.

The Protestant Reformation of the sixteenth century changed some aspects of the church's teaching but not the basic understandings of marriage and family. Luther and Calvin rejected the Catholic understanding of marriage as a sacrament and denied that celibacy was a higher calling than marriage. They also argued, on biblical grounds, that in very limited situations (e.g., adultery and desertion) divorce and remarriage were permissible, but Protestant theology continued to support a broad cultural consensus, that sex belongs only in marriage and marriage is for life. As in the medieval period, so too in the Reformers' thinking, romantic intimacy was a far less important purpose of marriage than economic partnership, the raising of children, and the provision of a legitimate context for sexual desires.

The Romantic movement of the nineteenth century changed that. Emphasizing human feelings, individual self-expression, and passion, the Romantics transformed marriage from a practical partnership to a romantic, emotional enterprise where the "romantic love" between the two people became more important than children or the marriage covenant. For a few decades, nineteenth-century Victorians managed to combine this romantic understanding with strong cultural taboos against promiscuity and divorce. But changing socioeconomic and cultural dynamics would soon prompt a radical departure from centuries of traditional practice, culture, and law.

In the earlier agricultural economy, wife and husband worked together as an economic team farming the land. The modern industrial world of the factory and office ended that economic partnership. Education and specialization prompted couples to move far from their home community, which in earlier times provided a supportive context discouraging promiscuity and divorce. Educated women no longer needed to stay married to avoid economic disaster.

Cultural ideas also began to change rapidly. Individualism has always been strong in American culture, but in the 1960s, an even stronger individualism joined with a developing relativism that moved from a small circle of academic thinkers to popular culture. The idea of romantic love merged with sweeping relativism and hyper-individualism to produce the sexual revolution of the 1960s. Personal self-fulfillment became the standard. Popular culture mocked and abandoned traditional views of sex and marriage. New birth-control techniques made nonmarital sex "safe," and many began to define family as any type of relationship or combination where two or more people chose to live together.

Not surprisingly, public law also soon changed dramatically. Within a ten-year period starting in 1969, virtually all states replaced laws requiring persons wanting a divorce to provide reasons (e.g., adultery, desertion) with "no-fault" divorce laws that allowed either partner to receive a divorce simply because the person no longer wanted to be married. In the next ten years, the divorce rate doubled. Today, in the United States, about 50 percent of all first marriages end in divorce—and 60 percent of all remarriages.[15]

Out-of-wedlock birthrates and cohabitation have skyrocketed along with the divorce rates. In 1960, unmarried moms gave birth to only 5 percent of all children born that year. In 2005, the out-of-wedlock birthrate was about 33 percent.[16] Today it is over 40 percent. In large cities like Baltimore, St. Louis, and Philadelphia, it is over 60 percent.[17]

As we saw earlier, these high divorce rates and high levels of single-parent families are devastating our children. Vast numbers of careful sociological studies now show that divorce and single parenthood create long-term, destructive havoc in the psyches and lives of children. As sociologist David Popenoe said in the *New York Times*, "I know of few other bodies of data in which the evidence is so decisively on one side of the issue: on the whole for children, two-parent families are preferable. . . . If our prevailing views on family structure hinged solely on scholarly evidence, the current debate would never have arisen."[18]

The evidence is clear: the sexual revolution of the sixties has been a disaster. I doubt that North American and European nations can survive for the long haul as decent, stable societies unless we can restore more widespread, wholesome marriages and families, in which moms and dads keep their marriage vows and together raise the children they bring into the world.

Historical experience, especially in the twentieth century, has taught us another set of things about marriage and family. Tyrannical and dictatorial governments wrongly try to monopolize and control all areas of life, including marriage and family, thus violating the biblical teaching that marriage and family are divinely established institutions independent of the state. Communist governments in the Soviet Union and China sought to prevent families from passing on their religious beliefs to their children. Forced sterilization and abortion deprived parents of the freedom to decide how many children to bring into the world.

The right of a married couple to choose whether to have children and how many children to have is a fundamental human right that governments have no authority to forcibly take away. That is not to condemn offering reasonable economic incentives that respect individual family decisions, either to encourage childbearing when the population is declining or to discourage large families when the population is problematically high, but the state has no right to dictate whether parents have children and how many they have.

Similarly, the state has no right to prevent parents from passing on their beliefs to their children. This means first of all that parents must have full religious freedom to teach their children their religious beliefs and have them participate in their religious activities and institutions. It also means something very basic about education. Since schools are one of the most basic places where one generation passes on its values to the next, parents must have the freedom to choose schools that share their values. The United Nations Universal Declaration of Human Rights (1948) correctly insists that "parents have a prior right to choose the kind of education that shall be given to their children" (Art. 26.3). This does not mean that the state should not pay for the education of all children. Justice for the poor, in fact, demands that the state does pay for quality education, at least for the poorer sectors of society. But the state can and should provide mechanisms that enable parents to choose the type of school their children attend. One way to do that—an approach widespread in Western Europe—is for tax dollars to pay for the costs of private schools chosen by parents up to an amount equal to that spent per pupil in government-operated schools.

The fact that parents, not the state, have the primary right and responsibility for raising children does not mean that the state should never intervene in the family. In situations of sexual abuse or major parental neglect that endangers the life or fundamental well-being of children, state agencies rightly intervene to protect children. But even then, they must always seek to strengthen parents, so they can resume their proper obligations, rather than replace parents.

So what should we do? What must the church and other religious institutions do? And what should Christians urge the state to do?

The most basic point is that restoring wholesome marriage and family life is first and foremost a task for the church, not the government. It is the church and other religious institutions that must teach biblical principles and nurture husbands and wives who will live according to biblical standards. Nothing the state can do will be very effective if the Christian church cannot persuade Christians to follow biblical norms in their marriages and families.

Does that mean that the state has no role? Some Christians have argued that since our society is so pluralistic, the state ought to withdraw completely from all legislation on marriage. Let churches, mosques, synagogues, and temples define their own standards on marriage and family, for their own members. The state, on the other hand, should remain entirely neutral about definitions and requirements for marriage and family, just as the state respects and does not interfere with the religious freedom, beliefs, and institutions of all citizens.

Would that be wise? Not really. As we saw earlier, marriage is not some human fabrication that persons can mold into any shape they choose. Every person, no matter what they may say or believe, has been made by the Creator in such a way that the biblical understanding of marriage and family works best. Of course, it is true that God has given persons freedom to reject God's way and to act apart from it, and human laws should provide the space for people to do that. But this does not mean that laws need to be neutral. God gives sinners the freedom to choose to disobey him in many ways, but the moral laws God has embedded in creation exact consequences for sinful behavior in our bodies, emotions, and relationships. In an analogous way, public law should provide freedom for wrong behavior without remaining neutral.

For example, public policy should define family as those persons related by blood, marriage, and adoption. It should resist efforts to broaden the definition of family (for example, two people cohabitating without benefit of marriage) without criminalizing nontraditional household units.

Probably the clearest illustration of the negative consequences of sinful behavior is the devastating impact of divorce and single parenthood on children. Large numbers of today's children have been painfully injured. The consequences for society as a whole are increasingly clear: higher suicide rates, school failure rates, crime rates, and prison rates all bring an increased cost to society. Our very future as a wholesome civilization is at risk. Society has a great deal at stake in what happens in our marriages and families. The state cannot wash its hands of what happens there precisely because what happens in our homes determines so much of what happens in the larger society.

Even very liberal persons like Cornel West and Sylvia Ann Hewlett agree that "government should get back into the business of fostering the values of marriage as a long-term commitment."[19] Given what we know from recent experience and social analysis about the importance of children growing up with their biological moms and dads, the state should provide economic incentives and encourage other cultural support that discourages divorce and strengthens marriage—especially when children are involved. The state can and should encourage wise behavior (abstinence until marriage, lifelong wholesome marriage) without making sexual promiscuity and divorce illegal. In so doing, the state acts in an analogous way with God, who permits sinful behavior but builds negative consequences for that behavior into the very structure of reality.

Several principles for political engagement emerge from this discussion of the biblical vision and human experience:

- The church, not the state, has the primary responsibility to nurture strong, wholesome marriages and families.
- Marriage and family are divinely created institutions, not creations of the state. Laws can recognize and support these God-given institutions, but they do not create them.
- Because stable, wholesome marriages and families are absolutely essential for a decent society, the state has a legitimate interest in encouraging such marriages and families and therefore rightly provides incentives that encourage wholesome, lifelong marriage, and discourage divorce.
- Parents, not the state, have the primary responsibility for raising children.

Reshaping Public Policy

In the United States, laws about marriage and divorce are the responsibility of each state. The primary way that federal policy impacts marriage and family is through laws on welfare and tax policies. What appropriate changes would strengthen marriage and family?

For some decades, federal laws on both welfare and taxation have actually harmed families. Welfare requirements that prohibited financial assistance if a husband lived in the home substantially discouraged marriage among poor Americans. And tax laws with a marriage penalty (two unmarried people living together paid lower taxes than if they were married) undermined marriage for everyone. Fortunately, in recent years, new welfare policies have sought to strengthen marriage. And most (but not all) the marriage penalties have been removed from the federal tax code.

Tax policy, however, could actually favor marriage. We should explore ways that the tax code could effectively encourage marriage and discourage divorce. Tax policy could also be changed to encourage one parent to stay at home when there are young children in the family.

Another important way that the state nurtures marriage and family is by promoting economic policies that enable one or both parents to earn an income that is generously sufficient for the family's economic needs. Parents need to be able to do this in ways that leave adequate time for parenting. Low wages (which compel parents to work excessively long hours), job insecurity, and lack of full-time work all undermine marriage and family. A job paying a family wage for everyone able to work is an essential component of a pro-family public policy.

How should we change state laws on marriage and divorce? Divorce should not be illegal. Even in the many situations where the church should not allow its members to divorce, the state must allow people the freedom to choose wrong behavior. But that in no way means the state should be neutral about marriage and divorce.

Laws regulating marriage licenses can include economic incentives for pre-marital counseling. State tax laws could include tax breaks to cover part of the cost of marriage enrichment and marriage counseling activities.

Divorce laws should be changed substantially. Today, no-fault divorce laws enable either party to seek divorce for any reason—or, more precisely, without stating any cause other than personal desire.

One way to discourage no-fault divorce is by offering marrying couples a more demanding option. In 1997, the state of Louisiana passed a covenant marriage law, and other states have since passed similar laws. Persons desiring a marriage license may still choose "marriage lite," which permits them to later choose a no-fault divorce. But the state also offers a "covenant marriage" license. In this case, the couple signs a formal statement of their decision to choose this approach. They must prove that they have had premarital counsel-ing, and they must agree that any subsequent divorce can only be based on some cause—that is, things like adultery, imprisonment for a felony, desertion, or sexual abuse of child or spouse. If they cannot show such "fault," they must demonstrate that they have not been living together for two years.

A second way to discourage divorce is to legislate much more stringent re-quirements for divorce whenever children are involved. (Children are involved in two-thirds of all divorces.) The sociological data overwhelmingly demonstrate that divorce devastates children. The state rightly acts to discourage parents with children from obtaining a divorce. The laws should require a lengthy waiting period (at least two years) and demand attendance at classes that explain divorce's negative impact on children. The law should either require mutual consent or require demonstration of fault (e.g., child or spousal abuse, persistent adultery). Gushee is right: "A unilaterally initiated divorce for the purpose of personal self-fulfillment or career advancement (or whatever) should not be permitted when children will be affected."[20]

This second approach is better than Louisiana's covenant marriage ap-proach, because in the former, covenant marriage is merely one option. Couples can still choose a marriage license that permits no-fault divorce even when children are involved. The second approach recognizes that "once children enter the picture, every marriage is, and must be, a covenant mar-riage, because bringing children into the world imposes covenantal obliga-tions on parents that they must not be permitted to evade in the quest for personal fulfillment."[21]

Finally, recent developments demand a discussion of "gay marriage." Court decisions in several states and countries have declared that failure to grant marriage licenses and the full legal status of marriage to gay couples represents discrimination and denial of legitimate civil rights.

How should Christians respond?[22] The first thing to say is that Christians should not abandon biblical norms about sexuality just because powerful segments of contemporary culture argue that homosexual practice is one of several equally valid personal lifestyle choices. Both biblical teaching and the long history of the church tell us that the only valid place for sexual intercourse is in a lifelong marriage covenant between a man and a woman. Homosexual practice is wrong.[23]

The second important point is to insist that Christians must condemn gay bashing and be leaders in decisive activity to end the ongoing physical attacks on gay people. Christians should insist that all citizens, whether or not they are living according to biblical moral standards, retain basic civil rights. Our stand against homosexual practice and gay marriage would be far more credible if we were known for defending the civil rights of gay persons.

Nor should the law criminalize homosexual activity between consenting adults or punish homosexual couples who live together. Both adulterous and homosexual sexual activity is sinful. If our laws require the police and the courts to discover and punish sinful sexual behavior (whether adultery or homosexual sex) between consenting adults, we will violate personal freedoms and move toward a police state. We will also be forgetting the fact that God has chosen to give people a great deal of freedom to choose misguided, destructive behavior without promptly denying them the good gifts of sun, rain, food, shelter, and life. That is what human freedom is all about.

None of the above, however, supports the claim that the state should grant the legal status of marriage to gay couples. Virtually every civilization for millennia has said that marriage is only between a man and a woman. One important purpose of marriage is the conception and raising of children by their biological parents. Gay couples cannot do these things and therefore cannot realize one of the most basic purposes of marriage.[24]

If two gay people should receive the legal status and benefits of marriage, then why not two women and one man or three men and one woman? If three men decide to live with one woman and ask that their relationship be granted all the rights of marriage, why is rejecting that request any less discriminating than denying marriage to gay couples? If personal choice is the decisive factor, then as the Manhattan Declaration (2009) says, we must grant the status of marriage to any number of relationships.[25]

But should the law not recognize polygamy, since the Old Testament did? The Old Testament allowed and regulated a number of things that were not the Creator's will. Jesus implicitly taught this when he acknowledged Moses's acceptance of divorce and then returned to the Creator's original intention.

However, Jesus's example and teaching about the full dignity and equality of women makes polygamy impossible. It is simply impossible for a wife married to a man with other wives to be a full and equal partner with her husband. Public law therefore rightly rejects polygamy.[26]

What about "gay unions"? Some gay people argue that gay relations would be less promiscuous and more permanent (surely desirable for society) if gay partners had some recognized legal status. They also point out that sometimes even partners who have lived together for many years find that they cannot visit a sick partner in the hospital, make medical decisions for their partner, or inherit a partner's property. Would a public law defining some status called "civil union" be something Christians should support or oppose?

I think it depends on the content of the law. Some gay activists want to use legislation on "civil unions" to legitimize the gay lifestyle. We should not support or acquiesce to such initiatives. We should certainly oppose legislation that explicitly or implicitly says that the status of a "civil union" is the same as the status of a "marriage." A civil union is not a marriage; it cannot perform some of the essential tasks that good societies urgently need from marriage. Society should not grant gay partners all the rights of marriage.

On the other hand, there are a number of things that a law on "civil unions" could rightly specify. Christians should affirm, not oppose, the right of gay partners to own property together, make medical decisions for each other, have full hospital visitation rights, and inherit each other's property. A law that specified concrete privileges of that sort—legal rights for gay and other couples who procured a state document that granted them the status of a civil union—would not undermine the definition or reality of the quite different publicly recognized status of marriage. If the legal status of civil union reduced promiscuity and encouraged longer-term gay partnerships rather than temporary ones, that would be good for society. One of the best clues as to whether the deepest motive is legitimizing gay lifestyle or securing the specific legal privileges I outlined would be shown by whether gay partners would accept a legal status of civil union that is explicitly not marriage and does not grant all the rights of marriage.

Through federal and state legislation and constitutional amendments, we should insist on the historic definition of marriage. Vastly more important, however, is the long, tough struggle to persuade heterosexual couples to keep their marriage vows and promises to their children. The right kind of legislation can help to some extent. More vigorous, biblically faithful teaching and discipling in our churches can do much more. Somehow, if our grandchildren are to live in good, just, healthy societies, we must find ways to restore wholesome, joyous, faithful marriages and families.

9

Religious Freedom, Church, and State

Freedom of religion is probably the most basic aspect of human freedom. Historically, believers fighting for religious freedom often led the way in what eventually became a much broader struggle, including freedom of speech, assembly, and emigration.

But what is religious freedom? For many today, religious freedom means some individualistic, self-centered right to create one's own truth and believe and act in whatever way one chooses. That is certainly not the Christian understanding of genuine freedom. Genuine freedom is the freedom to say yes to God's will and design. "You, my brothers and sisters, were called to be free. But do not use your freedom to indulge the sinful nature; rather serve one another humbly in love" (Gal. 5:13). The apostle Paul teaches that apart from Christ, people are in bondage to selfish desires. Only Christ can bring genuine freedom: "Where the Spirit of the Lord is, there is freedom" (2 Cor. 3:17).

So what is the connection between the genuine freedom to choose God's way and the modern notion that freedom means doing whatever one pleases? The connection is precisely the Creator's decision not to create automata compelled by their very nature to obey and glorify God. Instead, God chose to make free persons who could, without compulsion, willingly decide to love and submit to God. That meant, however, that God also created persons with the potential to disobey and thus foolishly embrace and glorify a distorted understanding of freedom as a personal right to do whatever we please. That is not what God desires. It is not genuine freedom (in part because it inevitably leads to bondage to harmful selfish desires). But its possibility flows from God's desire to be in personal relationship with persons who freely choose to love and obey him.

In an analogous way, societies that recognize the right of religious freedom do not thereby express a desire for a society full of a vast range of contradictory religious beliefs. But they do acknowledge that persons are free beings made by God to enjoy the freedom to obey or disobey their Creator. Therefore they insist that the state must protect the freedom of each person to embrace, practice, and share whatever religious beliefs they choose.

Biblical Foundations

At the beginning of the biblical story stands the divine decision to make human beings with the potential for two radically different outcomes. We are so intrinsically designed for right relationship with God that our hearts are forever restless until they rest in God. Yet we are also formed with the freedom that we can choose to embrace or turn away from our loving Creator. The natural world—sun, rivers, flowers, birds, and animals—all sing praises to their Creator. But they do so of necessity, not choice. God wanted human friends who would freely choose to obey and love him; that is the source and foundation of religious freedom. If God creates and treats persons that way, how dare society not also grant persons the same freedom?

God created the first human beings, revealed himself to them, and told them how to live in obedience and joy. They promptly used their freedom to doubt God's word and make their own rules. History, especially biblical history, records the long dialogue between the Creator, who keeps revealing himself and his way, pleading with us to believe and obey, and foolish persons, who sometimes respond faithfully, but at least as often choose to go their own way.

The history of Israel is an amazing illustration of that dialogue. Again and again—through Abraham, Moses, the judges, the prophets—God reveals more and more of himself and pleads with the people to obey. For a short time they do, but again and again they refuse. They make an idolatrous golden calf even while God is giving Moses the Ten Commandments. They worship Canaanite gods, even sacrificing their children to the idols, in spite of God's strict command to have no other gods beside Yahweh. It is true that God punishes them for their disobedience, but it is also crystal clear that God grants astonishing freedom to his chosen people—allowing them to choose whether or not to believe and obey what he has revealed. Although God eventually punishes with destruction and death, the important fact for our understanding of God's gift of freedom is that for centuries, God has continued to grant the good gifts of life, sun, rain, and food whether or not his people choose to embrace the truth he has revealed. The Old Testament is an astounding story of religious freedom.

Nowhere is that clearer than in the prophet Hosea. God commanded Hosea to act out in his own personal life the story of God's love for Israel and his longing for her to forsake all other gods and return to him. Like an unfaithful wife, Israel had committed adultery by worshiping false gods. So God told Hosea to marry and love a prostitute, and even return to her after she had betrayed him, as a sign that God still loved Israel and longed for her to choose to return to him. "The LORD said to me, 'Go, show your love to your wife again, though she is loved by another and is an adulteress. Love her as the Lord loves the Israelites, though they turn to other gods'" (Hos. 3:1). God continued to grant the people of Israel religious freedom even as they again and again broke his heart with their unbelief and disobedience. No one expresses this patient waiting of God who respects our freedom better than Paul: "Concerning Israel he says, 'All day long I have held out my hands to a disobedient and obstinate people'" (Rom. 10:21).

It is true that the Old Testament contains laws that are contrary to aspects of what today we consider basic elements of religious freedom. The penalty for blasphemy was death (Lev. 24:16). But it would be a mistake to focus on those texts and miss the larger picture in which God gives his people amazing freedom to embrace or reject his way.

Jesus deepens our understanding of God's gift of religious freedom, underlining the fact that God "causes his sun to rise on the evil and the good, and sends rain on the righteous and the unrighteous" (Matt. 5:45). Whether or not we respond to God in faith and obedience, God continues to give the good gifts necessary for human life.

Jesus's explanation of his parable of the wheat and weeds, as outlined in chapter 6, clearly points us to a societal framework in which all people enjoy religious freedom (Matt. 13:24–30). Jesus clearly says that the field where we should allow wheat and weeds to grow together is the world, that is, society as a whole. God wants everyone to enjoy the freedom to accept or reject the gospel until the end of the age.

The parable of the net thrown into the sea points in the same direction: The net gathers in good and bad fish, but the text explicitly says that it is "at the end of the age" when the angels will separate the evil from the righteous (Matt. 13:47–50). Until Christ's return both should enjoy freedom in society to embrace or reject God's way.

The New Testament describes a God who loves each person so much that God, in the person of the Son, suffers Roman crucifixion so that "whoever believes in him shall not perish but have eternal life" (John 3:16). God invites each person to accept or reject the divine invitation to live forever with the living God. He longs for every person to accept that invitation, "not wanting anyone to perish" (2 Pet. 3:9), but God does not force us to choose him. It is only those who choose to embrace Christ who are saved: "If you declare with your mouth, 'Jesus is Lord,' and believe in your heart that God raised him from the dead, you will be saved" (Rom. 10:9). The choice is ours. Indeed, even after persons have come to faith in Christ, after we "have tasted the heavenly gift . . . have shared in the Holy Spirit . . . have tasted the goodness of the word of God and the powers of the coming age" (Heb. 6:4–5), even after all that, Hebrews clearly teaches that we have the freedom to walk away from Christ ("to fall away") and depart eternally from him (v. 6). That is how serious God is about our freedom.

The nature of the incarnation underlines God's respect for our freedom. The Creator of the galaxies could have become flesh with such blazing splendor and overwhelming force that it would have obliterated our freedom and coerced our response. Instead, he came as a baby, then became an ordinary carpenter, and finally a wandering teacher. Throughout, there were powerful signs—birth by a virgin, miraculous healings—that someone highly unusual was present. Increasingly, he made astounding claims, not just to be the expected Messiah but to be the Son of God. And on Easter morning, he rose from the dead. But never was the evidence for his claims so overpowering that it overwhelmed human freedom. The risen Jesus could have visited Pilate and established permanent residence in the temple, compelling everyone to acknowledge who he was. Instead, he provided substantial evidence to reveal his identity and confirm his claims without overwhelming our freedom. Faithful to the pattern of the God we see in the Old Testament, Jesus wanted disciples who freely chose to believe and obey him.

Learning from History

For the first few centuries, the church lived out this vision. They were only a tiny minority in a powerful pagan empire, but they believed and taught that the risen carpenter was now Lord of all, King of the universe. This included the powerful Roman Empire where Caesar, who claimed to be divine, thought he was in charge. The early Christians announced that they would obey Jesus, rather than Caesar or any other earthly authority, when their commands conflicted. "We must obey God rather than human beings," the apostles insisted (Acts 5:29). They were clear that Jesus and the church's leaders must govern the church, not Caesar. Even though it meant martyrdom for thousands, the early Christians practiced their belief that the church had the right to be independent of the state. They simply refused to let Caesar run the church. At great cost, they practiced freedom of religion.

Again and again, over many centuries, the church has been a powerful voice for religious freedom simply by being the church. Confronted with ancient and modern dictators who tried to tell Christians what they could and could not believe and do, Christians regularly insisted that the church possessed a divine authority independent of the state and consequently defied unjust governments. "Thus the very existence of the Christian Church in society is an affirmation that there is to be human freedom within society, including the freedom to say no to the state when the Christian conscience dictates."[1] This was vividly clear in the first three centuries.

Things began to change when the emperor Constantine became a Christian in the early fourth century. At first, they were overwhelmed with gratitude to God for the new freedom to be Christians without persecution by the state, but the temptations of special privilege soon proved irresistible. Within one hundred years, even the great theologian Augustine called on the state to enforce Christian orthodoxy by executing heretics. The genuine religious freedom of the fourth century, in which Christians, pagans, and people of other beliefs all enjoyed basic religious freedom, soon disappeared. Not until the Second Vatican Council (1962–1965) did the Roman Catholic Church abandon its belief that "Christian" governments should enforce Christian belief with the sword.

The first major call to abandon the Constantinian union of church and state emerged in the early years of the Protestant Reformation. Some of Ulrich Zwingli's circle of Reformers in Zurich in the 1520s began to think that the New Testament taught that only believers should be baptized. Since they did not think infants could have saving faith, they rejected infant baptism and only baptized adults who believed. (Their critics said they rebaptized—hence the name Ana-[i.e., re-]baptists.) As Zwingli refused to move ahead with church reforms until the city government approved, the Anabaptists began to articulate a clear separation of church and state. They insisted that the state had no right to make decisions for the church. The church is that body of believing adults who have personally come to faith in Christ and now submit themselves to the leadership of officials selected by the church.[2]

In addition to this radical rejection of more than a millennium of the union of church and state, the Anabaptists also believed that Christians dare not kill and therefore cannot serve in any army. Not surprisingly, these two radical ideas provoked the wrath of all other Christians. As the Anabaptist movement spread rapidly throughout Europe in the decade after 1525, Catholics, Lutherans, and Calvinists all agreed that the state should execute these "heretics." Thousands died—drowned in rivers and lakes, burned at the stake, and executed with the sword.

The Anabaptists and their followers who later became known as Mennonites survived only in small isolated communities protected by rugged terrain or princes who appreciated their skills and hard work. One of those places was Calvinist Holland, which by the end of the sixteenth century began to allow some freedom to non-Calvinists. A thriving Mennonite community emerged and in the early seventeenth century welcomed some British Puritans who fled to Holland to escape Anglican persecution. The Dutch Mennonites convinced them that the New Testament teaches believer's baptism, so they underwent adult baptism. Their Baptist confession of faith of 1612 clearly affirmed the

Mennonite commitment to religious freedom for the individual conscience and thus the separation of church and state.[3]

A few decades later, some of these same Baptists returned to England from Holland with their Mennonite understanding of religious freedom and joined vigorously in the intense debates of the 1640s and 1650s. No one was more articulate than John Overton.[4] Overton published a blazing defense of religious freedom called *The Arraignment of Mr. Persecution*, citing Jesus's parable of the wheat and weeds to defend his call for religious freedom.[5] Slowly, over the course of the later seventeenth and early eighteenth centuries, both England and Holland granted increasing freedom to Christian groups that rejected the official Anglican or Calvinist state religion.

The Anabaptist/Baptist call for religious freedom had grown out of strong theological belief. But a second powerful movement for religious freedom emerged from a quite different source in the course of the seventeenth and eighteenth centuries. For almost 150 years after the Protestant Reformation divided Europe into Catholic, Lutheran, Reformed, and Anglican states, European nations fought bitter wars of religion. They were bloody, frequent, and devastating. Increasingly, European intellectuals turned away in revulsion, not just from the wars but from the Christian beliefs that seemed to motivate the warring armies. More and more "philosophers" of the eighteenth-century Enlightenment began to argue that we should replace passionate, historic Christian belief (which leads to intolerance and war) with a rational faith grounded in human reason. The result was an Enlightenment Deism that considered all the historic religions as equally good (or bad) and championed religious tolerance based on a rejection of the truth claims of specific religions. After all, was not 150 years of bloody wars of religion between Catholics and Protestants sufficient evidence that both must be wrong?

It was in America in the eighteenth century that these two streams—the Anabaptist/Baptist theological call for religious freedom and the Enlightenment plea based in revulsion from religious wars and growing suspicion of all religious belief—came together to produce the historic affirmation of full religious freedom in the First Amendment to the US Constitution in 1791.

In the 1630s, Roger Williams, an early Baptist leader, defended the right to religious freedom in the face of Puritan persecution in the Massachusetts Bay Colony,[6] but he was unsuccessful, so he fled to what is now Rhode Island and founded the town of Providence in 1644. In 1663, the new colony received a royal charter that granted toleration for all religions.[7] A little later, William Penn offered religious freedom in his Quaker-run Pennsylvania.

Others, like Thomas Jefferson, author of the American Declaration of Independence, also contributed to the historic declaration of religious freedom in the First Amendment. As an eighteenth-century Deist, Jefferson thought that human reason provided a universal, rational morality that should shape all public life and thereby free it from religious conflict. In fact, he expected that dogmatic religious beliefs like those integral to historic Christianity would wither away and eventually disappear. But in the meantime, he insisted on religious freedom for all religions as long as they accepted the understanding that religion should deal only with personal life, not the public realm.[8]

Together, these two streams—Anabaptist/Baptist/Quaker thought and Enlightenment Deism—created the First Amendment's sweeping affirmation of religious freedom. "Congress shall make no law respecting an establishment of religion, or prohibiting the free exercise thereof." Slowly, in the course of the next two hundred plus years, more and more countries either continued their slow progress toward full religious freedom—Great Britain, Holland—or moved more quickly to embrace it—Western Europe and the countries of the British Commonwealth in the nineteenth century, and then most countries around the world in the course of the twentieth century. Even in many places where governments significantly restrict religious freedom (e.g., China, Cuba), they officially recognize it.[9] It is a central affirmation of the UN Declaration of Human Rights. Only in some Muslim countries is religious freedom officially rejected today. The historical experience of the last two centuries has demonstrated that religious freedom contributes to, rather than undermines, societal peace and well-being.

Increasingly, throughout the world, there is widespread agreement on key elements of religious freedom: individuals should be free to believe, worship, and act in conformity with their religious beliefs (even convert to another religion) without interference from the state; religious institutions (churches, temples, mosques, synagogues, religious nonprofit organizations, etc.) should be free to organize and engage in activities in keeping with their mission without interference from the state.

Total Separation

Does that mean that "church and state" must be totally separate, totally unrelated? Is Thomas Jefferson's image of a "wall of separation" between church and state helpful?

No. Total separation of church and state is both practically impossible and theologically unacceptable.

If the state wants to be careful neither to establish religion nor hinder its free exercise, then the state must have some working definition of religion![10] If the state decides not to tax religious institutions (churches, synagogues, faith-based organizations), then it requires some legal definition of religion to distinguish the religious institutions it will not tax from nonreligious ones that it may tax. Precisely in order to respect religious freedom, the state must have some relationship with religious institutions.

The theological reasons for rejecting total separation are even more important. Jefferson's famous letter that contained the words "separation between church and state" also defined religion as something purely personal: "Religion is a matter which lies solely between man and his God."[11] Christianity, Judaism, and Islam all reject this exclusively personal, privatized view of religion.

For Christians, Jesus is Lord of all—King of kings and Lord of lords. That means that Christians must embrace and live out Christ's lordship not just in their personal lives and in church but also in every area of life. The very essence of Christian faith requires that it find expression in public life in many different ways.

There is a sense in which the church has some responsibility to shape every area of life: family, education, business, the arts, and the state. Since Christ is Lord of all these areas, Christians must reflect deeply on what it means to act in a Christlike way in all of these realms. The church must nurture individual believers and also specially focused organizations that understand how to do this and in fact do it well.

This task certainly includes shaping the state, but that does not mean the church should try to run the state. It is crucial to understand that church and state are two distinct institutions, both equally ordained by God, but enjoying different purposes. The purpose of the state is to nurture justice—i.e., right relationships between all the individuals and institutions in a given society—for our life here on earth until Christ returns. The purpose of the church is to preach and live the full gospel of the kingdom. This includes both preparing persons for life eternal and also teaching and modeling what it means to live now according to the norms of Jesus's messianic kingdom that has already begun to break into history. As the church does this second task, it necessarily teaches both its members, and anyone else who will listen, the basic principles that lead to justice and wholeness in every area of life including politics. Inevitably, therefore, the church interacts in fundamental ways with the state simply by carrying out its own mission to teach and live its confession that Jesus is Lord of all.

That does not mean, however, that we forget that the church and state have quite different mandates. It does not mean the church as an institution should seek to run the state. It does not mean that Christians should seek a constitutional amendment declaring, "Jesus is Lord." (That statement is certainly true, but it is not part of the state's mandate to comment in any way on that truth.) Proclaiming this truth is the task of the church, not the state.

One crucial implication of what we have just said about the different purposes of the church and state is that it is fundamentally misguided and exceedingly dangerous to speak of any nation, including the United States, as a "Christian nation." The purpose of every state is to promote the justice God wills for all its citizens, regardless of their religious beliefs, not to confess Christ's lordship. Partly for that reason, no state has a special relationship to

God, although some states at various times do a better job of promoting the justice God wills than do others. Furthermore, Christian theology teaches and history demonstrates that every nation is a complex mixture of good and evil. Christian values have indeed shaped the history of some nations more than others, but this in no way means either that some nations are "Christian" or that they have a special relationship to God.

American history is especially problematic at just this point.[12] One part of the New England Puritans' failure to practice religious freedom was that they saw their whole society as "God's new covenant people"—"a new Israel." Somehow, as the United States adopted religious freedom for all, the notion of God's new Israel was transferred to the nation. Many Americans, especially Christians, came to believe that God had a special covenant with America.[13] The result has frequently been a near-idolatrous nationalism that equates God and country, failing to make the basic distinction between church and state.

All this means that the relationship between church and state is complex. They must be separate in very important ways, but they must not, and cannot, be totally separate. Inevitably and rightly they will interrelate in numerous ways.

One important reason they must interrelate is because Christians insist that their faith in Christ must find expression not just in personal beliefs and individual private practices, but in the common life of the church, which is Jesus's new visible community. Simply in order to be the new kingdom community Christ calls his church to be, the church must be able to organize as a visible community, constructing buildings, and organizing programs and institutions (e.g., schools and hospitals) to minister to the many needs of people, especially the poor and needy. Since the task of the state is to promote justice for all the persons and institutions in society, it inevitably must relate to religious institutions.

Since Christians must let Christ be Lord of their whole lives, and since Christians are also citizens responsible in a democracy to shape the decisions of government, both individual Christians and the organized church must relate to the state in many different ways. Four are especially important: prayer, modeling, prophetic challenge, and political participation.[14]

Prayer. First Timothy 2:1–2 urges Christians to offer "petitions, prayers, intercessions . . . for kings and all those in authority." Karl Barth says prayer for the state is "the essential service which the Church owes the State."[15] Prayer for the state, Barth suggests, is perhaps the best way to both remind the state of its limits and remind the church of its freedom. Prayer for the state also includes all the other things Christians owe the state.

Modeling. The church also owes society, including the state, the gift that comes from simply being the church. The church is supposed to be Jesus's messianic community, a visible model now of what the kingdom will be like when Christ returns. The church should be a living, visible demonstration of the racial, economic, and social reconciliation that God wills for all humanity. The church should be leading the way, implementing God's special concern for the poor and needy.

Just by being the church—Christ's visible model now of the redeemed humanity that he will bring in its fullness at his return—the church deeply impacts society. Historically, it was the church that first sought to care for the sick and offer education to poor children. Impacted by this model, the state later built hospitals and organized universal education. On the other hand, Christian appeals to government in the absence of consistent modeling in the body of Christ are weak and ineffective. It is a farce to ask government to legislate what Christians refuse to live.[16]

Prophetic challenge. Christians know that Christ is Lord of all, even the state, though the state does not explicitly acknowledge that reality. Christians also know both God's standards about justice that apply to all societies and also the sad truth that sin has deeply corrupted every society. Therefore, Christians must raise voices of prophetic challenge that call attention to current instances of societal injustice.

Archbishop Desmond Tutu and other national and global Christian leaders rightly condemned the terrible evil of apartheid in South Africa. Bishop David Gitari rightly denounced undemocratic proposals and corruption by top government officials in Kenya.[17] Individual Christians, congregations, and denominations all act appropriately when they bring economic injustice, violations of freedom, sexual trafficking, indeed any injustice to the attention of society in general and political leaders in particular. Prophetic witness calling attention to the state's failure to implement justice is an important gift the church rightly offers to the state.

Political participation. There are many forms of political participation: formulating and promoting a biblically grounded framework for political engagement; holding open, bipartisan dialogues on specific issues, platforms, and candidates; supporting or opposing specific pieces of legislation; endorsing and working to elect specific candidates; running for and serving in an elected political office.

As citizens, individual Christians rightly do all of these things. It is also appropriate for groups of Christians to form organizations and institutions to do all these things, for Christians to act communally through a common vision.

Normally, however, it is better if church leaders (pastors, denominational leaders) and official church structures (congregations, national denominational bodies, etc.) not do some of these things. Why? For at least two reasons. First, it is not the proper task of the church to tell government what detailed policies it should follow. Second, if church officials and structures become immersed in detailed political bargaining and partisan activity, they lose their moral authority, weaken their ability to minister to the full range of church members who share sharply divergent political views, and easily are corrupted and used by politicians.

Normally, it is better for pastors and other church leaders not to run for political office.[18] It is not only illegal today in the United States but also generally unwise for church leaders and official church structures to endorse specific candidates. With care, on occasion, and after due process within a congregation or denomination, it is appropriate for a congregation or denomination to explicitly oppose or endorse a specific piece of legislation. On occasion, without a congregational or denominational process that authorizes church leaders to speak for the whole body, it is appropriate for church leaders to do the same—as long as they make it clear that they are only speaking for themselves as citizens and not for their churches. Most of the time, however, I think it is wiser for church leaders and official church structures to help their church members think about and engage wisely and faithfully in politics by articulating and promoting some general political principles rather than regularly endorsing specific legislation.

Embracing religious freedom for all and insisting that the state should neither establish nor hinder the full exercise of religion does not mean that there should be no interaction between church and state or that we should banish religious people and religious arguments from political life. Both political life and theological conviction demand substantial interaction. However, deciding exactly what kind of interaction, and how much of what kind, is a complex task that is never finished.

Current Debates

There will always be complicated questions that every new generation will have to resolve. Some will be fairly clear, others more ambiguous. Should the state declare (as the government of Zambia did) that Jesus Christ is Lord of the country? No. Christians know this is true, but it is a violation of religious freedom for the government officially to make such a declaration. (It is quite all right, however, for individual politicians to publicly state their belief that they consider themselves personally accountable in all their political decisions to Christ their Lord.)

Should government organize prayer in the public schools? No. Organized prayer is something for religious institutions to do, not the state. But a moment of silence in which individual students and teachers may pray if they choose violates no one's religious freedom.

What about "In God We Trust" on our coins or the reference to God in the pledge of allegiance? Or government-supported chaplains and official prayers in the Congress? Plausible arguments on both sides can be offered. I doubt that either retaining or abandoning these practices would be very significant, although the debates will undoubtedly continue.

There are other areas of current debate that are of greater significance. I will discuss two: the state's posting of the Ten Commandments and the question of whether the First Amendment should lead to "equal treatment" of all religious and nonreligious people or a much stricter separation of church and state so that no state money flows to religious organizations.

State Posting of Ten Commandments

In the last two decades, there has been intense debate in the United States about whether the state should post the Ten Commandments. This debate is not about whether publicly displaying the Ten Commandments is constitutional. Individuals and churches and a host of other non-state groups have every right to publicly display the Ten Commandments. The only issue in question is whether it is constitutional for the state to do so.

I find five arguments in favor of the state publicly displaying the Ten Commandments to carry some weight, even though I do not think they are finally convincing.

First, American society obviously is in desperate need of moral teaching. A quick look at the widespread moral decay in our nation underlines the fact that our society desperately needs to be reminded of fundamental moral laws such as the Ten Commandments' prohibition of lying, murder, adultery, and theft. The state, as well as the society as a whole, urgently needs a reversal of this widespread moral decay.

But just because societal well-being requires something does not mean that the state is the right agency to promote it. As a Christian, I am certain that societal well-being is significantly advanced when large numbers of people embrace Jesus Christ as Lord and Savior and experience the transforming power of the Holy Spirit who remakes their character so it conforms more and more to that of Christ. But that does not mean the state should promote Christian evangelism and conversion.

A second plausible argument is that the Ten Commandments have made an important historical contribution to American law and therefore the state rightly posts the Ten Commandments in recognition of that historical contribution.

One must be careful, however, not to overstate this point. Penalties against perjury, murder, and theft are part of virtually all legal systems, including very ancient ones not at all influenced by the Hebrews' Ten Commandments. American law against perjury, murder, and theft comes from the English common law, which in turn goes back to pre-Christian Germanic tribes whose law already prohibited perjury, murder, and theft before they knew anything about the Ten Commandments. Certainly, once the English embraced Christianity, the Ten Commandments became a further support for those pre-Christian laws, but we must be careful not to overstate this importance.

A third plausible argument starts with the very important fact that one of the most crucial foundations of freedom and a limited state is the belief that the state is finally accountable to a transcendent moral law. This is an extremely important issue. Does not the state's posting of the Ten Commandments promote this belief by showing that the state itself recognizes that it is accountable to a transcendent moral law grounded in God?

Again the concern is important, but the means are wrong. It is unnecessary for the state to officially declare that it is accountable to God in order for belief in that truth to be widespread and effective. The constitutional prohibition against the state endorsing any religious belief in no way prohibits vast numbers of citizens, religious groups, and politicians from publicly expressing their own religious conviction that all governments are in fact accountable to transcendent moral law and to God, the source of that law. (One example is the president's reference to God in a presidential address.) If large numbers of individual citizens, including prominent politicians, regularly express and act upon that belief, society will enjoy the benefits of this crucial conviction without the state itself asserting this truth.

A fourth plausible argument is that some secular people today are trying to remove all references to the role religion has played in shaping American history, and we must stop them.

Again the concern is valid. For example, there has been a widespread attempt to reduce or eliminate the discussion of religious beliefs and events in the textbooks used in public schools. We rightly insist that the history books be accurate.

But the mere fact that secularists are at work does not mean they are always wrong. We have to carefully examine each case.

A fifth—and I think the strongest—argument is that laid out vigorously by Justice Scalia in his scathing dissent from the Supreme Court's 5–4 rejection of the posting of the Ten Commandments in two Kentucky counties (Union of Kentucky et al., June 27, 2005). Scalia showed very clearly that historically the Congress has often passed laws that refer to God. The day after Congress proposed the First Amendment, the very same Congress officially asked the president to proclaim a day of thanksgiving and prayer to "Almighty God." Scalia is surely correct that historically US governments did not think that explicit, official state references to God violated the First Amendment.

It is less clear, however, that we should draw the same conclusion today at a time when American citizens have many different religious views—from historic Christianity to Hindu polytheism to atheism. Scalia himself admits that government acknowledgment of God cannot be "entirely nondenominational"—that is, government cannot publicly thank God "without contradicting the beliefs of some people." Scalia concludes that the establishment clause "permits this *disregard* of polytheists and believers in unconcerned deities just as it permits the *disregard* of devout atheists" (my italics).

I think this conclusion is highly problematic. The establishment clause means that official state actions should not normally include religious statements that support one particular religious view and reject another. I think there are decisive arguments against the state displaying the Ten Commandments.

First, the disestablishment clause of the First Amendment clearly means that the state must not advocate inherently religious beliefs and practices. Any casual reading of the Ten Commandments makes it perfectly clear that the explicit setting and the first four commandments are fundamentally religious. The setting for them all and the authority for them all is stated at the beginning: "I am the LORD your God, who brought you out of Egypt" (Exod. 20:2). The first few commandments prohibit polytheism, graven images of God, using God's name lightly, and working on the Sabbath. Clearly the Ten Commandments explicitly endorse monotheism (thus rejecting, to name a few alternative religious beliefs, atheism, Hindu polytheism, and those Buddhist traditions that do not believe in a personal God). The Ten Commandments not only endorse a belief in God, they endorse specific beliefs about God that significant numbers of US citizens reject. For the state to post and thus endorse these specific religious statements is clearly to violate the disestablishment clause.

Second, the free-exercise clause does not give Christians the right, as Carl Esbeck writes, "to seize the levers of government and employ the machinery of state in praying one's prayers and expounding one's Scriptures."[19] It does, of course, give Christians the right to publicly declare their beliefs with as large a public display of the Ten Commandments or any other part of the Bible that they want to erect on private property.

Third, when the state displays a religious text, it thereby endorses that text unless it is explicit and clear that that is not the case. For example, when a state school teaches a class on the history of religion and includes explicit religious texts from several different religions, it is clear that the posting of the several religious texts on the school website is not to endorse any of them, but to advance the neutral purpose of students studying all of them. Similarly, the pictures of Moses or the two tablets that appear in the Supreme Court building clearly do not constitute an endorsement of the Ten Commandments but rather represents the celebration of law and lawgivers because they appear with many other famous historical promulgators of law.

On the other hand, to install a large monument of the Ten Commandments as Judge Moore did in Alabama, or to organize a movement to have public schools display the Ten Commandments, is to wrongly ask the state to endorse what is a religious document.

At the heart of the meaning of the disestablishment clause is the demand that the state not discriminate in any way against any of its citizens on the basis of their religious beliefs or lack thereof. For the state to post (and thus endorse) a document that specifically advocates one set of religious beliefs that some citizens share and others reject is clearly to engage in discrimination and show disrespect for some citizens' beliefs. It thus runs the danger of promoting social conflict. The state should be neutral, not favor one religion over another. If we do not want the state to promote someone else's religion, we should not ask it to promote ours. If we do not want the state to promote Hindu polytheism or atheism, we should not ask it to promote theism.

No Aid or Equal Access?

One major recent debate over the meaning of the religious freedom clauses of the First Amendment has been whether the constitution calls for no state financial aid for social and educational programs run by religious organizations or rather demands equal access for all groups. (We are not talking about state funding of specifically religious activities like prayer, worship, Bible study, and evangelism. Everybody agrees that would be wrong and unconstitutional.) Ruling in a case on state funding for transportation to private religious primary and secondary schools, the Supreme Court decided (1947) that not a cent of state money should go to religious schools.[20] That was the rule for education for several decades.

At the same time, a number of religious social service organizations (including many pervasively religious ones) received substantial state funding.[21] It was not clear, however, how constitutional this practice was in light of the 1947 decision.

For the last two plus decades, however, the Supreme Court has increasingly moved away from the principle of no aid to religious organizations. In its place, the Supreme Court has adopted an equal access or neutrality approach.[22] This is clear in a number of cases, including *Widmar v. Vincent* (1981), *Agostini v. Felton* (1997), and the historic *Zelman v. Simmons-Harris* (2002) decision approving state-funded educational vouchers in Cleveland that enabled parents to choose religious schools.

In recent years, the debate over these issues has found a special focus over the "charitable choice" language in four bills signed by President Clinton and then the implementation of new faith-based initiatives by President George W. Bush and largely continued by President Obama. The charitable choice language in the 1996 welfare bill sought to enable all faith-based organizations to enjoy equal access to state funds for social service programs operated by non-state agencies. Specific provisions safeguarded both the religious freedom of clients and the religious character of faith-based social service agencies. The latter, even when they received state funds, could retain their religious identity and their right to hire staff that shared their religious beliefs.[23] Whether or not an organization was religious was no longer relevant; the only criteria were whether an organization could deliver the service effectively. Equal access—or neutrality with regard to the religious character of the organization—was the rule.

Understanding the current American context where there are many different types of social service organizations helps one see why equal access, rather than no aid to religious organizations, is the proper interpretation of the First Amendment. In the United States today, there are a vast array of non-state social service organizations: some are secular, others partially religious, and still others highly religious.[24] Many billions of dollars flow every year to many of these non-state social service organizations. If state funds only go to secular organizations, then religious social service organizations would have to compete in the same field, offering parallel services without state funds, with secular providers who enjoyed state funds. It hardly seems fair for the state to tax everyone—both religious and secular citizens—and then fund only allegedly secular programs.

There is also a second problem. These allegedly "secular" programs are not really as neutral as it is often claimed. It is true that there is no explicit teaching in these programs that philosophical naturalism is true and that nothing exists except the natural order. But *implicitly*, these programs support such a worldview. Implicitly, purely "secular" programs convey the message that all that is needed to address social problems such as drug addiction, low job skills, or single parenthood is nonreligious technical knowledge and skills. Implicitly, these programs teach that social problems can be solved solely through technical, materialistic, naturalistic procedures, with no reference to any spiritual dimension. Such a claim involves beliefs about the ultimate nature of reality and human existence. Instead of being religiously "neutral," this belief system actually serves the same function as religion. Whether it is advanced explicitly or implicitly, it thus represents one particular, contemporary religious worldview. In a context where state monies go only to allegedly "secular" programs that implicitly teach that religious faith is unnecessary to solve our social problems, the state ends up massively biased in favor of one particular quasi-religious perspective—namely philosophical naturalism.

In our kind of society, it is simply not possible for the state to carry out the "no-aid-to-religion" principle. If it ever tried to implement that principle consistently today in the funding of social services, it would end up offering aid almost exclusively to the quasi-religion of philosophical naturalism, even though that worldview would often be communicated in an implicit way. Charitable choice offers a better alternative that is fair to every religious perspective. Via charitable choice, the state offers equal benefits to any social service provider (faith-based or secular) as long as the nonprofit successfully provides social benefits desired by the state.[25]

The world has experienced an enormous expansion of religious freedom in the last one hundred years, but much remains to be done. Christians and others still experience persecution in many places, including China, North Korea, and most Muslim countries. The Orthodox Church sometimes seeks special privileges for itself from the state in places like Russia. Western Europe has to struggle anew with its commitment to religious freedom in light of a growing Muslim minority. Urgent struggles remain for all dedicated to genuine religious freedom for everyone.

10

Peacemaking, Just War, and Nonviolence

The historical record is a long, bloody plea for peace. For all of recorded history, political rulers and their underlings have slaughtered untold numbers of people in war, genocide, and massacres. Political decisions often led to widespread death by famine, forced migrations, and other atrocities. One scholar estimates that the numbers killed range from about 90 million to 260 million for the centuries before 1900.[1]

In a recent book by Jonathan Glover, the author estimates that another 86 million people died in wars fought from 1900 to 1989. That means 2,500 people every day, 100 people every hour, for ninety years.[2]

In addition to those killed in war, democide (i.e., genocide and mass murder by governments) killed approximately 120 million people just in the twentieth century—perhaps more than 80 million alone in the two communist countries of China and the Soviet Union.[3]

Behind those statistics stand hundreds of millions of mothers, fathers, wives, and children weeping for their loved ones. Out of this anguished history arises a longing for peace, for a time when "they will beat their swords into plowshares and their spears into pruning hooks," a time when "nation will not take up sword against nation, nor will they train for war anymore" (Isa. 2:4).

Biblical Foundations

The Bible does not contain one clear, unequivocal word on killing and war. Murder (unauthorized killing) is clearly forbidden (Exod. 20:13), but the Old

157

Testament prescribes the death penalty for a number of offenses. And there are numerous passages where the text says that God commanded the people of Israel to fight wars and even kill women and children captured in battle (Josh. 6:21; 8:24; 10:28–43; Judg. 1:17).

It is true that there is a strong, oft-repeated condemnation in the prophets of the way Israel trusted in horses and chariots rather than Yahweh. "Woe to those who go down to Egypt for help, who rely on horses, who trust in the multitude of their chariots and in the great strength of their horsemen, but do not look to the Holy One of Israel" (Isa. 31:1). Also, God frequently commanded the people of Israel to do nothing and allow Yahweh to protect them. To the terrified Israelites trapped between the sea and Pharaoh's approaching army, Moses said, "Do not be afraid. Stand firm and you will see the deliverance the Lord will bring you today. . . . The Lord will fight for you; you need only to be still" (Exod. 14:13–14).[4] How to interpret this complex Old Testament record on war is not entirely clear and obvious.

What is certain, however, is that there is a powerful set of Old Testament texts predicting a future messianic ruler, the Prince of Peace, who would bring shalom—right relationship with God, neighbors, and the earth. Isaiah in particular foretold a future messianic age when a Davidic Messiah would restore peace in all its richness.[5]

In the latter days (i.e., messianic time), the prophets foretold, all nations would learn God's ways, as quoted earlier:

> They will beat their swords into plowshares
>   and their spears into pruning hooks.
> Nation will not take up sword against nation,
>   nor will they train for war anymore.
>   Isaiah 2:4; Micah 4:3

The prophets expected the Messiah to usher in this age of peace. In "the latter time" (the messianic age), the boot of the tramping warrior and the battle garments rolled in blood will disappear (Isa. 9:5).

> For to us a child is born,
>   to us a son is given,
>   and the government will be on his shoulders.
> And he will be called
>   Wonderful Counselor, Mighty God,
>   Everlasting Father, Prince of Peace.
> Of the increase of his government and peace
>   there will be no end.
> He will reign on David's throne,
>   and over his kingdom,

> establishing and upholding it
>> with justice and righteousness
>> from that time on and forever.
>>>> Isaiah 9:6–7

Although the word *peace* is not used, the vision of messianic shalom in Isaiah 11 is at least as breathtaking. When the messianic shoot from the stump of Jesse comes forth, he will judge the poor with righteousness (v. 4). Peace and harmony will prevail throughout the earth.

> The wolf will live with the lamb,
>> the leopard will lie down with the goat,
> the calf and the lion and the yearling together;
>> and a little child will lead them. . . .
> They will neither harm nor destroy
>> on all my holy mountain,
> for the earth will be filled with the knowledge of the LORD
>> as the waters cover the sea.[6]
>>>> Isaiah 11:6, 9

Old Testament scholar Gerhard von Rad summarizes the Messiah's role in the prophetic hope for shalom: "The Messiah is the Guarantor and Guardian of peace in the coming messianic kingdom."[7]

In both these messianic passages, peace, justice, and righteousness are a central part of the expected messianic age. Elsewhere, Isaiah points out that peace is the result of justice and righteousness (32:16–17). The prophets, then, foresaw a time when God's Messiah would come to restore Israel and establish justice and peace.

The early church declared Jesus to be the fulfillment of these messianic prophecies. Matthew 4:15–16 quotes Isaiah 9:1–2 in connection with the beginning of Jesus's proclamation of the coming of the messianic kingdom. Paul refers to Isaiah 11:1, 10 in Romans 15:12. In Luke 1:68–79, Zechariah announces that John the Baptist will prepare the way for Jesus, the Messiah. Quoting Isaiah 9:2, Zechariah points with eager anticipation to the Messiah who will "guide our feet into the way of peace" (Luke 1:79 NRSV). When the angels (Luke 2:14) announce Jesus's birth with the choral shout "peace on earth," they simply confirm the fulfillment of the prophetic vision of messianic peace.[8]

Exactly the same claim appears in the church fathers of the first three centuries. Repeatedly they asserted that the messianic prophecies of Isaiah 2:4 and Micah 4:3 were fulfilled in Jesus's teaching on peace. "We have come in accordance with the counsels of Jesus to cut down our warlike and arrogant swords of dispute into ploughshares, and we convert into sickles the spears we formerly used in fighting. For we no longer take sword against nation, nor do we learn any more to make war."[9]

Almost all the Jews of Jesus's day longed for the time of the Messiah. But they had fundamentally contradictory ideas about how to prepare for his coming. The Essenes of the Qumran community had a ritualistic approach; ritual purity was the way to prepare for the messianic age. The Pharisees offered a legalistic strategy; if everyone would obey the law perfectly, the Messiah would come. The Zealots demanded violence; they genuinely believed that if they could persuade the entire Jewish nation to rebel against Rome, the Messiah would come.

The Zealots were not alone in expecting bloody conflict with the Romans. The "peaceful" Essenes opposed violent resistance to Rome for a time, but their War Scroll reveals violent expectations. When God himself would intervene at the end of the age, all the devout would join him in a holy war of total annihilation of the wicked. The unsophisticated masses, for their part, yearned for a military Messiah like David:

> How beautiful is the king, the messiah, who will arise from those who are of the house of Judah! He girds up his loins and goes forth and orders the battle array against his enemies and slays the kings along with their overlords, and no king or overlord can stand before him; he reddens the mountains with the blood of their slain, his clothing is dipped in blood like a winepress.[10]

The expectation of widespread violence at the appearance of the Messiah was prevalent. According to the unanimous judgments of the historians Josephus, Tacitus, and Suetonius, such martial messianic expectations were one of the major causes of the outbreak of the Jewish War (in AD 66).[11]

In fact, just before Jesus predicts the total destruction of Jerusalem, he weeps over the city. Sadly he laments, "If you, even you, had only known on this day what would bring you peace—but now it is hidden from your eyes" (Luke 19:42). Their failure to embrace Jesus's approach to peace will lead to their destruction.

Jesus's entire messianic understanding was radically different from most of his Jewish contemporaries. In both actions and words Jesus rejected lethal violence. At the triumphal entry Jesus clearly disclosed his nonviolent messianic conception. Both Matthew 21:5 and John 12:15 quote Zechariah 9:9 to underline their belief that Jesus's action fulfilled this Old Testament prophecy. Modern commentators agree that Jesus consciously chose to fulfill the eschatological prophecy of Zechariah precisely because it depicted a peaceful Messiah.[12] Zechariah's peaceful vision contrasts sharply with most messianic expectations:

> See, your king comes to you,
>   righteous and having salvation,
> lowly and riding on a donkey,
>   on a colt, the foal of a donkey.

> I will take away the chariots from Ephraim
> and the warhorses from Jerusalem,
> and the battle bow will be broken.
> He will proclaim peace to the nations.
> Zechariah 9:9–10

Here is a picture of the Messiah riding not a warhorse but a humble donkey. Echoing many prophets who had denounced Israel's reliance on chariots and cavalry, the text foresees the abolition of instruments of war. Messianic peace prevails. This is the messianic picture that Jesus chose to fulfill.

In the final crisis, Jesus persisted in his rejection of the sword. He rebuked Peter for attacking those who came to arrest him: "All who take the sword will perish by the sword" (Matt. 26:52 NRSV). Not even the defensive sword should be used. It is significant that Jesus's rebuke to Peter gives a general reason for not using the sword, not just an objection to use it in this special case. "He is obviously not thinking of just this special situation since he takes pains to lay down the general truth that they who take the sword shall perish with it."[13]

Similarly, Jesus informed Pilate that his kingdom was not of this world *in one specific way*—namely, that his followers do not use violence: "My kingdom is not of this world. If it were, my servants would fight to prevent my arrest by the Jewish leaders. But now my kingdom is from another place" (John 18:36). Jesus obviously did not mean that the messianic kingdom he had begun had nothing to do with this world. That would have contradicted the kingdom values he announced, and it would have made nonsense of the very prayer he taught his disciples: "Thy kingdom come . . . *on earth* as it is in heaven" (Matt. 6:10, emphasis added).

Jesus's high priestly prayer is perhaps the best commentary: "I have given them your word and the world has hated them, for they are not of the world any more than I am of the world. My prayer is not that you take them out of the world but that you protect them from the evil one" (John 17:14–15).

In this statement, as in John 18:36, the preposition *of* points to the source, not the location, of authority, methods, and norms. This gospel-of-the-Word-become-flesh would never have said that Jesus was not very much *in* this world, but his authority and methods did not derive from the fallen order. Here, Jesus rejects even defensive violence to prevent the most unjust arrest in human history! Jesus's followers must live according to the norms of the new messianic age.

Matthew 5:38–48 is, of course, Jesus's most famous teaching on peacemaking:

You have heard that it was said, "Eye for eye, and tooth for tooth." But I tell you, do not resist an evil person. If anyone slaps you on the right cheek, turn to them the other cheek also. And if anyone wants to sue you and take your shirt, hand over your coat as well. If anyone forces you to go one mile, go with them two miles. Give to the one who asks you, and do not turn away from the one who wants to borrow from you.

You have heard that it was said, "Love your neighbor and hate your enemy." But I tell you, love your enemies and pray for those who persecute you, that you may be children of your Father in heaven. He causes his sun to rise on the evil and the good, and sends rain on the righteous and the unrighteous. If you love those who love you, what reward will you get? Are not even the tax collectors doing that? And if you greet only your own people, what are you doing more than others? Do not even pagans do that? Be perfect, therefore, as your heavenly Father is perfect.

To a people so oppressed by foreign conquerors that over the previous two centuries they had repeatedly resorted to violent rebellion, Jesus gave the unprecedented command, "Love your enemies." New Testament scholar Martin Hengel believes that Jesus formulated this command to love one's enemies in conscious contrast to the teaching and practice of the Zealots.[14] Thus Jesus rejected one currently popular political method in favor of a radically different approach.

Jesus's command to love one's enemies contrasts sharply with widespread views that Jesus summarizes in verse 43: "You have heard that it was said, 'Love your neighbor and hate your enemy.'" The first part of this verse is a direct quotation from Leviticus 19:18: "love your neighbor as yourself." But who is one's neighbor? The first part of Leviticus 19:18 indicates that our neighbors are "sons of your own people" (ESV). This was the normal Jewish viewpoint. Pastor and scholar John Piper, in his extensive study of pre-Christian thinking about love for neighbor, shows that in Jewish thought the neighbor that one was obligated to love was normally understood to be a fellow Israelite.[15] This love for neighbor had clear ethnic and religious limitations. A different attitude toward gentiles was expected. Seldom, however, did the Old Testament command or sanction hatred of foreigners or enemies,[16] but Jewish contemporaries of Jesus did. The Zealots believed that "slaying of the godless enemy out of zeal for God's cause was a fundamental commandment, true to the rabbinic maxim "Whoever spills the blood of one of the godless is like one who offers a sacrifice." And the Qumran community's *Manual of Discipline* urged people to "love all the sons of light . . . and . . . hate all the sons of darkness."[17]

Jesus's way was radically different. Loving those who love you (Matt. 5:46), Jesus says, is relatively easy—even great sinners like tax collectors can do that. In fact, even the pagan gentiles act kindly toward the people in their own ethnic group. Jesus totally rejects that kind of ethnic or religious limitation on love.

For the members of Jesus's messianic kingdom, neighbor love must extend beyond the limited circle of the people of Israel, beyond the limited circle of the new people of God. This text says explicitly what the parable of the good Samaritan (Luke 10:29–37) suggests: all people everywhere are neighbors to Jesus's followers and therefore are to be actively loved. And that includes enemies—even violent, oppressive, foreign conquerors!

No image more powerfully contrasts Jesus's peaceful, messianic conception with violent contemporary expectations than that of the Suffering Servant. Popular Jewish thought hoped for a warlike, Davidic Messiah who would destroy the heathen oppressors. The early church taught that the Jewish messianic hope had been fulfilled in the humble Suffering Servant foreseen in Isaiah 53. The Old Testament passage spoke of a lowly servant who would suffer rather than kill: "He was wounded for our transgressions, He was bruised for our iniquities; the chastisement for our peace was upon Him, and by His stripes we are healed" (v. 5 NKJV). In his careful study, German New Testament scholar Joachim Jeremias concludes that from the beginning the early Christians saw Jesus as the fulfillment of Isaiah's "servant of God."[18]

Jeremias also holds that Jesus understood himself and his death in terms of Isaiah 53.[19] There are repeated indications in the Gospels that Jesus expected to die violently. Mark 10:45, which probably contains an allusion to Isaiah 53, indicates that he saw his death as a ransom for others. The word *ransom* probably refers to the offering for sin of Isaiah 53:10. At the Last Supper, Jesus spoke of his death for others in words that also likely allude to Isaiah 53. Understanding his messianic role in light of Isaiah 53, Jesus expected to die for others rather than to destroy the wicked.

Only in this context can we adequately understand Jesus's important teaching about peacemaking. It is the one who comes as Israel's true Messiah but then totally rejects all violent messianic visions, who rebukes Peter for using the sword. It is the one who faces the burning political question of his day and rejects violence as the way to usher in the messianic kingdom who says, "Turn the other cheek." It is the Messiah whose kingdom has already begun in dramatic acts of divine forgiveness who says, "Love your enemies . . . that you may be children of your Father in heaven" (Matt. 5:44–45).

Throughout history, Christians have disagreed about how to apply Jesus's example and teaching on peacemaking, but there can be no doubt that peacemaking was central to Jesus's vision and mission. He claimed to fulfill precisely the prophetic messianic passages that talked about a peaceful, non-warlike Messiah who would bring peace. He explicitly called his disciples to love even their enemies. Whatever Christians may finally conclude about the tough question of whether it is sometimes legitimate to restrain evil and correct injustice through lethal violence, all Christians must agree that our Lord Jesus summons us all to be active peacemakers who surprise even our enemies with love.

Christian History

Modern historical scholarship indicates that, for three centuries, every extant Christian writing that deals with the question of killing (both war and abortion) says that Christians must not kill.[20] In his careful scholarly study entitled *Christian Attitudes toward War and Peace*, Roland Bainton notes that, until the early fourth century, there is not a single existing Christian writing that supports Christian participation in warfare.[21] Paul Ramsey, a leading twentieth-century just-war theorist, has stated clearly that "for almost two centuries of the history of the early church, Christians were universally pacifists."[22] And Ramsey attributes their opposition to war to their theology of the cross: "How could anyone, who knew himself to be classed with transgressors and the enemies of God whom Christ came to die to save, love his own life and seek to save it more than that of his own enemy or murderer?"[23]

When the emperor Constantine made Christianity a legal religion in AD 313 things began to change. Within a century, Christianity became the official religion of the empire, and masses of people flocked into the church. Theologians developed arguments allowing Christians to fight for the "Christian" emperors. By the early fifth century, only Christians could serve in the army.

Even before Constantine, to be sure, there were some (we do not know how many) Christians in the army. Archaeologists have found a few epitaphs of soldiers who were Christians in the army in the late second and third centuries.[24] Writing in AD 197 Tertullian rebuked Christians who were in the army, thus acknowledging that some were there. Many, he added, withdrew at conversion.[25] Probably, however, their numbers were quite small in the second century, since the pagan author Celsus, writing in about AD 170, condemned Christianity on the grounds that if everyone became Christian, there would be no army![26]

By the late third century, more Christians were in the army. In the great persecution of 303–34, some of those martyred for their Christian faith were soldiers. By the early fourth century, there were clearly substantial numbers of Christians serving in the Roman army.[27]

There seems to be a disconnect between the consistent teaching of Christian writers that Christians dare never kill on the one hand and the growing number of Christian soldiers in the later third century. Part of the explanation may be that at that time many Roman soldiers did what was essentially police work. One prominent historian of the Roman army has said that "many a recruit need never have struck a blow in anger, outside a tavern."[28]

Some scholars have argued that the primary reason early Christian writers rejected Christian participation in the army was because of the idolatrous practices connected with military life. Careful analysis of the sources, however, indicates that this was one reason, but not the major one. The primary reason was opposition to killing.[29]

Again and again the sources make it clear the early church believed Jesus's teaching excluded killing. Tertullian (AD 160–220) taught that Jesus's summons to love enemies was the "principal precept."[30] He believed that in disarming Peter in the Garden of Gethsemane, Jesus "ungirded every soldier." He asked, "How shall a Christian wage war? Nay, how shall he even be a soldier in peacetime without the sword which the Lord has taken away?"[31]

In the middle of the third century, Origen (AD 183–254) said:

> We Christians no longer take up sword against nation, nor do we learn to make war anymore, having become children of peace for the sake of Jesus who is our leader. . . .
>
> To those who ask us where we have come from or who is our commander, we say that we have come in accordance with the counsels of Jesus to cut down our warlike and arrogant swords of dispute into plowshares, and we convert into sickles the spears we formerly used in fighting. For we no longer take sword against a nation, nor do we learn anymore to make war, having become sons of peace for the sake of Jesus who is our commander.[32]

In the middle of the previous century, Justin Martyr (martyred in AD 165) had said the same thing: "We who were filled with war and mutual slaughter and all wickedness have each and all throughout the earth changed our instruments of war, our swords into ploughshares and our spears into farming-tools, and cultivate piety, justice, love of mankind, faith and the hope which we have from the Father through the Crucified One."[33] A substantial number of Christian writers in the second and third centuries condemned Christian participation in war.[34]

In the one hundred years after the conversion of Constantine, however, the majority of Christians came to embrace a just-war position. Christian writers still emphasized peacemaking. They insisted that the use of lethal violence dare only be a last resort to correct injustice and repel attack, but the most influential Christian thinkers concluded that reluctantly, under certain limited circumstances, it was necessary to use the sword. In spite of a minority pacifist movement that surfaced with some vigor from time to time, this has been the majority view from the fifth century to the present.

St. Augustine (AD 356–430), followed by a long stream of Christian theologians over many centuries, slowly developed what became the just-war criteria for determining whether Christians should go to war and how they must fight.

What then are the criteria Christians in the just-war tradition use to determine under what circumstances war is justified?[35]

In *War and Conscience in America*, Edward L. Long offers an exceptionally lucid and concise statement of the just-war tradition.[36] Seven criteria, which pertain both to the cause for fighting and the means used in battle, are most common.[37]

1. *Last resort.* "All other means to the morally just solution of a conflict must be exhausted before resort to arms can be regarded as legitimate."[38] War must be the last resort, but that does not mean that an unjust solution must be accepted.

2. *Just cause.* "War can be just only if employed to defend a stable order or morally preferable cause against threats of destruction or the use of injustice."[39] The goals for which one fights must be just, and the opponent must be clearly unjust, even though one recognizes moral ambiguity even in oneself.

3. *Right attitude.* "War must be carried out with the right attitudes."[40] The intention must be the restoration of justice, not retaliation. Anger and revenge have no part in just wars.

4. *Prior declaration of war.* "War must be explicitly declared by a legitimate authority."[41] Individual citizens must not take up arms as self-appointed defenders of justice. A formal declaration of war must precede armed conflict so that the opponent has an opportunity to abandon unjust activity and prevent war.

5. *Reasonable hope of success.* "War may be conducted only by military means that promise a reasonable attainment of the moral and political objectives being sought."[42] If there is not a reasonable chance of success, then it is wrong to fight no matter how just one's cause. Nor does this simply mean that one must think one can win. There must be reasonable probability that the things for which one is fighting will not be destroyed in the process.

6. *Noncombatant immunity.* "The just war theory has also entailed selective immunity for certain parts of the enemy's population, particularly for non-combatants."[43] Noncombatants are all those not directly involved in the manufacture, direction, or use of weapons.[44] In a just war, no military action may be aimed directly at noncombatants. This is not to say that civilians may never be injured. If an army justly destroys a military target and nearby noncombatants are killed, that is an unintended side effect (called double-effect) that is permissible within limits. But the principle of proportionality applies here.

7. *Proportionality.* Finally, the principle of proportionality specifies that there must be a reasonable expectation that the good results of the war will exceed the horrible evils involved. This principle applies both to the whole enterprise of the war and to specific tactics in the course of battle.[45] For example, if the unintended double-effect of attacking a legitimate military target involves killing a disproportionate number of noncombatants, then the action is immoral.

According to the just-war tradition, a particular war is justified only if all the above criteria are met. Both the cause for which one goes to war and the methods by which one fights must be just.

Critics of the just-war tradition have asked whether those who embrace the tradition actually apply the criteria faithfully.[46] If in any given war, one side has a just cause for fighting, then presumably the other side does not. Across the centuries, however, "Christian" nations fought each other again and again, and very seldom did Christian citizens on either side argue that their own nation was fighting an unjust war. If the just-war tradition is to have integrity, Christians who stand within the tradition must rigorously apply the criteria and regularly oppose wars proposed by national leaders that fail to meet the tradition's rigorous criteria.

The debate and division between pacifist and just-war Christians in the church continue to the present. The pacifist minority includes Mennonites, Quakers, and small numbers of Catholics and other Protestants. The Pentecostal movement argued for pacifism on biblical grounds in its earlier years. In fact, the Assemblies of God denomination was officially pacifist until 1967.[47] As in the previous sixteen centuries, however, the majority of Christians remain within the just-war tradition.

Recently, however, a number of prominent Christian theologians and ethicists from both traditions have developed what is often called a third approach: just peacemaking. This approach starts by combining key arguments from both pacifists and just-war Christians with some basic historical facts.

Pacifists have claimed they have an alternative to war. If so, they ought to demonstrate that claim in active peacemaking rather than withdraw to some peaceful countryside.

Just-war Christians have insisted they dare never go to war unless fighting is a last resort. That means that all reasonable nonlethal alternatives must first be tried. Over the centuries, however, we have discovered many highly successful ways to resolve conflicts nonviolently. Settling disagreements between gentlemen with a duel (swords or pistols) used to be common. Many died. Today we settle the same disputes nonviolently through the courts. Improving international diplomacy and multilateral negotiations and structures has also reduced armed conflict.

Some of the most striking examples of nonviolent conflict resolution have come in the growing adoption of the techniques of Mahatma Gandhi and Martin Luther King Jr.[48] Gandhi's nonviolent campaign to end colonial rule successfully defeated the British Empire. (It took a little longer than the Algerians' violent revolution against French colonialism, but a million Algerians were killed [1 in 10], whereas only 8,000 [about 1 in 400,000!] Indians died.)[49] Martin Luther King Jr.'s nonviolent civil rights movement changed American history. Hundreds of thousands of nonviolent Filipino marchers overthrew President Marcos's decades-long dictatorship in 1986.[50] Solidarity's nonviolent tactics resisted the Soviet Empire and eventually helped win Poland's freedom. In the 1980s, hundreds of nonviolent, short-term teams organized by Witness for Peace helped to defeat Ronald Reagan's attempt to overthrow the Nicaraguan government by funding an armed rebellion by the "contras."[51]

In the last two decades, Christian Peacemaker Teams (CPT; originally founded by Mennonites, Quakers, and people from the Church of the Brethren) has grown into a small but effective organization using the tactics of nonviolent direct action to intervene in areas of conflict on several continents. Especially important, perhaps, has been its presence in Hebron in the West Bank. In Hebron, a small Jewish settlement protected by Israeli soldiers exists in the midst of an overwhelmingly Palestinian city. Hatred and mistrust are everywhere. Violence and killing are frequent. For more than ten years small groups from Christian Peacemaker Teams have lived in Hebron seeking to understand and befriend both Israelis and Palestinians. CPT personnel intervene in hostile confrontations to prevent violence, seek to stop the illegal demolition of houses, and accompany young children traveling to school through dangerous neighborhoods.[52] Recently, Jonathan Kuttab, a prominent Palestinian Christian committed to nonviolence, has called for one thousand Christian Peacemaker Teams to locate all around the West Bank. Kuttab believes those teams could dramatically reduce conflict in the West Bank.

This brief sketch of strikingly successful, twentieth-century nonviolent campaigns to oppose injustice and reduce killing demonstrates an important fact: nonviolence frequently works! Even without much preparation and training, even without a large investment of money and personnel, nonviolent direct action has frequently been highly effective. One wonders what might be accomplished if all parts of the Christian church (in cooperation with all others who are interested) would get serious about investing resources, time, money, and people to explore what more could be done nonviolently to end injustice and prevent war.[53]

One wonders what might have happened if very prominent Catholic, Orthodox, and Muslim leaders had led a few thousand of their peaceful, praying followers into Bosnia or Kosovo before the ethnic cleansing began. Their message to all would have been: "We come in the name of God. We will stay to pray and stand between warring parties until the killing ends." Might that have been more successful than soldiers and bombs?

We could do the same in other unjust, violent situations waiting to explode. Cardinals, archbishops, patriarchs, and others could lead hundreds of followers into the West Bank. Archbishop Tutu could lead hundreds to Zimbabwe demanding an end to injustice and calling for democracy. The list of potential areas for intervention is long.

Top Christian leaders from both the just-war and pacifist traditions must decide that now is the time to vastly expand groups like Christian Peacemaker Teams. We need thousands of praying, peaceful team members to travel and deploy in dozens of dangerous situations. Pacifists need not abandon their belief that killing is always wrong. Just-war proponents can continue to insist that killing is sometimes necessary. But both traditions *demand* that they vigorously do as much as possible in nonviolent ways. After decades when nonviolence has often enjoyed stunning success even without much preparation, we must now invest tens of millions of dollars in the first serious effort in human history to explore how much can be done to reduce injustice and war through the techniques of nonviolent direct action.

The techniques used by Christian Peacemaker Teams, however, represent only one set of ways to work at peacemaking in nonviolent ways. The scholars who have developed the third way of just peacemaking delineated here agreed on ten important steps.[54]

1. "Support nonviolent action."[55] That means a massive expansion of the techniques of King and Gandhi that we have just discussed.
2. "Take independent initiatives to reduce threat."[56] Even when two strong, visible enemies cannot agree on major negotiations, one side can announce a series of visible, verifiable smaller steps that it intends to take to build trust and invite reciprocity. Sometimes that leads to a negotiated breakthrough. For example, after Presidents Eisenhower and Kennedy unilaterally halted atmospheric testing, the 1963 Atmospheric Test Ban Treaty with the Soviet Union became possible.
3. "Use cooperative conflict resolution."[57] President Jimmy Carter demonstrated this approach at Camp David, and the result was a dramatic peace agreement between Israel and Egypt.
4. "Acknowledge responsibility for conflict and injustice; seek repentance and forgiveness."[58] South Africa's Truth and Reconciliation Commission provides a striking example of this approach.
5. "Promote democracy, human rights, and religious liberty."[59] In the twentieth century, no democracy has gone to war against another democracy.
6. "Foster just and sustainable economic development."[60] Widespread, devastating poverty in a world where others enjoy enormous wealth will inevitably create conflict.
7. "Work with emerging cooperative forces in the international system."[61] International networks in many areas—communication, travel, missions, and businesses—are increasing international understanding. That can lead to less conflict.
8. "Strengthen the United Nations and international efforts for cooperation and human rights."[62] Many problems today—unfair trade, debt, pollution, global warming, and international terrorism—simply cannot be solved by one nation acting alone. Global cooperation through international structures like the United Nations is essential. (That does not mean the United Nations should become an all-powerful global institution; centralized power in a fallen world always leads to abuse. It does, however, mean we should somewhat strengthen global institutions like the United Nations and at the same time balance their power with strong nation-states and other smaller centers of power.)
9. "Reduce offensive weapons and weapons trade."[63] The world would be safer if we negotiated further reductions of nuclear weapons and

dramatically reduced the importation of weapons by developing nations. Developing nations spend $200 billion on defense each year—more than they spend on education.[64]

10. "Encourage grassroots peacemaking groups and voluntary associations, especially churches."[65] These non-state groups can teach just peacemaking theory and challenge governments to take more vigorous steps toward peace. International networks of such groups, especially within the one worldwide body of Christ, can help everyone overcome nationalistic blindness. That is why the official public policy document "For the Health of the Nation" (unanimously approved by the board of the National Association of Evangelicals representing 30 million American evangelical Christians) invites "Christians outside the United States to aid us in broadening our perspectives on American life and action."[66]

Every Christian who seeks to follow Christ must be an active peacemaker. "Blessed are the peacemakers," Jesus said, "for they will be called children of God" (Matt. 5:9). Being peacemakers today involves many things. It involves continuing the dialogue between pacifist and just-war Christians. It involves rigorously applying the just-war criteria to any new proposed, potential, or present war. (Pacifists can join just-war persons in that task.)

Perhaps most important, at this point in history, being faithful Christian peacemakers means vigorously expanding an aggressive effort to do as much as possible via nonviolent approaches. The new consensus document of the National Association of Evangelicals (also signed by such leaders as Charles Colson, James Dobson, Richard Land, and Rick Warren) is crystal clear:

> We urge governments to pursue thoroughly nonviolent paths to peace before resorting to military force. . . . As followers of Jesus, we should, in our civic capacity, work to reduce conflict by promoting international understanding and engaging in nonviolent conflict resolution.[67]

11

Creation Care

Our present behavior threatens the well-being of the entire planet. We are destroying our air, forests, land, and water so rapidly that, unless we change, our grandchildren and their grandchildren will face disastrous problems.

The scientific evidence is now clear. The burning of fossil fuels has already increased global temperatures, and they will continue to rise dangerously in the next one hundred years unless we dramatically reduce our carbon emissions. The result will be climate change, more extreme storms, rising sea levels, loss of coastal land, and increasing disease. The poor will suffer the most. The national scientific academies of the United States, Great Britain, France, Germany, Japan, Canada, Italy, and Russia all accept the scientific fact of global warming.

Tragically, some evangelicals ignore the scientific evidence.[1] Wayne Grudem, prominent evangelical theologian and author of the recent textbook, *Politics according to the Bible*, dismisses the growing scientific agreement that dangerous, human-induced global warming is happening. Grudem claims that "more scientists *reject* than embrace the idea of dangerous man-made global warming."[2] A loving Creator, he argues, would not have made such a fragile world. After quoting a biblical text that says God provides the rain and harvest, he suggests that "the underlying cause of fears of dangerous global warming might not be science but rejection of belief in God."[3] For "much of the environmentalist movement," "'Mother Earth' rather than the one true God is their highest object of devotion."[4] Finally, he charges that "the controversy over global warming is to a very large degree a controversy over human liberty versus government control."[5] Environmentalists are just liberal statist political folk who want to use government to control our lives.

This is bad science, bad theology, and inaccurate slander. To suggest that most environmentalists worship Mother Earth rather than the true God is simply false. Most North American environmentalists—including the rapidly growing number of younger evangelicals committed to creation care—are Christians. To suggest that a small group of environmentalists with bizarre religious ideas represent most environmentalists is simply slander. To say that we can dismiss our best scientists' predictions of destructive climate change because God would not make such a fragile earth is like saying that a loving Creator would not allow the bubonic plague, which wiped out perhaps a third of the population in medieval Europe.

We face a serious, dangerous environmental crisis.

We pollute our air, contribute to global warming (climate change), exhaust our supplies of freshwater, overfish our seas, and destroy precious topsoil, forests, and unique species lovingly shaped by the Creator. In many countries, chemicals, pesticides, oil spills, and industrial emissions degrade air, water, and soil. "Is it not enough for you to feed on the good pasture?" the Creator asks. "Must you also trample the rest of your pasture with your feet? Is it not enough for you to drink clear water? Must you also muddy the rest with your feet?" (Ezek. 34:18).

Biblical Foundations

The Bible offers a solid theological framework for thinking about the nonhuman creation and the relationship of human beings to it. In fact, biblical faith provides the best foundation for being an environmentalist; God's revelation demands that we actively care for creation.

Five biblical principles are especially important. First, whereas a one-sided view of either God's transcendence or immanence compounds our problems, a biblical view of both points the way through our dilemmas. If we focus only on God's immanence (his presence in the world) we end up in pantheism, which declares that everything is divine and good as it is. If we talk only about God's transcendence (his radical separateness from creation), we may end up seeing nature as a mere tool to be used at human whim.

The biblical God is both immanent and transcendent. He is not a cosmic watchmaker who wound up the global clock and now lets it run on its own. God continues to work in the creation. In Job we read that God gives orders to the morning (38:12), that the eagle soars at God's command (39:27), and that God provides food for the ravens when their young cry out in hunger (38:41). The Creator, however, is also radically distinct from the creation. Creation is finite, limited, dependent; the Creator is infinite, unlimited, and self-sufficient.

Second, we should gratefully learn all we can from the book of nature without in any way abandoning biblical revelation. Matthew Fox is a radical Roman Catholic theologian (the Vatican has disciplined him) who has urged that we turn from a theology centered on sin and redemption and develop a "creation spirituality." Nature is our primary revelation. When Fox tells us that we can get most or all the revelation we need from creation, our firm response must be that the biblical revelation of redemption from sin through Jesus Christ is as true and essential as ever in our environmental age.

Third, human beings are both interdependent with the rest of creation and unique within it, because we alone have been created in the divine image and given stewardship over the earth. Christians have at times forgotten our interdependence with the rest of creation. Our daily existence depends on water, sun, and air. Everything is interdependent in the global ecosystem. The emissions from our cars contribute to the destruction of trees—trees that convert the carbon dioxide we exhale into the oxygen we need to survive. Christians today must recover an appreciation of our dependence on the trees and flowers, the streams and forests. Unless we do, we shall surely perish.

But the Bible insists on two other things about humanity: human beings alone are created in the image of God, and we alone have been given a special "dominion" or stewardship. It is a biblical truth, not speciesism, to say that only human beings—and not trees and animals—are created in the image of God (Gen. 1:27). This truth is the foundation of our God-given mandate to have dominion over the nonhuman creation (Gen. 1:28; Ps. 8).

Tragically—and arrogantly—we have distorted dominion into domination. Lynn White, the historian who, several decades ago, wrote a famous essay blaming Christianity for environmental decay, was partly correct. But it is a misunderstanding of the Bible, not God's word itself, that is at fault here.

Genesis 2:15 says the Lord put us in the garden "to work it and take care of it." The word *'abad*, translated "work," means "to serve." The related noun actually means "slave" or "servant." The word *shamar*, translated "take care of," suggests watchful care and preservation of the earth. In fact, *shamar* is the word used five times in Psalm 121 to describe the wonderful way God constantly "watches over" us without ever sleeping:

> I lift up my eyes to the mountains—
>   where does my help come from?
> My help comes from the LORD,
>   the Maker of heaven and earth.
> He will not let your foot slip—
>   he who watches over you will not slumber;
> indeed, he who watches over Israel
>   will neither slumber nor sleep.
> The LORD watches over you—
>   the LORD is your shade at your right hand;

the sun will not harm you by day,
    nor the moon by night.
The LORD will keep you from all harm—
    he will watch over your life;
the LORD will watch over your coming and going
    both now and forevermore.

Psalm 121

What an awesome task we have to watch over the earth the way God watches over us! We are to serve and watch lovingly over God's good garden, not destroy it.

The Old Testament offers explicit commands designed to prevent exploitation of the earth. Every seventh year, for instance, the Israelites' land was to lie fallow because "the land is to have a year of sabbath rest" (Lev. 25:4). Failure to provide this sabbatical for the land was one reason for the Babylonian captivity (Lev. 26:34, 42–43). "I will remember the land," Yahweh declares.

God summons us to both watch over and care for the nonhuman creation and recognize our unique status. If we have no different status from that of animals and plants, we cannot eat them for food or use them to build civilizations. We do not need to apologize to brother carrot when we have lunch. We are free to use the resources of the earth for our own purposes. Created in the divine image, we alone have been placed in charge of the earth. At the same time, our dominion must be the gentle care of a loving gardener, not the callous exploitation of a self-centered lord. So we should not wipe out species or waste the nonhuman creation. Only a careful, stewardly use of plants and animals by human beings is legitimate.

Fourth, a God-centered, rather than a human-centered, worldview respects the independent worth of the nonhuman creation. Christians have too easily, and too often, fallen into the trap of supposing that the nonhuman creation has worth only as it serves human purposes. This, however, is not a biblical perspective.

Genesis 1 makes it clear that all creation is good—good, according to the story, even before our first ancestors arrived on the scene. Colossians 1:16 reveals that all things are created *for* Christ, and according to Job 39:1–2, God watches over the doe in the mountains, counting the months of her pregnancy and watching over her when she gives birth! The first purpose of the nonhuman creation, then, is to glorify God—not to serve us. "The heavens declare the glory of God; the skies proclaim the work of his hands. Day after day they pour forth speech; night after night they display knowledge. They have no speech, they use no words; no sound is heard from them. Yet their voice goes out into all the earth, their words to the end of the world" (Ps. 19:1–4).

It is important to note that God has a covenant not only with persons but also with the nonhuman creation. After the flood, God made a covenant with the animals as well as with Noah: "I now establish my covenant with you and with your descendants after you and with every living creature that was with you—the birds, the livestock and all the wild animals, all those that came out of the ark with you—every living creature on earth" (Gen. 9:9–10). Jesus recognized God's covenant with the whole of creation when he noted how God feeds the birds and clothes the lilies (Matt. 6:26–30). The nonhuman creation has its own worth and dignity apart from its service to humanity.

Insisting on the independent dignity of the nonhuman creation does not mean that we ignore the biblical teaching that it has been given to us for our stewardship and use. Always, however, our use of the nonhuman creation must be a thoughtful stewardship that honors creation's dignity and worth in the eyes of the Creator.

Finally, God's cosmic plan of redemption includes the nonhuman creation. This fact provides a crucial foundation for building a Christian theology for an environmental age. The biblical hope that the whole created order—including the material world of bodies, rivers, and trees—will be part of the heavenly kingdom confirms that the created order is good and important.

The Earth's Hope

The Bible's affirmation of the material world can be seen most clearly in Christ himself: not only did the Creator enter his creation by becoming flesh and blood to redeem us from our sin, but the God-man was resurrected *bodily* from the tomb. The goodness of the created order is also revealed in how the Bible describes the coming kingdom: the marriage supper of the Lamb, where we will feast on bread, wine, and all the glorious fruit of the earth. The material world is so good that we delight in the fruit of the earth, not just now but even in the coming kingdom!

Christians have sometimes ignored the significance of the body and the material world, focusing all their energy on preparing the soul for some future, immaterial, invisible existence in a spiritual heaven. Interestingly, there are striking parallels between such Christians and Eastern monists who tell us that the material world is an illusion to be escaped, so that we can discover the divine spark within and eventually merge with the All and lose individual identity. Neither view would be of much help to environmentalists. If the material world is evil or an illusion, why worry about it?

Biblical faith, however, is radically different. Every part of the material world comes from the loving hand of the Creator, who calls it into being out of nothing and declares it very good. Unlike the Creator, the creation is finite and limited, but it is not an illusion. Nor is it a result of blind, materialistic chance; the Creator lovingly nurtured it into existence over the course of a long evolutionary history.

The prophets often spoke of the impact of human sin on nature (Gen. 3:17–18; Isa. 24:4–6; Hos. 4:3). But they also foresaw that in the messianic time nature would share in the wonderful fruit of salvation: "In that day I will make a covenant for them with the beasts of the field, the birds in the sky and the creatures that move along the ground" (Hos. 2:18; see also Isa. 55:12–13; Hos. 2:16–23).

In biblical faith, the material world is so good that the Creator of the galaxies actually became flesh in the time of Caesar Augustus. Indeed, the material world is so good that not only did Jesus devote much time to restoring broken bodies, he also arose bodily from death and promised to return to complete his victory over every form of brokenness in persons, nature, and civilization.

According to biblical faith, God's cosmic plan of restoration includes the whole creation, not just individual "souls." In Colossians 1:15–20, we read that God intends to reconcile all things, "whether things on earth or things in heaven" (v. 20) through Jesus Christ. That does not mean that everyone will be saved; rather, it means that Christ's restoration will finally extend to all of creation. The fall's corruption of every part of creation will be corrected.

Paul says that, at the end of history as we now experience it, Christ will return not only to usher believers into a life of restored bodily existence in the presence of God but also to restore the whole nonhuman creation. "The creation itself will be liberated from its bondage to decay and brought into the freedom and glory of the children of God" (Rom. 8:21).

The last book of the Bible uses a beautiful metaphor about the tree of life growing beside an unpolluted river, pure as crystal, that purges human civilization of its brokenness and evil so that the glory and honor of the nations may enter into the holy city of the future (Rev. 21:22–22:2). Unlike Christian Platonists and Hindu Monists who see the material world as evil or as an illusion to escape, biblical people believe that it matters so much that the Creator will eventually restore its broken beauty. Knowing God's grand design, Christians work to initiate now what God will later complete.

The Christian hope for Christ's return must be joined with our doctrine of creation. Knowing that we are summoned by the Creator to be wise gardeners caring for God's good earth, knowing the hope that someday the earth will be restored, Christians should be vigorous participants in creation care.

A Framework for Change

Restoring environmental integrity is a task for individuals and governments, children and adults, churches and businesses.[6] It can be worked on at every level. Each family can make a difference by practicing the three Rs: reduce, reuse, and recycle (in that order). Churches can teach biblical principles—like temperance, patience, justice, and self-restraint—which are essential if we are to develop a sustainable society. Businesses must prepare to shoulder more costs, and politicians must dare to adopt more courageous public policies.

The basic direction we need to travel is fairly clear. We want to make decisions now that will allow our grandchildren and their grandchildren to have a decent, sustainable life. We want their future to be one where they can continue to rejoice in the earth's goodness and splendor. Therefore, we must end the degradation of the environment by making changes in the way we think, believe, and act. Some changes, such as using public transportation and buying a fuel-efficient vehicle, are a matter of individual choice.[7] Other changes (e.g., the availability of good public transportation) involve forces and institutions that no individual or family can change by themselves. All these changes are necessary, and they all will be difficult.

The good news is that not just scientists but also business leaders have come to the conclusion that we must act vigorously to combat climate change. A cover story in *Business Week* (August 16, 2004) pointed out that business is "far ahead of Congress and the White House." "We accept that the science on global warming is overwhelming," said the CEO of Exelon Corp. And he added, "There should be mandatory carbon constraints." It is also good business. DuPont has cut its greenhouse-gas emissions 65 percent since 1990—and saved hundreds of millions of dollars!

Momentum is building to correct our environmental problems, although the economic recession of 2007 and the slow economic growth in the following years has undermined the political will to make major changes. There is much to be done if we want to pass on a sustainable world to our grandchildren.

This is not the place to detail the specifics of how to do that. What is important here is to provide a framework and sketch the principles (especially those relevant to public policy) that should guide our action. Six are especially important.

First, persons are more important than animals, birds, and plants. If we have to choose between losing an endangered species of birds and killing human beings, the choice is clear. Persons are created in the image of God, and birds are not. That, however, is virtually never the choice that confronts us. Almost always, the choice is between destroying an endangered species and temporarily having a little less affluence. In those situations, we should normally choose not to exterminate forever a species lovingly crafted by the Creator. Instead, we should make sure, through things like unemployment insurance and job retraining, that we all share the modest burden of costs such as temporary loss of jobs.

Second, we should be sure that caring for creation is a task for all institutions in society. Individuals, families, churches, civic institutions, businesses, and the state all must play their part. It is wrong to think that the state is the only institution that can work to renew and protect the environment.

Third, however, we must understand that government action is essential. Without rules that apply to all, businesses that invest in pollution controls and environmental sanity are at a competitive disadvantage with callous competitors who continue dumping on everyone. In the short run, the market ignores environmental costs. Therefore, legislation that justly compels all businesses to end pollution places all competitors on an even playing field.

Fourth, international structures are also essential. In its consensus document on public policy, the National Association of Evangelicals insists that "government has an obligation to protect its citizens from the effects of environmental degradation. . . . We urge governments to encourage fuel efficiency, reduce pollution, encourage sustainable use of natural resources, and provide for the proper care of wildlife and their natural habitats."[8] Pollution, however, does not respect international boundaries. For many countries, a great deal of the pollution degrading their nation comes from abroad, and they in turn export much of the pollution they produce. So if one country decides to spend the money to reduce pollution, and surrounding nations refuse, the investment improves the lives of selfish neighbors as well as its own citizens.

International standards are essential. Some things can be done only by strengthened global institutions like the United Nations. Obviously, it would be unwise to centralize vast power in any one global agency, but that does not mean that we can ignore the need for a strengthened United Nations to deal with our inextricably interrelated countries on planet Earth. While we do that, however, we must be careful both to do all we can on a local level and to make sure there are careful checks and balances for the centralized global institutions that the environmental crisis requires.

No one country or even continent can solve the huge problem of global warming by itself. The United States, China, Europe, and Japan produce the largest amount of carbon emissions, but Brazil, India, and other rapidly developing nations are also quickly expanding their consumption of fossil fuels. Only a global agreement (with the richest nations bearing the bigger share of the costs) will be workable and just.

Fifth, state regulations, as much as possible, should be market friendly. It is possible for governments to design environmental laws that work well in a market framework. For example, one way to dramatically reduce carbon emissions from the burning of fossil fuels would be for nations to impose a heavy carbon tax. The tax on gasoline, coal, and natural gas could be high enough to double or triple the prices of these products. Market mechanisms would then take over to influence people's choices; many people would choose more fuel-efficient cars and other forms of transportation. Renewable sources of energy (wind, sun, water) would suddenly become much more competitive and replace more fossil fuels.

Finally, wealthy nations must be ready to slow their economic growth, if it is necessary, to restore a sustainable environment for our grandchildren. We do not know enough yet to identify how much continuing economic growth is compatible with preserving a sustainable environment. There is no question about the need for major economic growth in all of Africa, and much of Asia and Latin America. To dramatically reduce poverty, those nations must have major economic growth in the next several decades, but does another expensive gadget or another thousand-dollar raise really add significantly to the genuine happiness of already wealthy North Americans or Europeans? We must reevaluate the good life and place more emphasis on caring today for this endangered planet that God has entrusted to our stewardship. It will not be easy, but it can be done, in our time, in a way that will bless our grandchildren and honor the Creator.

12

Nation-States
and International Affairs

Are national boundaries sacred? Are they ordained by God? Do the citizens of a rich nation have the right to use their abundant resources just for themselves? Or to keep out immigrants from poor nations who seek greater economic opportunity? Does one nation ever have the right to intervene in the internal affairs of another nation? If so, what are the criteria? Should the United States serve as the global policeman? Can a world of competing, sovereign nation-states solve the problems of our ever more interconnected planet? Do we need a stronger United Nations? Should the United States and other nations give up substantial sovereignty to some global political structure? What should the role of religion be in international affairs?

These questions point to enormously complicated problems that cannot be solved in one chapter, one book, or even a whole lifetime of reflection and work. Here I can only sketch out briefly a basic framework that can help us struggle with these crucial issues.

Contrary to the predictions of secular thinkers, religion is becoming more powerful in shaping international politics.[1] Some people deplore this development, believing that religion inevitably breeds intolerance and violence. On the other hand, the historical record also demonstrates that religion nurtures peace and justice. Furthermore, as we saw earlier, every political decision is finally grounded in some normative framework that ultimately rests on religious and philosophical foundations. Since it is impossible to prevent religion from shaping global politics, we need to work hard to encourage religious political influences that nurture freedom, human rights, peace, justice, and life for all.[2]

Every morning newspaper and every evening news report underlines the way all parts of our little planet are increasingly interconnected. International trade links producers and buyers in every continent and every country. Modern communications technology almost instantly transmits news to every part of the globe. Cultural values from one country and continent invade the others. Environmental problems are global, as each nation's pollution spreads around the world. Immigrants from one country and continent enter, legally and illegally, into countries on the other side of the globe. International terrorism threatens people on every continent. Increasingly, we live in one interconnected, interdependent global village.

But the world is still ruled largely by sovereign nation-states. Since the Treaty of Westphalia in 1648, first Europe and then later the whole world has been governed by nation-states that possess total sovereignty within their national boundaries. Each nation acts in the world, making and breaking treaties with other sovereign nations, according to its own national self-interest. The military and economic power of each nation determines what it can do in the world. And the shifting balance of power produces whatever order and peace emerge.[3] That, at least, is the realist perspective on how international affairs work.

Nationalism is a powerful component of the modern nation-state. French, Chinese, British, and American citizens all take special pride in their own country. Frequently citizens make sweeping claims about the unique goodness, beauty, and virtue of their own nation. "Love it [America] or leave it" or "My country, right or wrong" are widespread attitudes. Three thousand American deaths matter much more to Americans than three million Africans, Arabs, or Asians. Citizens of one nation often confuse their own national self-interest with the well-being of the world.

American evangelicals have been especially tempted to adopt a thoughtless nationalism that uncritically embraces as God's will for the world whatever US foreign policy their president promotes. This uncritical nationalism is deeply rooted in a long-standing, widespread notion of American exceptionalism—the idea that America has a unique calling from God to renew the world. The roots of this thinking go back to the Puritans, who saw themselves as a new Israel, God's chosen people. The specific religious formulation of the Puritan vision slowly disappeared, but vast numbers of Americans embraced a secular version.[4] Albert Beveridge, a prominent US senator in the first decade of the twentieth century, expressed it well: "He [God] has marked the American people as His chosen nation to finally lead in the redemption of the world."[5]

James Skillen is almost certainly right that this long tradition of American exceptionalism, of America as God's chosen nation, played a central role in President George W. Bush's response to the terrible terrorist attack on

September 11, 2001. In his 2002 National Security Strategy (an important document in which presidents spell out their understanding of America's role in the world and the means with which they will protect national security), he declared that "the United States will use this moment of opportunity to extend the benefits of freedom across the globe."[6] It was, of course, *America's* definition of freedom mixed with *America's* national self-interest that he intended to promote. The document went on to say that the United States intended to maintain global military superiority "beyond challenge" by any other nation or group of nations. It spelled out absolute United States sovereignty, rejecting the jurisdiction (for American citizens) of the International Criminal Court, which the United States had helped design. And, as shown by the largely unilateral invasion of Iraq (contrary to the wishes of the United Nations and most American allies), President Bush reserved the right to invade other nations whenever America so chooses. "The unstated implication is that the world will henceforth know only one truly sovereign state—the United States."[7]

There are two fundamental problems with this vision for America. It is both immoral and unworkable. It is unjust for one nation to unilaterally dictate to other nations. And, in spite of the double fact that the United States has the most powerful economy in the world and is more dominant militarily than any other nation since the Roman Empire, a unilateral American attempt to dictate to the rest of the world simply will not work in the long run. There are a vast variety of other nations and other centers of power in the world that will resist and reject American unilateralism. The Arab world with its vast oil reserves, the rapidly developing nations of China and India, Russia with its vast natural resources, Latin America, Europe, and Japan—the list goes on and on. All of these centers of power demand to be partners in the shaping of international affairs.

In the months after the terrorist attacks of 9/11, the United States enjoyed enormous support around the world, but the subsequent unilateral policy of the United States led to a rapid loss of respect and support for America in almost all nations on the planet. Not even the most powerful sovereign state in human history can unilaterally shape international affairs.

With the installation of President Barack Obama in 2009, American foreign policy changed significantly. President Obama articulated and sought to implement a more multilateral approach. The United States, he said, must seek to cooperate where possible with all other nations. He also expressed greater support for the United Nations.

Recent American experience, including the reaffirmation of near absolute American sovereignty under President George W. Bush, should prompt us to evaluate carefully the whole idea of the sovereign nation-state. Is the international political system of the last several hundred years God's will for the world? Or would it be better to limit national sovereignty and have a stronger United Nations? How should a Christian evaluate the modern nation-state?

Evaluating the Nation-State

It would be fundamentally wrong to dismiss as a total mistake the modern nation-state and the patriotic affection that its people share. In several important ways, the modern nation-state plays a positive role.

Persons are made for community. When a group of people share a common culture, a common geography, and a common history, they come to enjoy a deep sense of community. As they work and play together, do business together, and intermarry, strong communal bonds naturally and rightly develop. It is right for us to develop a deep love and affection for the hills and valleys, the rivers and mountains, the lakes and sandy beaches where as children we first experienced the earth's splendor and as adults continue to deepen our appreciation of its gorgeous beauty. As finite persons, we rightly form special attachments to specific people and places. Special affection for one's particular nation and its people is natural and good. Patriotism—if understood as the "steady willing of the true good of one's nation"—is something to celebrate.[8]

It is also true that the modern nation-state has contributed to order and peace in significant ways. Within its own borders, the nation-state (especially democratic nations that respect the rule of law) has often restrained evil and promoted justice. Internationally, a balance of power based on shifting alliances of sovereign nation-states has sometimes (for example, in Europe for much of the nineteenth century) restrained outside interference and produced substantial peace.[9]

Further, it is important to remember that a good deal of the wealth of any nation-state has resulted from the hard work, common labor, and communally developed technologies of its people. They have a substantial right to enjoy the wealth that their own effort and ingenuity have created.

Tragically, there is another side to all these positive features. Genuine patriotism, which wills the *true* good of one's nation, often degenerates into a deadly jingoism that uncritically embraces whatever one's country does. Peaceful balances of power between competing nation-states easily dissolve into bloody conflicts like the two world wars. In fact, the twentieth century, dominated by sovereign nation-states, was the bloodiest century in human history.

Nor is it right for a nation to keep all its wealth (even if it created all that wealth in entirely just ways) exclusively for its own use. The Bible regularly condemns people who are rich but fail to share with the poor (e.g., Ezek. 16:49–50; Luke 16:19–31).[10] Jesus's parable of the rich man and Lazarus does not accuse the rich man condemned to hell of becoming rich unjustly; it simply says he failed to share. The papal encyclical *Populorum Progressio* (1967) puts it well: "While it is proper that a nation be the first to enjoy the God-given fruits of its own labour, no nation may dare to hoard its riches for its own use alone. Each and every nation must produce . . . so that it may contribute to the common development of the human race."[11]

Both key biblical themes and historical experience should move Christians to raise serious questions about the way the sovereign nation-state has functioned in the modern world.

The most basic point is that, according to the Bible, every single human being is my brother or sister. In his great speech at Athens, the apostle Paul pointed out both that we are all God's children and that we are all descendants of Adam. "We are God's offspring" (Acts 17:29) and "from one man he made all the nations" (v. 26). Paul insisted that every person on the planet has the same heavenly Father and the same earthly father. That means we are all family. We must treat all other persons on the planet as brothers and sisters. As we remember that the heavenly Father has created every person in the divine image and loves every person equally, we grasp more of the meaning of the fact that everyone in the world is our beloved sister or brother.

That biblical truth fundamentally undermines exclusive nationalism. *Populorum Progressio* rightly insists that legitimate national pride must be tempered by "love for the whole family of man."[12] This unity of the whole human family compels us to promote the common good of everyone, not just the citizens of our country.[13]

A second biblical, theological truth is also important. All believers in Jesus Christ are part of his global body. Furthermore, our allegiance to Christ and his one global body far transcends all other human allegiances—whether to biological family or to one's native country.

Jesus vigorously insisted that his disciples must be willing to forsake mother or father (Matt. 10:37). The early church saw themselves as strangers and sojourners (Heb. 11:13–16; 1 Pet. 2:11), people without a country—precisely because their highest loyalty was to Christ's body in which they possess a true citizenship. In fact, Christians are strangers in this world and ambassadors of Christ's kingdom (2 Cor. 5:20).

The early Christian *Letter to Diognetus* (later second century) captures this truth beautifully. The writer points out that Christians are living in many different countries and cultures where they follow the local customs as long as they do not contradict Jesus's teaching.

> While living in Greek and barbarian cities . . . and following the local customs both in clothing and food and the rest of life, they show forth the wonderful and confessedly strange character of the constitution of their own citizenship. They dwell in their own fatherlands, but as if sojourners in them. . . . Every foreign country is their fatherland, and every fatherland is a foreign country. They marry as all men, they bear children, but they do not expose their offspring. They offer free hospitality, but guard their purity. . . . They pass their time upon the earth, but they have their citizenship in heaven (Phil. 3:20).[14]

The early Christians understood that God invites all people everywhere to embrace Christ's salvation and join his one universal body. And they looked forward to Christ's return when people of all races, nations, and classes would unite together singing praises to the Lamb (Rev. 7:9).

This understanding of the church demands that Christians have a much higher loyalty to the one body of Christ, and thus to all Christians around the world, than to the citizens of one's particular nation-state. National loyalty is legitimate up to a point, but commitment to the global body of Christ must be a far more important loyalty.[15]

A third theological point is crucial. There is simply no biblical or theological basis for "American exceptionalism," for the notion that the United States has some special divine calling and relationship to God that no other nation has. There has been only one "chosen nation," the ancient people of Israel described in the Old Testament. With the coming of Christ, the people of God are no longer one ethnic group living in a specific geography, but rather the world-wide body of Christ. No nation has any special relationship with God. God summons all nations to do justice, and to the extent that they do that, God is pleased and they accomplish God's will. But God does not play favorites and love one nation more than another. It is blasphemous idolatry to claim that the United States—or any other nation—is God's new Israel to redeem the world.

Christians must be extremely vigilant against the ongoing temptations of idolatrous nationalism. Christians in the United States are especially prone to embrace this evil, but the temptation lurks in every nation. Many Christian thinkers—not least Reinhold Niebuhr and Pope John Paul II—have rightly warned against this danger.[16] "It is idolatry to vote, participate in parties, and make all political judgments in terms of primary loyalty to a nation."[17]

The biblical and theological truths discussed in this section have wide implications. They should prompt Christian citizens in rich nations to urge their political leaders to be more generous in giving economic foreign aid to poor nations and promoting international trade that benefits developing countries. They should lead Christian citizens to urge their political leaders to think not just about national self-interest, but rather about the common good of all nations. In fact, the list of significant issues affected by these principles is very long. Here I will briefly discuss two: immigration policy and global political structure.

Immigration Policy

Does a rich nation have the moral right to refuse entry to poor immigrants from needy nations seeking economic opportunity?

There is nothing sacred about current national boundaries. They have emerged over time as the result of wars, often fought because of human greed and pride.[18] There is no biblical or theological reason for saying that they dare not be changed or crossed.

It is true that, to a significant degree, the wealth of a particular country has been created by the labor of its citizens and they therefore have some right to enjoy that wealth without others demanding an equal share. But it is also true in every particular situation that injustice has also contributed to the nations' wealth. (In the case of the United States, that injustice included centuries of slavery, the theft of the continent from native Americans, and a long history of unfair patterns of international trade.)[19] As we have seen, however, we are obligated to share our wealth with needy people, even if we earned it all justly by our labor. Every needy immigrant is a brother or sister. Many of them are also brothers and sisters in Christ. Since biblical faith calls us to generously share our resources with needy people, Christians in rich nations ought to promote generous immigration policies that make it easier, rather than harder, for poor immigrants to enter their country legally to seek work.

Other biblical teachings support this claim. The Old Testament frequently commanded God's people to have a special concern for the "stranger" and "alien"—that is, the people who are not citizens. Both because God loves the stranger and because the Israelites were to remember that they once were mistreated noncitizens, the biblical texts called them to have a special concern for aliens: "For the Lord your God . . . defends the cause of the fatherless and the widow, and loves the foreigners residing among you, giving them food and clothing. And you are to love those who are foreigners, for you yourselves were foreigners in Egypt" (Deut. 10:17–19). Jesus himself was a refugee in Egypt (Matt. 2:15). Indeed, as Matthew 25 reveals, Christ the Lord is present himself, somehow, in the poor, needy immigrant.

The Catholic bishops of the United States and Mexico have drawn some proper conclusions about immigration. Sovereign nations, they argue, do not have any absolute right to close their borders to needy people. They must also weigh the needs of poor people wanting to enter as immigrants.[20] Working out specific legislation for a particular country at a particular moment will always be complex, but Christian citizens and politicians involved in such decisions must start with the knowledge that the poor persons wishing to enter their country are also brothers and sisters of the one heavenly Father who has given the wealth of this world to promote the common good of all people.

Global Political Structure

There are three basic answers today to the question, How should we structure the international political order?[21]

Realists want to retain the full sovereignty of the nation-state. Order will emerge as competing, sovereign nation-states promote their own self-interest through a variety of alliances. Economic and military might are the decisive forms of power.

Globalists want one powerful global political structure with a monopoly on the use of force and thus the power to enforce global laws.

Pluralists affirm a plurality of power centers. They want to combine a strengthened (but not too powerful) global political entity with strong nation-states that surrender some of their sovereignty. In addition, a variety of other international actors (multinational corporations, global religious structures, nongovernmental organizations like Amnesty International, the World Trade Organization) join with nation-states and a global political entity to offer a wide variety of power centers that diversify and decentralize power.

There are three basic problems with the view of the realists.

First, today we face many severe problems that cannot be solved satisfactorily by nation-states because the problems are global. Pollution (especially the carbon dioxide emissions that fuel global warming) comes from every country and damages every other country. Only a global solution will work.

The spread of weapons of mass destruction similarly threatens everyone. Global terrorism cannot be prevented by one or a few nations. Disease that begins in one continent can quickly threaten people in every other continent. International trade today affects the well-being of every country on the planet. These and other problems cannot be solved adequately by sovereign nation-states.

Second, the world has already moved away from sovereign nation-states in at least two significant ways. The European Union is a new political entity in which the member states have surrendered substantial national sovereignty to a new European political structure with legislative, judicial, and administrative powers. In fact, many Christian thinkers and politicians consciously worked hard to create the European Union because they wanted to limit absolute sovereignty, promote the principle of subsidiarity, and strengthen cooperation across national borders.[22] In addition, there has been a growing belief in the last two decades that "humanitarian intervention" in the affairs of "sovereign nations" is sometimes justified and necessary.[23] Repeatedly, in the past fifteen years, an international force (frequently sanctioned by the United Nations) has intervened against the will of "sovereign" nations: the former Yugoslavia, Haiti, Liberia, Afghanistan, Iraq (1991), and Libya.[24]

Third, the notion of an absolutely sovereign state is morally unacceptable. Such a notion affirms the legitimacy of a human institution with no moral responsibility to anybody or anything beyond itself—with no responsibility even to a moral order that transcends the state. That, as Daniel Philpott notes, is "an idolatrous claimant to godlike status."[25]

Christians, I believe, dare not embrace the realist option of the sovereign nation-state.

What then of the globalist position? On the surface, it may appear attractive. Christians want structures that can promote the common good of all humanity. Theoretically, a powerful global political entity could do just that.

But there is a huge problem: sin. If we have learned anything in the last century, it is that Lord Acton was right: power tends to corrupt and absolute power corrupts absolutely. In a fallen world, it would be exceedingly dangerous to develop a centralized global political structure with the power to dominate all other centers of power. This global center would almost certainly abuse that power, act in a totalitarian way, and use its power to oppress people. The word *antichrist* might indeed become highly appropriate. Christians should clearly reject the globalist proposal.

That leaves the pluralist model. Hopefully, we can find ways to do three things simultaneously:

1. Strengthen the United Nations sufficiently so that it has more ability to deal effectively with problems that can only be solved at the global level.
2. Maintain strong nation-states (even as we somewhat reduce their sovereignty) so that they remain centers of real power able to provide a counterbalance to a somewhat strengthened United Nations.
3. Nurture the emergence of a vast array of other powerful global structures, some of which are independent both of the United Nations and of nation-states and thus are able to serve as counterweights to both.

Some of these global structures would be political structures, in that they would be instruments of the United Nations and the nation-states. One thinks of the World Trade Organization, the World Bank, and the International Monetary Fund. An effective structure dealing with the environment is needed. Other global structures exist or will be created by the United Nations, groups of nation-states, or both, working together. More regional political groups like the European Union will also probably be created by groups of nation-states.

In addition, very large, very diverse groups of strong, global nongovernmental organizations would be a crucial part of a free, decentralized global community. One thinks of a strong, international voice for labor; global human rights organizations; international organizations supporting the rule of law; global networks of journalists; international relief and development structures—the list goes on and on. The fact that these global networks of international civil society are independent of both nation-states and any global political authority enables them to be counterweights to political power and thus strong forces for freedom.

The pluralist model embraces the moral truth that there is one global family. The structures of the United Nations and many of the global non-state organizations would be able to promote the common good of all humanity. At the same time, the pluralist model recognizes the fact of human sin and the danger of centralized power. It offers a genuine decentralization of power at the same time that it promotes enough centralized structure to accomplish what can only be done at the global level. Lawrence Adams put it well: such a system "recognizes an international realm that speaks of global good and checks exclusive interests while it gives room for particular interests within a larger framework. . . . It provides a means for restraining states and their pursuit of national interests at the expense of others while providing checks on the excessive accumulation of power in a global tyranny."[26]

As early as *Pacem in terris* (1963), Pope John XXIII noted global problems that could only be solved, he believed, by a global public authority. But he insisted that the principle of subsidiarity—when a larger entity like a national government steps in to help smaller entities like local governments and families, it must strengthen rather than weaken or replace them—must apply to the relationship between the global public authority and nation-states. The global public authority rightly seeks solutions to problems that affect the universal common good. "But it is no part of the duty of universal authority to limit the sphere of action of the public authority of individual states, or to arrogate any of their functions to itself. On the contrary, its essential purpose is to create world conditions in which the public authorities of each nation, its citizens, and intermediate groups, can carry out their tasks, fulfill their duties and claim their rights with greater security."[27]

This is not the place to spell out the details either of the exact shape a somewhat strengthened United Nations should take or the complicated process required to achieve it. Brilliant scholars and political practitioners are working on both.[28] Making progress will be a gradual process.

But the basic direction we need to go is clear. In the words of the recent Project on National Security, the present international system "is broken."[29] We have desperately urgent global problems that need international solutions, but the United Nations is dreadfully ineffective. United States policy under President George W. Bush has demonstrated that unilateralism breeds resentment, fear, and resistance. It simply does not work for the world's lone superpower to try to dictate to the world even when it defends its actions as merely the promotion of freedom and democracy for all. Our world desperately needs a more humble United States to help lead the world to a genuinely multilateral approach to global problems. That will mean that the United States (and other nations too) must give up some—but not too much—sovereignty so that they can strengthen the United Nations. Above all, it will mean ensuring the existence of many strong, independent centers of power. This kind of pluralist international structure offers the best hope for nurturing life, justice, freedom, and peace for the entire human family.

PART 4

Loving One's Neighbor through Faithful Political Engagement

Contemporary Christians have an enormous opportunity to use politics to shape a better world. A few basic facts underline this truth: More than one-third of the world's people claim to be Christians. That one-third of the global population controls two-thirds of the world's wealth.

If even a quarter of the world's Christians truly followed biblical norms in their politics, we would fundamentally change history.

To do that, we must embrace a biblically balanced political agenda, understand the different ways that we appropriately shape public policy, and learn how to combine humility and confidence.

13

Biblical Balance, Historic Opportunity

In this book, we have seen that the God of the Bible cares about the poor and the family, about peacemaking and the sanctity of human life, about freedom and creation care. Any political engagement that claims to be Christian must be concerned with the full range of things that the Bible says God cares about. We dare not pick out one or two issues that suit our personal preference or some narrow political agenda—whether family and abortion or economic justice and environmental concern—and neglect the others.

"For the Health of the Nation," the recent (2004) statement adopted unanimously by the board of the National Association of Evangelicals in the United States, says pointedly, "The Bible makes it clear that God cares a great deal about the well-being of marriage, the family, the sanctity of human life, justice for the poor, care for creation, peace, freedom, and racial justice." The conclusion? "Faithful evangelical civic engagement must champion a biblically balanced agenda."[1] The declaration goes on to delineate seven crucial areas for evangelical political activity: religious freedom, family, the sanctity of human life, justice for the poor, human rights, peace, and creation care. All are essential because God's revealed word teaches that they all matter a great deal to God—therefore we cannot pick and choose. We must embrace them all. If our politics is to be Christian, we must adopt a biblically balanced agenda.

Of course that does not mean that every individual Christian must spend equal time on every issue. Individuals rightly specialize. Nor does it mean that Christian organizations focused on one issue (whether poverty or abortion) are wrong. But it does mean that all Christians must speak and act in such a way that everyone knows that they are not "one-issue" or "two-issue" people. It means that church leaders will teach their people how faithful Christians can develop and promote a biblically balanced political agenda. It means that when Christians vote and when they work full-time in politics, they will strive to encourage a concern for that same balanced agenda. If Christian political engagement focuses on just one or two issues, it is misguided, unfaithful, and unbiblical.

The Many Ways to Shape Public Policy

To seize our current opportunity, we must also understand the many different ways that we can have political impact and be clear on which of these ways are appropriate or inappropriate for different groups of Christians.[2]

Just being the church. The first way Christians should influence politics is by being a living model of Jesus's dawning kingdom. Tom Skinner used to say that the church should be a little picture now of what heaven will be like. When the church simply lives out a visible model of transformed social, racial, and economic relations, it profoundly influences society.

In previous centuries, as the church cared for the sick and built hospitals to offer healing, the larger society slowly realized that was the right thing to do. As the church started Sunday schools to teach poor kids (who had to work on the other six days) how to read and write, the larger society began to see the importance of universal education. If the church in South Africa had simply lived out a powerful, visible model of racial integration and justice, apartheid would have collapsed. The common life of the church—where we nurture virtuous persons and model an alternative reality—should be the first way Christians impact political life.

Prayer. Earlier, we quoted Karl Barth as saying that prayer is the church's most important contribution to political life. The Bible calls us to pray for our political leaders. We ought to pray passionately for politicians who vigorously promote justice and life, freedom and peace, family and creation care. Jesus made some astounding statements about the power of prayer. If he is right, asking God to send us good, wise politicians and just, effective political decisions has immense importance.

Shaping culture. To a great extent, broad cultural assumptions determine what is politically possible. Abraham Lincoln allegedly told the clergy of his day that "the church sets the boundaries within which politics has to function."[3] Christians help shape the cultural norms in society first by their common life, then by their ideas, writings, and artistic productions. Popular books, movies, music, and art that convey Christian values create a cultural climate where good political decisions are possible. Conversely, popular culture that promotes immoral ideas increases the probability of destructive decisions. Consider the recent case of marriage in the United States. For a decade, conservative Christians have regularly won legislative votes and referenda on marriage. But the dominant secular media have powerfully promoted destructive values on sex and marriage that are rapidly changing the culture. That cultural change increases the probability that more politicians will do what some have already done, revising earlier votes that retain the historic understanding of marriage. If we win current political battles but lose the struggle to shape the larger culture, we will soon also suffer defeat in the political debate.

Educating church members to think biblically and wisely about politics. Unless church leaders help their people develop a biblically informed way to think about political life, church members will simply borrow their political values from secular sources. It is crucial that pastors and denominational leaders develop careful programs and excellent materials to help all their members embrace a faithful methodology for politics and a biblically balanced agenda. This would involve sermons, Sunday school classes, and study groups where church members come to understand the biblical foundations for economic and racial justice, respect for the dignity and sanctity of human life—in short, all the components of a biblically balanced agenda.

This does not mean that the pastor or denominational leader should regularly promote a specific political proposal. This does not mean preaching—as one prominent TV evangelist did in the 1980s—a ten-part series promoting President Ronald Reagan's controversial program of "Star Wars" (to develop the ability to fight nuclear battles in space).[4]

Ed Dobson (formerly a vice president of Jerry Falwell's Moral Majority and later longtime pastor of the largest evangelical church in Grand Rapids, Michigan) once explained why he felt so strongly that a pastor should not take explicit political stands. Apparently Ed was under pressure from prominent evangelical political voices to publicly endorse and promote state-funded educational vouchers for private schools. Ed's response? He told me that as he looked down from his pulpit, he saw a good church member who had spent millions to fund private charter schools. Right beside him sat a man who had invested millions to put educational vouchers on the ballot. And next to him sat the city's superintendent of public schools, then a top official in the state department of education, who was then also a homeschooler. "How," Ed Dobson asked, "can I take a specific political stand on educational vouchers from the pulpit and still truly pastor all of these sincere members of my congregation?"[5]

When church leaders regularly take specific political stands, they make it impossible to effectively pastor their diverse congregations. They also presume to act in an area where they normally lack training and expertise, and they run the great risk of politicizing the church and dividing it along political lines.

Instead, church leaders should help their members develop a faithful approach to politics. They should provide settings within the congregation where church members with different political views learn how to dialogue with civility, honesty, and humility. They should encourage all their members to be active politically and nurture a few to devote themselves full-time to politics. Normally, however, church leaders should not take specific public political stands themselves.

Occasionally, unusual circumstances may require church leaders to publicly embrace specific political goals. When the South African government silenced almost all political opposition to its policies of apartheid, Archbishop Tutu rightly used his freedom as a prominent church leader to speak out.[6] Occasionally, pastors may feel such clarity and urgency that they rightly (if they make it clear they speak only for themselves) publicly urge a specific political approach. But that should not be the normal pattern.

Being the church, praying for politicians, shaping the culture, and educating church members are all important but indirect ways of shaping the political life of the nation. But there are also other more direct ways to do that. Five are especially important: occasional official church pronouncements; educating the public on specific political issues; lobbying elected officials; promoting the election of specific candidates; and running for political office.

Occasional official church pronouncements. Church leaders dare not make political pronouncements in the name of their church when they only speak for themselves, but the situation is quite different when the congregation or the denomination goes through a careful process to develop an official congregational or denominational position on a political issue. This dare not be done hastily, nor should it be done constantly. But from time to time, it is important and right. When that process produces a duly authorized statement, then church leaders rightly speak to political leaders in the name of their church.[7] If done well, this kind of official church pronouncement can have a substantial political impact.

Educating the public on specific political issues. In political education, people seek to inform a group of citizens (whether church members or others) about particular issues, the reasons for taking a specific stand, the current state of the political debate on the issues, and how best to impact the outcome.

Christians may do this in several types of organizations. Many denominations have social action departments that do political education on specific issues. Far too often, these structures go beyond their mandate and endorse specific proposals without proper authorization. If the denominational structures have taken official action that authorizes education on a specific issue or legislative proposal, however, such activity is appropriate. A second possibility is to work through the large number of parachurch organizations formed to do education on political issues. These organizations have a Christian rationale and motivation but are one step removed from specific church structures and thus are less likely to inappropriately politicize the church. A third way for Christians to do political education is to work with secular public policy organizations promoting agendas that agree with at least some portion of a biblically informed agenda.

Lobbying elected officials. Here it is even more crucial that denominational social action agencies do this kind of work only when denominational structures have had a clear process and given concrete authorization so that church agencies can speak in the name of the denomination. However, parachurch organizations (and of course secular lobbying agencies) are better able to lobby politicians without politicizing the church.

Promoting the election of specific candidates. In the United States, public law forbids congregations and other official church structures from endorsing specific political candidates. Even if it did not, church leaders should not endorse candidates except in extremely unusual and rare circumstances. Normally church leaders should help educate their members on how to think and act publicly and then urge each individual member to make his or her own decisions about specific candidates. Individual Christians should be encouraged to join the debate over specific candidates and work to elect their preferred candidates.

Running for political office. Congregations should encourage members with the interests and gifts to be candidates for political office. Caring church leaders and other members of the congregation are the ideal people to help Christian political candidates (and elected officials) to develop platforms that reflect a biblically balanced agenda, to think and speak honestly, and to retain integrity in public life. We need far better, more concrete structures for a loving, tough-minded process of both personal support and genuine accountability for Christians who embrace the difficult calling of public office. None of this means that a congregation should publicly endorse a respected church member running for political office. It does, however, mean a congregation should quietly and privately provide prayer, counsel, and a structure of accountability.

In all this political engagement, it is crucial that Christians understand that the church and the state are two separate institutions. Their interests and agendas frequently intersect, but their respective spheres of authority and action must remain clearly distinct. H. M. Kuitert puts it well:

> Politics must be done through politics and not through church channels. . . . The church is the church and must not want to take part in the power struggle between political parties, any more than the authorities or the political parties can ever or must ever take the place of the church.[8]

Acting with Humility and Integrity

Nothing undermines Christian political engagement as much as dishonesty, selfishness, corruption, and arrogance.

Politics offers powerful temptations to twist the truth and to distort the views of opponents and smear their character. Whenever that happens, it belittles and undermines political life. But when Christian political activists do it, the name of Christ and the reputation of Christian faith suffer great damage. Christians must be ready to lose politically rather than engage in dishonesty or corruption. Christians in politics should have the universal reputation of being the people whose word and action can always be trusted.

There is a dramatically noticeable difference between a politician whose primary goals are selfish ambition and personal power and a politician whose primary goals are justice for all and service to neighbor. For the Christian politician, "justice is the goal, and as one subordinates personal needs and desires to pursue that goal, one becomes a servant."[9]

Another essential mark of faithful Christian politicians will be that they emphasize seeking justice for others at least as much, if not more, than demanding the rights of Christians. There is nothing wrong with insisting that Christians in every nation be treated fairly, but Christian politicians deeply shaped by the Scriptures will be a powerful voice for the poor and forgotten. They will be the voice of the voiceless. They will even be a voice for unpopular minorities—for example, Muslims in a nation where the vast majority claim to be Christians. That kind of unselfish servanthood should be the normal hallmark of all Christian political engagement.

Christians in politics must also seek the right mix of confidence and humility. No politician can succeed without self-confidence, and Christian faith does not condemn that, but it does denounce an arrogance that refuses to admit mistakes or makes excessive claims to wisdom and competence. Christian politicians should remember that they are both finite and sinful. As finite beings, we can never know all the relevant facts. Our knowledge is always dreadfully imperfect. Hence our conclusions will always be imperfect and frequently wrong.

Remembering how even the best Christian leaders of the past made great mistakes, they will realize that they too are undoubtedly enmeshed in confusion and error. Because they know that God forgives them, as they trust in Christ's mercy, this awareness of failure does not immobilize or paralyze. They continue to advocate strongly what they believe is right, but they do it with a humility that recognizes wisdom, even in their opponents' views, and displays a readiness to change when new data or altered circumstances require it.

A Historic Opportunity

Imagine the impact if even a quarter of the total Christian community—or even a quarter of today's evangelical Christians—embraced a new political engagement that truly reflected a biblically balanced agenda and was conducted in an honest and confident, yet humble, way.

In Africa, south of the Sahara, professed Christians represent a substantial majority of all voters. The same is true in most of Latin America and the Philippines. In many countries in Asia, there is a rapidly growing Christian minority.

In the United States, the world's only superpower, the vast majority of citizens claim to be Christians. Because of its unique global power today, the United States could become a powerful force to reduce poverty, to promote freedom and peace, to care for creation, and to respect the sanctity of human life and the importance of the family—if a strong minority of American citizens would decide to act vigorously and wisely to promote a biblically balanced political agenda.

One recent development is especially striking and potentially momentous. The new evangelical declaration, "For the Health of the Nation: An Evangelical Call to Civic Responsibility," now represents the official stance of the National Association of Evangelicals (the largest evangelical network in the United States). Prominent evangelical leaders like Charles Colson, Rick Warren, Richard Land, and James Dobson have also signed it.

Evangelical ethicist David Gushee has recently argued that "For the Health of the Nation" represents an emerging "evangelical center" that goes far beyond the National Association of Evangelicals. It includes evangelical colleges and universities, *Christianity Today*, prominent evangelical publishing houses, Evangelicals for Social Action, and evangelical relief and development agencies. Especially important, Gushee argues, is that the broader, biblically balanced agenda "is winning the hearts and minds of younger evangelicals and this represents the likely future of evangelicalism."[10]

What is especially striking is that the policy proposals of the National Association of Evangelicals and the larger emerging evangelical center are overwhelmingly parallel to the official public policy agenda of Roman Catholics.[11] Both communities' official teaching promote a pro-poor, pro-life, pro-peace, pro-family, pro-freedom, and pro-creation care agenda. Evangelicals constitute probably more than one-quarter of all American voters.[12] Catholics make up another one quarter. If these two communities, representing at least half of all American voters, discover how to work together over a couple of decades to promote their common framework for public life, they will transform American politics.

Similar things could happen in sub-Saharan Africa, Latin America, and the Philippines. Thus, it is absolutely essential that evangelicals and Roman Catholics learn how to cooperate more deeply and effectively.

Wise, honest, and biblically balanced political activity by Christians could dramatically transform our world in the next twenty-five years. We could substantially reduce poverty around the world. We could increase respect for the sanctity of human life and renew and strengthen the family. We could care for creation and pass on a sustainable planet to our grandchildren. We could reduce injustice, violence, and war. All of that is worth vigorous, sustained effort on the part of devout, biblical Christians.

We should not, however, expect utopia or exaggerate the importance of politics. Even the most successful, most faithful Christian political engagement will not bring in the kingdom. Christ will do that when he returns. Sin, injustice, and violence will continue, but biblically grounded Christian political engagement could save tens of millions of our neighbors from agony and death. It could create a better planet for our grandchildren to inhabit.

Above all, let us never forget that politics is not the Christian's only responsibility. It is not even the most important. Let us never forget to be the church, to worship our Lord, and to share the gospel with those who have never heard. Politics is important because it can nurture a better, more wholesome life for billions of neighbors for their brief sojourn on this gorgeous planet, but sharing the gospel leads not only to life abundant now but also life eternal. As we rejoice in the important but limited results that flow from faithful political engagement, let us revel in the eternal blessings that flow from embracing the gospel.

Bibliography

A Place at the Table. Washington, DC: USCCB Publishing, 2002.

Adams, Lawrence E. *Going Public: Christian Responsibility in a Divided Nation*. Grand Rapids: Brazos, 2002.

Alexander, Paul. *Peace to War: Shifting Allegiances in the Assemblies of God*. Scottdale, PA: Herald Press, 2009.

Ashcroft, John, and Christopher Townsend. *Political Christians in a Plural Society: A New Strategy for a Biblical Contribution*. Cambridge: Jubilee Policy Group, 1994.

Atkinson, David J., and David H. Field, eds. *New Dictionary of Christian Ethics and Pastoral Theology*. Downers Grove, IL: InterVarsity, 1995.

Augustine. *The City of God*. Translated by Marcus Dods. New York: The Modern Library, 1950.

Ball, Jim. *Global Warming and the Risen Lord: Christian Discipleship and Climate Change*. Washington, DC: Evangelical Environmental Network, 2010.

Balmer, Randall H. *Thy Kingdom Come: How the Religious Right Distorts the Faith and Threatens America*. New York: Basic Books, 2006.

Bammel, Ernst, and C. F. D. Moule, eds. *Jesus and the Politics of His Day*. Cambridge: Cambridge University Press, 1984.

Bandow, Doug. *Beyond Good Intentions: A Biblical View of Politics*. Westchester, IL: Crossway, 1988.

Barth, Karl. *Community, State and Church*. Gloucester, MA: Peter Smith, 1968.

Bauckham, Richard. *The Bible in Politics: How to Read the Bible Politically*. Louisville: Westminster/John Knox, 1989.

Beisner, E. Calvin. *Prosperity and Poverty: The Compassionate Use of Resources in a World of Scarcity*. Westchester, IL: Crossway, 1988.

Benson, Bruce Ellis, and Peter Goodwin Heltzel, eds. *Evangelicals and Empire: Christian Alternatives to the Political Status Quo*. Grand Rapids: Brazos, 2008.

Berger, Peter L., and Richard John Neuhaus. *To Empower People: The Role of Mediating Structures in Public Policy*. Washington, DC: American Enterprise Institute for Public Policy Research, 1977.

Bernbaum, John A., ed. *Economic Justice and the State: A Debate between Ronald H. Nash and Eric Beversluis*. Grand Rapids: Baker, 1986.

Black, Amy E. *Beyond Left and Right: Helping Christians Make Sense of American Politics*. Grand Rapids: Baker Books, 2008.

———. *For the Sake of the Children: Reconstructing American Divorce Policy*. Crossroads Monograph Series on Faith and Public Policy, vol. 1, no. 2. Wynnewood, PA: Crossroads, 1995.

Bonino, Jose Miguez. *Toward a Christian Political Ethics*. Philadelphia: Fortress Press, 1983.

Boyd, Greg. *The Myth of a Christian Nation*. Grand Rapids: Zondervan, 2005.

Bratt, James D., ed. *Abraham Kuyper: A Centennial Reader*. Grand Rapids: Eerdmans, 1998.

Brunner, Emil. *Justice and the Social Order*. Translated by Mary Hottinger. New York: Harper & Brothers, 1945.

Budziszewski, J. *The Revenge of Conscience: Politics and the Fall of Man*. Dallas: Spence, 1999.

———. *Written on the Heart: The Case for Natural Law*. Downers Grove: InterVarsity, 1997.

Butler, Jennifer. *All This in Just Two Years? Faith in Public Life's Second Year a Success*. Washington, DC: Faith in Public Life, 2007.

Cahn, Steven M., ed. *Classics of Modern Political Theory: Machiavelli to Mill*. New York: Oxford University Press, 1997.

Calvin, John. *Calvin: Institutes of the Christian Religion*. Edited by John T. McNeill. Translated by Ford Lewis Battles. 2 vols. Philadelphia: Westminster, 1960.

Campolo, Tony. *Red Letter Christians: A Citizen's Guide to Faith and Politics*. Ventura, CA: Regal Books, 2008.

Carter, Stephen L. *The Culture of Disbelief: How American Law and Politics Trivialize Religious Devotion*. New York: Basic Books, 1993.

———. *God's Name in Vain: The Wrongs and Rights of Religion in Politics*. New York: Basic Books, 2000.

Charles, J. Daryl. *Returning to Moral First Things: The Natural Law Tradition and its Contemporary Application*. Grand Rapids: Eerdmans, 2008.

Cizik, Richard, ed. *The High Cost of Indifference: Can Christians Afford Not to Act?* Ventura, CA: Regal Books, 1984.

Claiborne, Shane, and Chris Haw. *Jesus for President: Politics for Ordinary Radicals*. Grand Rapids: Zondervan, 2008.

Colson, Charles W. *God and Government: An Insider's View on the Boundaries between Faith and Politics*. Grand Rapids: Zondervan, 2007.

Colson, Charles W., and Nancy Pearcey. *How Now Shall We Live?* Wheaton: Tyndale House Publishers, 1999.

Coppenger, Mark T. *A Christian View of Justice*. Nashville: Broadman, 1983.

Cromartie, Michael, ed. *A Public Faith: Evangelicals and Civic Engagement*. New York: Rowman & Littlefield, 2003.

Curran, Charles E., and Richard A. McCormick, eds. *Readings in Moral Theology No. 5: Official Catholic Social Teaching*. New York: Paulist Press, 1986.

Daly, Lew. *God's Economy: Faith-Based Initiatives and the Caring State*. Chicago: University of Chicago Press, 2009.

Davis, Harry R., and Robert C. Good, eds. *Reinhold Niebuhr on Politics*. New York: Scribner's Sons, 1960.

Demy, Timothy J., and Gary P. Stewart, eds. *Politics and Public Policy: A Christian Response*. Grand Rapids: Kregel, 2000.

Dengerink, Jan. *The Idea of Justice in Christian Perspective*. Toronto: Wedge Publishing Foundation, 1978.

Deutsch, Karl W. *Politics and Government: How People Decide Their Fate*. Boston: Houghton Mifflin, 1970.

DiIulio, John J. *Godly Republic: A Centrist Blueprint for America's Faith-Based Future*. Berkeley: University of California Press, 2007.

Dionne, E. J., Jr., *Souled Out: Reclaiming Faith and Politics after the Religious Right*. Princeton: Princeton University Press, 2008.

Dionne, E. J., Jr., Jean Bethke Elshtain, and Kayla M. Drogosz, eds. *One Electorate Under God? A Dialogue on Religion and American Politics*. Washington, DC: Brookings Institution Press, 2004.

Dorrien, Gary. *Economy, Difference, Empire: Social Ethics for Social Justice*. New York: Columbia University Press, 2010.

Duchrow, Ulrich. *Two Kingdoms: The Use and Misuse of a Lutheran Theological Concept*. Geneva: Lutheran World Federation, 1977.

————, ed. *Lutheran Churches—Salt or Mirror of Society?* Geneva: Lutheran World Federation, 1977.

Dunning, William Archibald. *A History of Political Theories Ancient and Mediaeval*. London: Macmillan, 1919.

Eberly, Don E. *American Promise: Civil Society and the Renewal of American Culture*. Lanham, MD: Rowan and Littlefield, 1998.

————. *Restoring the Good Society: A New Vision for Politics and Culture*. Grand Rapids: Baker, 1994.

Edgar, Robert. *Middle Church: Reclaiming the Moral Values of the Faithful Majority from the Religious Right*. New York: Simon and Schuster, 2006.

Ellul, Jacques. *The Politics of God and the Politics of Man*. Translated and edited by Geoffrey W. Bromiley. Grand Rapids: Eerdmans, 1972.

Elshtain, Jean Bethke. *Augustine and the Limits of Politics*. South Bend, IN: University of Notre Dame Press, 1995.

Esbeck, Carl H., Stanley W. Carlson-Thies, and Ronald J. Sider. *The Freedom of Faith-Based Organizations to Staff on a Religious Basis*. Washington, DC: The Center for Public Justice, 2004.

Evans, Robert A., and Alice Frazer Evans. *Human Rights: A Dialogue between the First and Third Worlds*. Maryknoll, NY: Orbis Books, 1983.

Faithful Citizenship: A Catholic Call to Political Responsibility. Washington, DC: USCCB Publishing, 2003.

Fea, John. *Was America Founded as a Christian Nation? A Historical Introduction*. Louisville: Westminster John Knox Press, 2011.

Figgis, John Neville. *Political Thought from Gerson to Grotius: 1414–1625*. New York: Harper & Brothers, 1960.

Forrester, Duncan B. *Christian Justice and Public Policy*. Cambridge: Cambridge University Press, 1997.

Forster, Greg. *The Contested Public Square: The Crisis of Christianity and Politics*. Downers Grove, IL: IVP Academic, 2008.

Freston, Paul. *Evangelicals and Politics in Asia, Africa, and Latin America*. Cambridge: Cambridge University Press, 2001.

———, ed. *Evangelical Christianity and Democracy in Latin America*. New York: Oxford University Press, 2006.

Friesen, Duane K. *Christian Peacemaking and International Conflict: A Realist, Pacifist Perspective*. Scottdale, PA: Herald Press, 1986.

Galbraith, John Kenneth. *The Good Society: The Humane Agenda*. New York: Houghton Mifflin, 1996.

Galston, William A. *Justice and the Human Good*. Chicago: University of Chicago Press, 1980.

George, Robert P. *The Clash of Orthodoxies: Law, Religion and Morality in Crisis*. Wilmington, DE: ISI Books, 2001.

Gerson, Michael J. *Heroic Conservatism: Why Republicans Need to Embrace America's Ideals (And Why They Deserve to Fail if They Don't)*. New York: HarperOne, 2007.

Gerson, Michael J., and Peter Wehner. *City of Man: Religion and Politics in a New Era*. Chicago: Moody, 2010.

Gilgoff, Dan. *The Jesus Machine: How James Dobson, Focus on the Family and Evangelical America are Winning the Culture War*. New York: St. Martin's Press, 2007.

Gitari, David. *In Season and Out of Season: Sermons to a Nation*. Oxford: Regnum, 1996.

Goodin, Robert E., and Philip Pettit, eds. *Contemporary Political Philosophy: An Anthology*. Oxford: Blackwell, 1997.

Green, Chris, ed. *A Higher Throne: Evangelicals and Public Policy*. Downers Grove, IL: InterVarsity, 2008.

Green, John. *Fourth National Survey of Religion and Politics*. Akron, OH: Bliss Institute, University of Akron, 2004.

Gregory, Eric. *Politics and the Order of Love: An Augustinian Ethic of Democratic Citizenship*. Chicago: University of Chicago Press, 2010.

Gushee, David P. *The Future of Faith in American Politics: The Public Witness of the Evangelical Center*. Waco: Baylor University Press, 2008.

————, ed. *Christians and Politics Beyond the Culture Wars: An Agenda for Engagement*. Grand Rapids: Baker, 2000.

Harper, Lisa Sharon. *Evangelical ≠ Republican . . . or Democrat*. New York: The New Press, 2008.

Harper, Lisa Sharon, and D. C. Innes. *Left, Right and Christ*. Boise, ID: Russel Media Web, 2011.

Hauerwas, Stanley. *After Christendom? How the Church Is to Behave if Freedom, Justice and a Christian Nation Are Bad Ideas*. Nashville: Abingdon, 1991.

Hays, Richard B. *The Moral Vision of the New Testament: A Contemporary Introduction to New Testament Ethics*. San Francisco: HarperSanFrancisco, 1996.

Heltzel, Peter Goodwin. *Jesus and Justice: Evangelicals, Race, and American Politics*. New Haven: Yale University Press, 2009.

Hendricks, Obery M., Jr. *The Politics of Jesus*. New York: Doubleday, 2006.

Hertzke, Allen D. *Freeing God's Children: The Unlikely Alliance for Global Human Rights*. New York: Rowman & Littlefield, 2004.

Heslam, Peter S. *Creating a Christian Worldview: Abraham Kuyper's Lectures on Calvinism*. Grand Rapids: Eerdmans, 1998.

Himes, Kenneth R., ed. *Modern Catholic Social Teaching: Commentaries and Interpretations*. Washington: Georgetown University Press, 2005.

Holland, Joe. *Modern Catholic Social Teaching: The Popes Confront the Industrial Age 1740–1958*. New York: Paulist Press, 2003.

Hollenbach, David. *Claims in Conflict: Retrieving and Renewing the Catholic Human Rights Tradition*. New York: Paulist Press, 1979.

————. *Justice, Peace, and Human Rights: American Catholic Social Ethics in a Pluralistic Context*. New York: Crossroad, 1988.

Hollinger, Dennis P. *Choosing the Good: Christian Ethics in a Complex World*. Grand Rapids: Baker, 2002.

Hopfl, Harro, ed., *Luther and Calvin on Secular Authority*. Cambridge: Cambridge University Press, 1991.

Horn, Wade F. *Father Facts*. Lancaster, PA: The National Fatherhood Initiative, 1995.

Horsley, Richard A. *Religion and Empire: People Power and the Life of the Spirit*. Minneapolis: Fortress Press, 2003.

Hughes, Richard T. *Christian America and the Kingdom of God*. Champaign, IL: University of Illinois Press, 2009.

Hunter, James Davison. *To Change the World: The Irony, Tragedy and Possibility of Christianity in the Late Modern World*. New York: Oxford University Press, 2010.

Hunter, Joel C. *Right Wing, Wrong Bird: Why the Tactics of the Religious Right Won't Fly with Most Conservative Christians*. Longwood, FL: Distributed Church Press, 2006.

Joireman, Sandra Fullerton, ed. *Church, State, and Citizen: Christian Approaches to Political Engagement*. New York: Oxford University Press, 2009.

Jones, Robert P. *Progressive and Religious: How Christian, Jewish, Muslim and Buddhist Leaders are Moving Beyond the Culture Wars and Transforming American Public Life*. Lanham, MD: Rowman & Littlefield, 2008.

Jungel, Eberhard. *Christ, Justice and Peace: Toward a Theology of the State*. Edinburgh: T&T Clark, 1992.

Kegley, Charles W., ed. *Reinhold Niebuhr: His Religious, Social, and Political Thought*. New York: Pilgrim, 1984.

Kemeny, P. C., ed. *Church, State and Public Justice: Five Views*. Downers Grove, IL: IVP Academic, 2007.

Kennedy, D. James, and Jerry Newcombe. *How Would Jesus Vote? A Christian Perspective on the Issues*. Colorado Springs: WaterBrook Press, 2008.

King, Martin Luther, Jr. *Letter from Birmingham Jail*. Atlanta: The King Center, 2003.

Koopman, Douglas L., ed. *Serving the Claims of Justice: The Thought of Paul B. Henry*. Grand Rapids: Paul B. Henry Institute, 2001.

Koyzis, David T. *Political Visions and Illusions: A Survey and Christian Critique of Contemporary Ideologies*. Downers Grove, IL: InterVarsity, 2003.

Kraynak, Robert P. *Christian Faith and Modern Democracy: God and Politics in the Fallen World*. South Bend, IN: University of Notre Dame Press, 2001.

Kubassek, Erika. *One Moment to Midnight*. Columbus, GA: Brentwood Christian, 2003.

Kuitert, H. M. *Everything Is Politics but Politics Is Not Everything*. Translated by John Bowden. Grand Rapids: Eerdmans, 1986.

Kuyper, Abraham. *The Crown of Christian Heritage*. Mussoorie, U.P., India: Nivedit Good Books Distributors, 1994.

———. *The Problem of Poverty*. Edited by James W. Skillen. Grand Rapids: Baker, 1991.

Land, Richard. *The Divided States of America? What Liberals and Conservatives are Missing in the God-and-Country Shouting Match!* Nashville: Thomas Nelson, 2007.

Lebacqz, Karen. *Six Theories of Justice*. Minneapolis: Augsburg, 1986.

Lehmann, Paul. *The Transfiguration of Politics*. New York: Harper & Row, 1975.

Lerner, Natan. *Religion, Beliefs, and International Human Rights*. Maryknoll, NY: Orbis Books, 2000.

Lindsay, D. Michael. *Faith in the Halls of Power: How Evangelicals Joined the American Elite*. New York: Oxford University Press, 2007.

Lugo, Luis E., ed. *Religion, Pluralism, and Public Life: Abraham Kuyper's Legacy for the Twenty-first Century*. Grand Rapids: Eerdmans, 2000.

———. *Sovereignty at the Crossroads? Morality and International Politics in the Post–Cold War Era*. New York: Rowman & Littlefield, 1996.

Lumsdaine, David Halloran, ed. *Evangelical Christianity and Democracy in Asia*. New York: Oxford University Press, 2006.

MacIntyre, Alasdair. *After Virtue*. 2nd ed. South Bend, IN: University of Notre Dame Press, 1984.

Marshall, Ellen Ott. *Christians in the Public Square: Faith that Transforms Politics.* Nashville: Abingdon, 2008.

Marshall, Paul. *God and the Constitution: Christianity and American Politics.* New York: Rowman & Littlefield, 2002.

———. *Thine Is the Kingdom: A Biblical Perspective on the Nature of Government and Politics Today.* Grand Rapids: Eerdmans, 1984.

———, ed. *Religious Freedom in the World.* Lanham, MD: Rowman and Littlefield, 2008.

Marty, Martin E. *The Public Church: Mainline—Evangelical—Catholic.* New York: Crossroad, 1981.

Massaro, Thomas. *Living Justice: Catholic Social Teaching in Action.* 2nd ed. Lanham, MD: Rowman and Littlefield, 2012.

McElroy, Robert W. *The Search for an American Public Theology: The Contribution of John Courtney Murray.* New York: Paulist Press, 1989.

Mead, Sidney E. *The Nation with the Soul of a Church.* Macon, GA: Mercer University Press, 1985.

Milbank, John. *Theology and Social Theory Beyond Secular Reason.* Cambridge, MA: Basil Blackwell, 1990.

Mitchell, Basil. *Law, Morality, and Religion in a Secular Society.* London: Oxford University Press, 1970.

Moltmann, Jürgen. *God for a Secular Society: The Public Relevance of Theology.* Minneapolis: Fortress Press, 1999.

Monsma, Stephen V. *Healing a Broken World: Christian Perspectives on Public Policy.* Wheaton: Crossway Books, 2008.

———. *Pursuing Justice in a Sinful World.* Grand Rapids: Eerdmans, 1984.

———. *When Sacred and Secular Mix.* Lanham, MD: Rowman & Littlefield, 1996.

Monsma, Stephen V., and J. Christopher Soper. *The Challenge of Pluralism: Church and State in Five Democracies.* 2nd ed. Lanham, MD: Rowman and Littlefield, 2009.

Mott, Stephen Charles. *A Christian Perspective on Political Thought.* New York: Oxford University Press, 1993.

Mouw, Richard J. *The God Who Commands.* South Bend, IN: University of Notre Dame Press, 1990.

———. *Politics and the Biblical Drama.* Grand Rapids: Eerdmans, 1976.

———. *When the Kings Come Marching In: Isaiah and the New Jerusalem.* Grand Rapids: Eerdmans, 2002.

Nash, Ronald H. *Freedom, Justice and the State.* Lanham, MD: University Press of America, 1980.

———. *Social Justice and the Christian Church.* Lima, OH: First Academic Renewal Press, 2002.

Neuhaus, Richard John. *America Against Itself: Moral Vision and the Public Order.* South Bend, IN: University of Notre Dame Press, 1992.

———. *Christian Faith and Public Policy: Thinking and Acting in the Courage of Uncertainty.* Minneapolis: Augsburg, 1977.

————. *The Naked Public Square: Religion and Democracy in America*. Grand Rapids: Eerdmans, 1984.

Niebuhr, Reinhold. *An Interpretation of Christian Ethics*. New York: World, 1935.

————. *The Nature and Destiny of Man*. 2 vols. New York: Scribner's Sons, 1964.

Noll, Mark A. *One Nation Under God: Christian Faith and Political Action in America*. San Francisco: Harper & Row, 1988.

————. *The Scandal of the Evangelical Mind*. Grand Rapids: Eerdmans, 1994.

Noll, Mark A., and Luke E. Harlow, eds. *Religion and American Politics: From the Colonial Period to the 1980s*. 2nd ed. New York: Oxford University Press, 2007.

Novak, Michael. "The Moral Spirit of Capitalism." In *The Institute on Religion and Democracy*, September 16, 2002.

O'Donovan, Oliver. *Common Objects of Love: Moral Reflection and the Shaping of Community*. Grand Rapids: Eerdmans, 2001.

————. *The Desire of the Nations: Rediscovering the Roots of Political Theology*. Cambridge: Cambridge University Press, 1996.

O'Donovan, Oliver, and Joan Lockwood O'Donovan, eds. *From Irenaeus to Grotius: A Sourcebook in Christian Political Thought, 100–1625*. Grand Rapids: Eerdmans, 1999.

Paris, Peter J. *The Social Teaching of the Black Churches*. Philadelphia: Fortress Press, 1985.

Patterson, Eric. *Christianity and Power Politics Today: Christian Realism and Contemporary Political Dilemmas*. New York: Palgrave Macmillan, 2008.

Peachey, Paul, ed. *Peace, Politics, and the People of God*. Philadelphia: Fortress Press, 1986.

Penner, Archie. *The New Testament, the Christian, and the State*. Scottdale, PA: Herald, 1959.

Plant, Raymond. *Politics, Theology and History*. Cambridge: Cambridge University Press, 2001.

Pohl, Christine D. *Making Room: Recovering Hospitality as Christian Tradition*. Grand Rapids: Eerdmans, 1999.

Pontifical Council for Justice and Peace. *Compendium of the Social Doctrine of the Church*. Washington, DC: United States Conference of Catholic Bishops, 2004.

Ranger, Terence O., ed. *Evangelical Christianity and Democracy in Africa*. New York: Oxford University Press, 2006.

Ray, Stephen G., Jr. *Do No Harm: Social Sin and Christian Responsibility*. Minneapolis: Fortress Press, 2003.

Reformed Ecumenical Synod Testimony on Human Rights. The Reformed Ecumenical Synod. Grand Rapids: Reformed Ecumenical Synod, 1983.

Reichley, A. James. *Religion in American Public Life*. Washington, DC: The Brookings Institution, 1985.

Ryan, John A. *Economic Justice: Selections from* Distributive Justice *and* A Living Wage. Edited by Harlan R. Beckley. Louisville: Westminster John Knox, 1996.

Sandel, Michael. *Liberalism and the Limits of Justice.* Cambridge: Cambridge University Press, 1982.

Sanders, Cheryl J. *Empowerment Ethics for a Liberated People: A Path to African American Social Transformation.* Minneapolis: Fortress Press, 1995.

Savage, Barbara Dianne. *Your Spirits Walk Beside Us: The Politics of Black Religion.* Cambridge: Belknap Press, 2008.

Schluter, Michael, and John Ashcroft, eds. *Jubilee Manifesto: A Framework, Agenda, and Strategy for Christian Social Reform.* Downers Grove, IL: InterVarsity, 2005.

Schrey, Heinz-Horst, Hans Hermann Walz, and W. A. Whitehouse. *Ecumenical Biblical Studies No. 3: The Biblical Doctrine of Justice and Law.* London: SCM, 1955.

Schroeder, Christopher O. *History, Justice and the Agency of God: A Hermeneutical and Exegetical Investigation on Isaiah and Psalms.* Boston: Brill, 2001.

Sherratt, Timothy R., and Ronald P. Mahurin. *Saints as Citizens.* Grand Rapids: Baker, 1995.

Sider, Ronald J. *The Early Church on Killing: A Comprehensive Sourcebook on War, Abortion, and Capital Punishment.* Grand Rapids: Baker Academic, 2012.

———. *Fixing the Moral Deficit: A Balanced Way to Balance the Budget.* Downers Grove, IL: InterVarsity, 2012.

———. *Good News and Good Works.* Grand Rapids: Baker, 1996.

———. *Rich Christians in an Age of Hunger.* 5th ed. Nashville: W Publishing Group, 2005.

———, ed. *The Chicago Declaration.* Carol Stream, IL: Creation House, 1974.

Skillen, James W. *In Pursuit of Justice: Christian Democratic Explorations.* Lanham, MD: Rowman and Littlefield, 2004.

———. *Recharging the American Experiment: Principled Pluralism for Genuine Civic Community.* Grand Rapids: Baker, 1994.

———. *The Scattered Voice: Christians at Odds in the Public Square.* Grand Rapids: Zondervan, 1990.

Smidt, Corwin E., et al. *The Disappearing God Gap? Religion in the 2008 Presidential Election.* New York: Oxford University Press, 2010.

Smidt, Corwin E., ed. *In God We Trust? Religion and American Political Life.* Grand Rapids: Baker, 2001.

Smith, Christian. *Christian America? What Evangelicals Really Want.* Berkeley: University of California Press, 2002.

Smith, Gary Scott, ed. *God and Politics: Four Views on the Reformation of Civil Government.* Phillipsburg, NJ: Presbyterian and Reformed, 1989.

Spencer, Nick, and Jonathan Chaplin, eds. *God and Government.* London: SPCK, 2009.

Stackhouse, Max L. *Creeds, Society, and Human Rights: A Study in Three Cultures.* Grand Rapids: Eerdmans, 1984.

———. *Public Theology and Political Economy: Christian Stewardship in Modern Society.* Grand Rapids: Eerdmans, 1987.

Stassen, Glen H. *Just Peacemaking: Transforming Initiatives for Justice and Peace.* Louisville: Westminster John Knox, 1992.

————, ed. *Just Peacemaking: Ten Practices for Abolishing War*. Cleveland: Pilgrim, 1998.

Stassen, Glen H., and David P. Gushee. *Kingdom Ethics: Following Jesus in Contemporary Context*. Downers Grove, IL: InterVarsity, 2003.

Stewart, Robert. M., ed. *Readings in Social and Political Philosophy*. 2nd ed. Oxford: Oxford University Press, 1996.

Stiller, Brian C. *From the Tower of Babel to Parliament Hill: How to Be a Christian in Canada Today*. Toronto: Harper Collins, 1997.

Storkey, Alan. *Jesus and Politics: Confronting the Powers*. Grand Rapids: Baker, 2005.

Sullivan, Amy. *The Party Faithful: How and Why Democrats are Closing the God Gap*. New York: Scribner, 2008.

Temple, William. *Christianity and Social Order*. New York: Seabury, 1976.

————. *Christianity and the State*. London: Macmillan, 1928.

The Bible and Law. Occasional Papers No. 3. Elkhart, IN: Council of Mennonite Seminaries, Institute of Mennonite Studies, 1982.

Thielicke, Helmut. *Theological Ethics: Politics*. Grand Rapids: Eerdmans, 1979.

Thiemann, Ronald F. *Constructing a Public Theology: The Church in a Pluralistic Society*. Louisville: Westminster John Knox, 1991.

Thomas, Cal, and Ed Dobson. *Blinded by Might: Can the Religious Right Save America?* Grand Rapids: Zondervan, 1999.

Unruh, Heidi Rolland, and Ronald J. Sider. *Saving Souls, Serving Society: Understanding the Faith Factor in Church-Based Social Ministry*. New York: Oxford University Press, 2005.

Volf, Miroslav. *A Public Faith: How Followers of Christ Should Serve the Common Good*. Grand Rapids: Brazos, 2011.

Wallis, Jim. *Faith Works: Lessons from the Life of an Activist Preacher*. New York: Random House, 2000.

————. *God's Politics: Why the Right Gets It Wrong and the Left Doesn't Get It*. San Francisco: HarperSanFrancisco, 2005.

————. *The Great Awakening: Reviving Faith and Politics in a Post-Religious Right America*. New York: HarperOne, 2008.

————. *Rediscovering Values: On Wall Street, Main Street, and Your Street*. Riverside, NJ: Howard Books, 2010.

Walzer, Michael. *Spheres of Justice: A Defense of Pluralism and Equality*. New York: Basic Books, 1983.

Weigel, George. *Catholicism and the Renewal of American Democracy*. New York: Paulist Press, 1989.

Williamson, Rene De Visme. *Independence and Involvement: A Christian Reorientation in Political Science*. Baton Rouge: Louisiana State University Press, 1964.

Wiser, James L. *Political Philosophy: A History of the Search for Order*. Upper Saddle River, NJ: Prentice-Hall, 1983.

Wogaman, J. Philip. *Christian Perspectives on Politics*. Philadelphia: Fortress Press, 1988.

Wolf, Frank R., and Anne Morse. *Prisoner of Conscience: One Man's Crusade for Global Human and Religious Rights.* Grand Rapids: Zondervan, 2011.

Wolfe, Alan. *The Future of Liberalism.* New York: Knopf, 2009.

Wolterstorff, Nicholas. *Until Justice and Peace Embrace.* Grand Rapids: Eerdmans, 1983.

Wright, Christopher J. H. *An Eye for an Eye: The Place of Old Testament Ethics Today.* Downers Grove, IL: InterVarsity, 1983.

———. *God's People in God's Land: Family, Land, and Property in the Old Testament.* Grand Rapids: Eerdmans, 1990.

———. *Human Rights: A Study in Biblical Themes.* Grove Booklet on Ethics 31. Cambridge: Grove, 1979.

Wright, N. T. *Jesus and the Victory of God.* Minneapolis: Fortress Press, 1996.

Yoder, John Howard. *The Christian Witness to the State.* Institute of Mennonite Studies Series 3. Newton, KS: Faith and Life, 1964.

———. *Discipleship as Political Responsibility.* Translated by Timothy J. Geddert. Scottdale, PA: Herald Press, 2003.

———. *For the Nations: Essays Public and Evangelical.* Grand Rapids: Eerdmans, 1997.

———. *Politics of Jesus.* Grand Rapids: Eerdmans, 1972.

Notes

Preface to the Second Edition

1. Wayne Grudem, *Politics according to the Bible* (Grand Rapids: Zondervan, 2010), 368.

Chapter 1 Tragic Failure, New Opportunity

1. Jerry Falwell, quoted in Richard John Neuhaus, *The Naked Public Square* (Grand Rapids: Eerdmans, 1984), 10.

2. Tim LaHaye, "Leaders of the Christian Right Announce Their Next Step," in *Christianity Today*, December 13, 1985, 65.

3. See "The Chicago Declaration of Evangelical Social Concern" (1973) in Ronald J. Sider, ed., *The Chicago Declaration* (Carol Stream, IL: Creation House, 1974); and Richard J. Mouw, *Politics and the Biblical Drama* (Grand Rapids: Eerdmans, 1976).

4. Paul Freston, *Evangelicals and Politics in Asia, Africa, and Latin America* (Cambridge: Cambridge University Press, 2001), 285.

5. Paul Freston, "Evangelicals and Politics in the Third World," in David P. Gushee, ed., *Christians and Politics: Beyond the Culture Wars* (Grand Rapids: Baker, 2000), 109.

6. Ibid., 126.

7. Frederick Chiluba, quoted in Isabel Apawo Phiri, "President Frederick Chiluba and Zambia," in Terence O. Ranger, ed. *Evangelical Christianity and Democracy in Africa* (New York: Oxford University Press, 2006), chap. 3.

8. Richard Cizik, "A History of the Public Policy Resolutions of the National Association of Evangelicals," in Ronald J. Sider and Diane Knippers, eds., *Toward an Evangelical Public Policy* (Grand Rapids: Baker, 2005), 42.

9. See Phiri's lengthy chapter (see n7) and Freston, "Evangelicals and Politics in the Third World," 115–20.

10. Freston, "Evangelicals and Politics," 315.

11. Ibid., 126.

12. Ralph Reed, *Active Faith: How Christians Are Changing the Soul of American Politics* (New York: Free Press, 1996), 23.

13. Personal correspondence with Ed Dobson.

14. Cal Thomas and Ed Dobson, *Blinded by Might: Can the Religious Right Save America?* (Grand Rapids: Zondervan, 1999), 105, 165.

15. Michael L. Cromartie, "The Evangelical Kaleidoscope," in Gushee, ed., *Christians and Politics*, 25.

16. Don Eberly, quoted in Lawrence E. Adams, *Going Public: Christian Responsibility in a Divided Nation* (Grand Rapids: Brazos, 2002), 104.

17. Douglas L. Koopman, *Serving the Claims of Justice: The Thoughts of Paul B. Henry* (Grand Rapids: The Paul B. Henry Institute, 2001), 79.

18. Mark Noll, *The Scandal of the Evangelical Mind* (Grand Rapids: Eerdmans, 1994), 166.

19. Ibid., 173.

20. Os Guinness, quoted in ibid., 23.

21. Ibid., 221–27. See also David P. Gushee and Dennis P. Hollinger, "Toward an Evangelical Ethical Methodology," in Sider and Knippers, eds., *Toward an Evangelical Public Policy*, chapter 6. In fact, there have been dozens of books on politics written by evangelicals in the last decade; see the bibliography for books by Lawrence Adams, Stephen Carter, Michael Cromartie, Don Eberly, Allen D. Hertzke, David T. Koyzis, Luis E. Lugo, Paul Marshall, Stephen Monsma, Stephen Mott, Oliver O'Donovan, Timothy Sherratt and Ronald P. Mahurin, James Skillen, Corwin Smidt, Jim Wallis, and others.

22. Noll, *Scandal*, 22.

23. See especially Kenneth R. Himes, et al., eds., *Modern Catholic Social Teaching: Commentaries and Interpretations* (Washington, DC: Georgetown University Press, 2005); and Pontifical Council for Justice and Peace, *Compendium of the Social Doctrine of the Church* (Washington, DC: United States Conference of Catholic Bishops, 2004).

24. See the bibliography for books by Emil Brunner, Jean Bethke Elshtain, Charles Kegley, Paul Lehmann, Reinhold Niebuhr, Max L. Stackhouse, William Temple, Ronald Thiemann, and J. Philip Wogaman.

25. A partial exception to this generalization is provided by the books on Abraham Kuyper and recent authors inspired by Kuyper (especially James Skillen) and the Reformed thinkers shaped by Calvin College (e.g., Richard Mouw and Stephen Monsma).

26. David Gushee, *The Future of Faith in American Politics* (Waco, TX: Baylor University Press, 2008).

27. Matthew 19:8–9.

28. See chap. 1, n14.

29. Gushee and Hollinger, "Evangelical Ethical Methodology," 117–21.

30. See Freston (n4) and the three volumes by Oxford University Press on evangelical Christianity and democracy in Asia (ed. David H. Lumsdaine), Latin America (ed. Paul Freston), and Africa (ed. Terence O. Ranger).

Chapter 2 Developing a Faithful Methodology

1. Oliver O'Donovan and Joan Lockwood O'Donovan, eds., *From Irenaeus to Grotius: A Sourcebook in Christian Political Thought, 100–1625* (Grand Rapids: Eerdmans, 1999), 14.

2. Robert W. McElroy, *The Search for an American Public Theology: The Contribution of John Courtney Murray* (New York: Paulist Press, 1989), 22.

3. Augustine, *City of God*, trans. Marcus Dods (New York: The Modern Library, 1950). See also O'Donovan and O'Donovan, *Sourcebook*, 137–63.

4. Jean Bethke Elshtain, *Augustine and the Limits of Politics* (South Bend, IN: University of Notre Dame Press, 1995). See Jose Miguez Bonino's valid point that Augustine balances

order and justice in a way that preferences the status quo: *Toward a Christian Political Ethics* (Philadelphia: Fortress Press, 1983), 82–84.

5. See Stephen J. Pope, "Natural Law in Catholic Social Teachings," in Himes, ed., *Modern Catholic Social Teaching*, 43–45, and the literature cited there.

6. John Courtney Murray, quoted in McElroy, *The Search for an American Public Theology*, 96. See also John A. Ryan, *Economic Justice: Selections from* Distributive Justice *and* A Living Wage, ed. Harlan R. Beckley (Louisville: Westminster John Knox, 1996), xix.

7. Harro Hopfl, ed., *Luther and Calvin on Secular Authority* (Cambridge: Cambridge University Press, 1991), 11.

8. Ibid., 9.

9. Martin Luther, quoted in Duncan B. Forrester, *Christian Justice and Public Policy* (Cambridge: Cambridge University Press, 1997), 213.

10. Helmut Thielicke, *Theological Ethics: Politics* (Grand Rapids: Eerdmans, 1979), 17.

11. Ibid., 144.

12. Forrester, *Christian Justice and Public Policy*, 214; Karl Barth, *Community, State and Church: Three Essays* (Gloucester, MA: Peter Smith, 1968), 101–48.

13. Hopfl, ed., *Luther and Calvin on Secular Authority*, 49.

14. Ibid., 50.

15. Mark A. Noll, *One Nation Under God: Christian Faith and Political Action in America* (San Francisco: Harper & Row, 1988), 25.

16. H. Richard Niebuhr, *Christ and Culture* (New York: Harper, 1951).

17. Schleitheim Confession (1527), article 6 in O'Donovan and O'Donovan, *Sourcebook*, 635 (my italics).

18. See my *The Early Church on Killing: A Comprehensive Sourcebook on War, Abortion and Capital Punishment* (Grand Rapids: Baker Academic, 2012).

19. See, John Howard Yoder, *Discipleship as Political Responsibility*, trans. Timothy J. Geddert (Scottdale, PA: Herald Press, 2003).

20. Duane Friesen, *Christian Peacemaking and International Conflict: A Realist, Pacifist Perspective* (Scottdale, PA: Herald Press, 1986), 44.

21. See Himes, ed., *Modern Catholic Social Teaching.*

22. See Stathis N. Kalyvas, *The Rise of Christian Democracy in Europe* (Ithaca, NY: Cornell University Press, 1996), and Michael P. Fogarty, *Christian Democracy in Western Europe* (South Bend, IN: University of Notre Dame Press, 1957).

23. See, for example, Reinhold Niebuhr, *An Interpretation of Christian Ethics* (New York: World, 1935); and *The Nature and Destiny of Man* (New York: Scribner's Sons, 1964).

24. See, for example, the writings of Jean Bethke Elshtain, Max Stackhouse, Ronald Thiemann, and Philip Wogaman.

25. See Stephen V. Monsma, *Pursuing Justice in a Sinful World* (Grand Rapids: Eerdmans, 1984). Richard J. Mouw, *The God Who Commands* (South Bend, IN: University of Notre Dame Press, 1990); *Politics and the Biblical Drama* (Grand Rapids: Eerdmans, 1976); and *When the Kings Come Marching In: Isaiah and the New Jerusalem* (Grand Rapids: Eerdmans, 2002). Paul Marshall, *God and the Constitution: Christianity and American Politics* (New York: Rowman & Littlefield, 2002); *Thine Is the Kingdom: A Biblical Perspective on the Nature of Government and Politics Today* (Grand Rapids: Eerdmans, 1984). And James W. Skillen, *Recharging the American Experiment: Principled Pluralism for Genuine Civic Community* (Grand Rapids: Baker, 1994); *The Scattered Voice: Christians at Odds in the Public Square* (Grand Rapids: Zondervan, 1990).

26. For example, Jose Miguez Bonino, *Toward a Christian Political Ethic* (Philadelphia: Fortress Press, 1983); Jose Porfiro Miranda, *Marx and the Bible* (Maryknoll, NY: Orbis Books, 1974); and Gustavo Gutierrez, *A Theology of Liberation: History, Politics, and Salvation*, trans. and ed. Caridad Inda and John Eagleson (Maryknoll, NY: Orbis Books, 1973).

27. Stephen Charles Mott, *A Christian Perspective on Political Thought* (New York: Oxford University Press, 1993).

28. Doug Bandow, *Beyond Good Intentions* (Westchester, IL: Crossway, 1988); Ronald H. Nash, *Freedom, Justice, and the State* (Lanham, MD: University Press of America, 1980).

29. See, for example, books by Greg L. Bahnsen (e.g., *Theonomy in Christian Ethics* [Nacogdoches, TX: Covenant Media Press, 2002]), R. J. Rushdooney, and Gary North.

30. See chap. 2, n25.

31. Mott (see chap. 2, n27).

32. Yoder (see chap. 2, n19).

33. A first step in this direction can be seen in "For the Health of the Nation: An Evangelical Call to Civic Responsibility" (unanimously adopted by the board of the National Association of Evangelicals in October 2004); for the process, background papers, and the document itself, see Sider and Knippers, eds., *Toward an Evangelical Public Policy*.

34. Alexis de Tocqueville, quoted in Lawrence E. Adams, *Going Public: Christian Responsibility in a Divided Nation* (Grand Rapids: Brazos, 2002), 67.

35. Max L. Stackhouse, *Public Theology and Political Economy: Christian Stewardship in Modern Society* (Grand Rapids: Eerdmans, 1987), 160.

36. Richard John Neuhaus, *The Naked Public Square: Religion and Democracy in America* (Grand Rapids: Eerdmans, 1984), 152–53. See also Ronald F. Thiemann, *Constructing a Public Theology: The Church in a Pluralistic Society* (Louisville: Westminster John Knox, 1991), 38.

37. Peter Singer, *Practical Ethics*, 2nd ed. (Cambridge: Cambridge University Press, 1993), chaps. 6–7 (esp. p. 172).

38. For a brief discussion of M. Foucault and J. Derrida, see Raymond Plant, *Politics, Theology, and History* (Cambridge: Cambridge University Press, 2001), 100.

39. Ibid., 353.

40. Some evangelicals are attracted to this position. See Paul Henry in Koopman, ed., *The Thoughts of Paul B. Henry*, 86; David L. Weeks, "The Uneasy Politics of Modern Evangelicalism," *Christian Scholars Review*, 30, no. 4 (Summer 2001), 403–18; and, carefully, J. Budziszewski, *Written on the Heart: The Case for Natural Law* (Downers Grove, IL: InterVarsity, 1997). For a classic Catholic example, see John A. Ryan, *Economic Justice*, ed. Harlan R. Beckley (Louisville: Westminster John Knox, 1996), xix.

41. See Weeks's helpful summary of major objections (and a critique of the objections), "Uneasy Politics of Modern Evangelicalism," 412–15.

42. Emil Brunner, *Justice and the Social Order*, trans. Mary Hottinger (New York: Harper & Brothers, 1945), 91; and Carl Henry, cited in nn. 41–42 of Weeks's "Uneasy Politics."

43. Bonino, *Toward a Christian Political Ethic*, 80–86.

44. Karl Barth, *Community, State and Church* (Gloucester, MA: Peter Smith, 1968), 163 (also 29, 147).

45. See the helpful comments by Budziszewski, *Written on the Heart*, 179–86.

46. For this overview and critique of Rawls, see Paul A. Brink, "Selves in Relation: Theories of Community and the Imago Dei Doctrine," in Thomas W. Heilke and Ashley

Woodiwiss, eds., *The Re-Enchantment of Political Science: Christian Scholars Engage Their Discipline* (Lanham, MD: Lexington Books, 2001), 85–123.

47. See the lengthy discussion in Plant, *Politics, Theology, and History*, 331–47.

48. Michael Sandel, *Liberalism and the Limits of Justice* (Cambridge: Cambridge University Press, 1982), e.g., 62–64.

49. See Ashley Woodiwiss, "Rawls, Religion, and Liberalism," chapter 3 in Heilke and Woodiwiss, eds., *Re-Enchantment of Political Science.*

50. John Milbank, *Theology and Social Theory: Beyond Secular Reason* (Oxford: Blackwell, 1991), 380.

51. My argument is parallel to that of James W. Skillen in *Recharging the American Experiment* (Grand Rapids: Baker, 1994), see, for example, 122–23. My proposal rejects any suggestion that public theology must use only arguments that are independent of a particular faith (see, for example, David Tracy, *The Analogical Imagination: Christian Theology and the Culture of Pluralism* (New York: Crossroad, 1981). See also Ronald Thiemann's helpful critique of Tracy: *Constructing a Public Theology*, 20–21. Ashley Woodiwiss makes a proposal similar to mine in calling for a Christian political approach in which Christians first define the Christian community's identity and interests and then negotiate with other communities in our multicultural, pluralistic society. "Deliberation or Agony? Toward a Post-Liberal Christian Democratic Theory," chapter 6 in Heilke and Woodiwiss, eds., *Re-Enchantment of Political Science.*

52. Richard John Neuhaus, *America Against Itself: Moral Vision and the Public Order* (South Bend, IN: University of Notre Dame Press, 1992), 188. At other places, however, Neuhaus seems to take a different position. He condemns the Religious Right for entering politics and "making public claims on the basis of private truths. . . . A public argument is trans subjective. It is not derived from sources of revelation" (*Naked Public Square*, 36).

53. Neuhaus, *America against Itself*, 188.

54. This section is adapted from Sider, "Toward an Evangelical Political Philosophy," in Gushee, ed., *Christians and Politics*, 82–84.

55. Oliver O'Donovan, *The Desire of the Nations: Rediscovering the Roots of Political Theology* (Cambridge: Cambridge University Press, 1996), 22.

56. See a brief critique of the theonomists in John M. Frame, "Penultimate Thoughts on Theonomy," *IIIM Magazine Online* 3, no. 34 (August 20–26, 2001).

57. *Political Christians in a Plural Society: A New Strategy for a Biblical Contribution* (Cambridge: Jubilee Centre, 1994), 58. For further discussion of this paradigmatic approach, see C. J. H. Wright, "The Use of the Bible in Social Ethics," *Transformation* 1, no. 1 (April 1984), 11–20; and *Living as the People of God* (Leicester: Inter-Varsity, 1983). See also the somewhat parallel argument in Brunner, *Justice and the Social Order*, 118–23.

58. Noll, *One Nation Under God*, 172; William Temple, *Christianity and the State* (London: Macmillan, 1929), 3–5.

59. That, of course, raises the complex question: Which sociology, and which social science? Liberation theologians have been especially insistent on this question (see, for example, Bonino, *Toward a Christian Political Ethic*, chap. 3). They have also been too quick to adopt a Marxist sociology and economics. Christians must be aware of secular and other non-Christian bias that often creeps into so-called neutral methodologies. See, for example, James Skillen's attempt to develop a Christianly informed method for political science in "Toward a Comprehensive Science of Politics," *Political Theory and Christian Vision* (Lanham, MD: University Press of America, 1994), 57.

60. See Ronald J. Sider, *Just Generosity: A New Vision for Overcoming Poverty in America,* 2nd ed. (Grand Rapids: Baker, 2007), for an example in the arena of domestic economic justice; Ronald J. Sider, *Rich Christians in an Age of Hunger,* 5th ed. (Nashville: W Publishing Group, 2005), for global poverty; and Ronald J. Sider, *Fixing the Moral Deficit: A Balanced Way to Balance the Budget* (Downers Grove, IL: InterVarsity, 2012), for the American debt crisis.

61. See Ronald J. Sider, "A Plea for More Radical Conservatives and More Conserving Radicals," *Transformation,* January–March 1987, 11–16.

62. Temple, *Christianity and the State,* 108.

63. Lawrence E. Adams, *Going Public: Christian Responsibility in a Divided Nation* (Grand Rapids: Brazos, 2002), 23.

64. Ibid.

65. Ibid., 24.

66. Roger Lundin, quoted in Adams, *Going Public,* 25.

67. Harry R. Davis and Robert C. Good, eds., *Reinhold Niebuhr on Politics* (New York: Scribner & Sons, 1960), 92–94.

Chapter 3 Politics and the Biblical Story

1. Gutierrez, *Theology of Liberation,* 154–60.

2. Oliver O'Donovan, *The Desire of the Nations: Rediscovering the Roots of Political Theology* (Cambridge: Cambridge University Press, 1996), 22.

3. See, for example, Richard J. Mouw, *Politics and the Biblical Drama* (Grand Rapids: Eerdmans, 1976).

4. Philip J. Wogaman, *Christian Perspectives on Politics* (Philadelphia: Fortress Press, 1988), 118.

5. See Ronald J. Sider, "Tending the Garden without Worshipping It," in Stan LeQuire, ed., *The Best Preaching on Earth* (Valley Forge, PA: Judson, 1996), 32–33.

6. See Paul Ramsey, *Basic Christian Ethics* (New York: Scribner's Sons, 1950), 250–89; and Paul A. Brink's use of these two traditions in developing his political philosophy in "Selves in Relation: Theories of Community and the *Imago Dei* Doctrine," in Heilke and Woodiwiss, eds., *Re-Enchantment of Political Science,* chap. 4.

7. See Oliver O'Donovan's discussion of how, in the face of communal disobedience, faithful individuals represented God's will. The result was a growing emphasis on the individual. O'Donovan, *Desire of the Nations,* 73ff.

8. Brunner, *Justice and the Social Order,* 84; and O'Donovan, *Desire of the Nations,* 254.

9. See Moltmann's comment that every declaration of human rights is grounded in the biblical affirmation of the dignity of the individual person. Jürgen Moltmann, *God for a Secular Society: The Public Relevance of Theology* (Minneapolis: Fortress Press, 1999), 179.

10. See chapter 5 on justice and also Sider, *Rich Christians in an Age of Hunger,* chap. 4.

11. Brunner, *Justice and the Social Order,* 40–42.

12. See, for example, the critiques of Western liberalism by Mary Ann Glendon, *Rights Talk: The Impoverishment of Political Discourse* (New York: Free Press, 1991); Jean Bethke Elshtain, "The Family and Civic Life," in her *Power Trips and Other Journeys* (Madison: University of Wisconsin Press, 1990), 49–56; and Michael Sandel, *Liberalism and Its Critics* (New York: New York University Press, 1984).

13. *Political Christians in a Plural Society,* 100 (emphasis added).

14. Temple, *Christianity and the State*, 89.

15. For one brief summary of Reinhold Niebuhr's thought on this, see Davis and Good, eds., *Reinhold Niebuhr on Politics*, 72–74.

16. See Ronald J. Sider, *Good News and Good Works: A Theology for the Whole Gospel* (Grand Rapids: Baker, 1999), 33–36.

17. J. Philip Wogaman, *The Great Economic Debate: An Ethical Analysis* (Philadelphia: Westminster, 1997), 43.

18. See Skillen, *Recharging the American Experiment*, esp. chap. 4.

19. Moltmann, *God for a Secular Society*, 84.

20. See chapter 6 of Sider, *Rich Christians in an Age of Hunger*. Probably no theologian has explored the reality of social evil more extensively than Reinhold Niebuhr. See his *Moral Man and Immoral Society* (New York: Scribner's, 1960); and *Nature and Destiny of Man*, 2 vols. (New York: Scribner's, 1964).

21. John Paul II, *Sollicitudo Rei Socialis* (December 30, 1987), sec. 36.

22. See undoubtedly the best recent book on Jesus's proclamation of the gospel of the kingdom: N. T. Wright, *Jesus and the Victory of God* (Minneapolis: Fortress Press, 1996).

23. See ibid., 308 and elsewhere; and O'Donovan, *Desire of the Nations*, 22–25.

24. N. T. Wright, *The Challenge of Jesus* (Downers Grove, IL: InterVarsity, 1999), 132.

25. The literature is vast, and Wright cites a great deal of it in *Jesus and the Victory of God*.

26. Brunner, *Justice and the Social Order*, 112, 256.

27. Wright, *Jesus and the Victory of God*, 207ff., 321, 361ff.; and chapter 10 of his *New Testament and the People of God* (Minneapolis: Fortress Press, 1992).

28. Wright, *Jesus and the Victory of God*, 321.

29. The following two paragraphs are adopted from Sider, *Good News and Good Works*, 205.

30. See Ronald J. Sider, *Christ and Violence* (Scottdale, PA: Herald Press, 1979), 50–57, and the literature cited there. See also the three-volume work by Walter Wink, *Naming the Powers* (Minneapolis: Fortress Press, 1984); *Unmasking the Powers* (Minneapolis: Fortress Press, 1986); *Engaging the Powers* (Minneapolis: Fortress Press, 1992).

31. See Albert van den Heuvel, *The Rebellious Powers* (Naperville: SCM Book Club, 1969), 44.

32. Wright, *Challenge of Jesus*, 131.

33. O'Donovan, *Desire of the Nations*, 241.

34. Wright, *Challenge of Jesus*, 132.

35. Richard J. Mouw, *When the Kings Come Marching In: Isaiah and the New Jerusalem* (Grand Rapids: Eerdmans, 2002), 18. Mouw rejects this view.

36. Evangelical New Testament scholar F. F. Bruce comments, "If words mean anything, these words of Paul denote not the annihilation of the present material world . . . but the transformation of the present universe." F. F. Bruce, *The Epistle of Paul to the Romans* (Grand Rapids: Eerdmans, 1963), 170.

37. David Lawrence, *Heaven: It's Not the End of the World* (Valley Forge, PA: Scripture Union, 2003). See also Craig S. Keener's statement: "Western Christendom has inherited an allegorical view of heaven from the Platonism of some of its early interpreters, but the New Testament emphasizes resurrection for bodily existence, ultimately on the new earth." *Revelation: The NIV Application Commentary* (Grand Rapids: Zondervan, 2000), 502. See also the literature cited in ibid., 502n80.

220

Notes

38. James Skillen, "Living in Tune with Christ's Supremacy," in Timothy J. Demy and Gary P. Stewart, eds., *Politics and Public Policy* (Grand Rapids: Kregel, 2000), 72.

39. See Al Wolters, "Worldview and Textual Criticism in 2 Peter 3 v. 10," *Westminster Theological Journal* 49 (1987): 405–13; and Paul Marshall and Lela Gilbert, *Heaven Is Not My Home: Learning to Live in God's Creation* (Nashville: Word, 1998), 236–38.

40. Duncan B. Forrester, *Christian Justice and Public Policy* (Cambridge: Cambridge University Press, 1997), 249.

41. Ibid., 248. Tragically, Forrester is not very hopeful that in our time, the Christian hope can sustain major movements of social change, 257ff.

42. Ronald J. Sider, "Resurrection and Liberation," in Robert Rankin, ed., *The Recovery of Spirit in Higher Education* (New York: Seabury, 1980), 171–74.

Chapter 4 The State: Its Nature, Purposes, and Limits

1. Wogaman, *Christian Perspectives on Politics*, 13. Pacifist and nonpacifist Christians disagree over whether God *wants* the state to use lethal violence as it compels compliance, but it is a matter of historical fact that most, if not all, states over the course of human history have done so.

2. James W. Skillen, "Toward a Comprehensive Science of Politics," in Jonathan Chaplin and Paul Marshall, eds., *Political Theory and Christian Vision: Essays in Memory of Bernard Zylstra* (Lanham, MD: University Press of America, 1994), 72.

3. Temple, *Christianity and the State*, 66.

4. In this section I use parts of my chapter "Justice, Human Rights and Government" in Sider and Knippers, eds., *Toward an Evangelical Public Policy*, 185–92.

5. Paul Marshall, *Thine Is the Kingdom* (Grand Rapids: Eerdmans, 1984), 43–45.

6. Temple, *Christianity and the State*, 108.

7. James Skillen, drawing especially on Abraham Kuyper and Herman Dooyeweerd, regularly develops this basic approach. See, for example, his "Toward a Comprehensive Science of Politics," 67–73.

8. Temple, *Christianity and the State*, 88.

9. Marshall, *Thine Is the Kingdom*, 42.

10. For example, Doug Bandow, *Beyond Good Intentions*, and Carl F. H. Henry, *Aspects of Christian Social Ethics* (Grand Rapids: Eerdmans, 1964), 160. Henry argues that modern theological liberalism's submerging of God's wrath in God's love has led to a parallel disaster in society. Both in God and in society, according to Henry, love and justice are very different and should never be confused. The state should be responsible for procedural justice, while the church is responsible for love. In dire emergency (the Great Depression, for example), it may be proper for the government to assist the poor and jobless, but normally voluntary agencies like the church should perform such acts of love or benevolence without assistance or interference from the state. "In the New Testament view," Henry argues, "the coercive role of the state is limited to its punitive function." Henry is surely right that the biblical God is both holy and loving. The one attribute dare not be collapsed into the other. But does that mean love is not connected with societal justice? Does it mean that societal justice exists as long as procedural justice prevents fraud, theft, and violence? As I show in chapter 4, several aspects of biblical teaching point to a broader role for government, beyond the guaranteeing of just procedures and the restraint of evil. Frequently the words for *love* and *justice* appear together in close relationship. Biblical justice has a dynamic,

restorative character. The special concern for the poor running throughout the Scriptures moves beyond a concern for unbiased procedures. Restoration to community—including the benefit rights that dignified participation in communities requires—is a central feature of biblical thinking about justice.

11. John Calvin, *Institutes of the Christian Religion*, ed. John McNeill (Philadelphia: Westminster, 1960), 4.20.3, 4, 22 (1488, 1490, 1510); Cf. Harro Hopfl, *The Christian Polity of John Calvin* (Cambridge: Cambridge University Press, 1982), 44–46. Similarly for Luther, government is an inestimable blessing of God and one of God's best gifts; compare W. D. J. Cargill Thompson, *The Political Thought of Martin Luther*, ed. P. Broadhead (Sussex: Harverster, 1984), 66.

12. Cf. 1 Peter 2:14: Government officials are sent by God "to punish those who do wrong and to praise those who do right" (NRSV).

13. Marshall, *Thine Is the Kingdom*, 42.

14. Ibid.

15. O'Donovan, *Desire of the Nations*, 146–47.

16. Yoder, *Discipleship as Political Responsibility*, 21–22. One need not accept Yoder's claim that the text says this is the *only* purpose of the Roman state.

17. Ibid., 20.

18. O'Donovan, *Desire of the Nations*, 137.

19. Ibid., 148–49.

20. See Mouw, *When the Kings Come Marching In*.

21. Marshall, *Thine Is the Kingdom*, 48–49.

22. George Sabine, *History of Political Theory* (New York: Holt, Rinehart, and Winston, 1961), 180; cited in Marshall, *God and the Constitution*, 117. See ibid., 134n7 for similar comments.

23. The following section is adapted from my *Fixing the Moral Deficit* (Downers Grove: InterVarsity Press, 2012), 60–62.

24. John Mason, "Assisting the Poor: Assistance Programmes in the Bible," *Transformation*, April–June, 1987, 9 (see all of pp. 1–14).

25. Ronald J. Sider and Diane Knippers, *Toward an Evangelical Public Policy* (Grand Rapids: Baker Books, 2005), 366.

26. David Beckman, *Exodus from Hunger* (Louisville: Westminster John Knox, 2010), 11.

27. The position presented here has parallels to that developed in the Roman Catholic social tradition's principle of subsidiarity. See, for instance, David Hollenbach, *Justice, Peace and Human Rights: American Catholic Social Ethics in a Pluralistic Context* (New York: Crossroad, 1988), 81.

28. See, for example, Skillen, *Recharging the American Experiment*, 65–82.

29. Thielicke, *Politics*, 158–59.

30. Monsma, *Pursuing Justice*, 47.

31. The literature is vast. See, for example, Sider, *Christ and Violence*; Ronald J. Sider and Richard Taylor, *Nuclear Holocaust and Christian Hope* (Downers Grove, IL: InterVarsity, 1982), chaps. 5–8; all of John Howard Yoder, especially *The Politics of Jesus* (Grand Rapids: Eerdmans, 1972); and Richard B. Hays, *The Moral Vision of the New Testament* (San Francisco: Harper, 1996), chap. 14.

32. See chap. 2, n17.

33. "That YHWH used Assyria's troops to chastise his own people (Isa. 10:6–34) did not make those deeds into good works, nor were the Israelites called to celebrate them or

to help with them. That God reserves vengeance to himself and may then 'delegate' that vengeance to Cyrus or to Caesar (Rom. 13:2, 4 and Isaiah 45) is grounds for his people to renounce human vengeance (Rom. 12:19 but also Deut. 32:35) rather than claiming to be his instruments. The same applies to the place of Pilate in the crucifixion" (John Howard Yoder, *For the Nations: Essays Public and Evangelical* [Grand Rapids: Eerdmans, 1997], 245).

34. Ibid., 35.

35. Ronald J. Sider, *Non-Violence: An Invincible Weapon?* (Dallas: Word, 1989), 76.

36. See Gene Sharp, *Exploring Nonviolent Alternatives* (Boston: Porter Sargent, 1971), 25–26; Brian Martin, *Social Defence, Social Change* (London: Freedom, 1993), 89–95; Dave Jackson, *Dial 911: Peaceful Christians and Urban Violence* (Scottdale, PA: Herald Press, 1981); Howard Zehr, *The Christian as Victim* (Akron, PA: Office of Criminal Justice, Mennonite Central Committee, 1982); and Zehr's bibliography.

37. John Howard Yoder is right that "most of what a public order (i.e., government) does is not violent" (*For the Nations*, 36).

38. This and several following paragraphs are adapted from Ronald J. Sider, "The Anabaptist Perspective," in Gary W. Deddo, ed., *Church, State and Public Justice: Five Views* (Downers Grove, IL: InterVarsity, 2007), 183–87.

39. See, for example, Jonathan Schell, *The Unconquerable World: Power, Nonviolence, and the Will of the People* (New York: Holt, 2003).

40. Karl Deutsch, *The Analysis of International Relations* (Englewood Cliffs, NJ: Prentice-Hall, 1978), 17–18; quoted in Friesen, *Christian Peacemaking*, 38.

Chapter 5 Justice

1. Large parts of this chapter come from Ronald J. Sider, "Justice, Human Rights and Government," in Sider and Knippers, eds., *Toward an Evangelical Public Policy*, 164–84.

2. Nicholas Wolterstorff, "Justice and Peace," in David J. Atkinson et al., eds., *New Dictionary of Christian Ethics and Pastoral Theology* (Downers Grove, IL: InterVarsity, 1995), 17. Justice, of course, refers not only to rights but also to responsibilities.

3. The obligation to give persons their due applies to every sphere of life: family, church, state, etc. In this chapter, the primary focus is on what is owed to persons and institutions in the public realm, especially that area properly in the control of the state.

4. Emil Brunner, *Justice and the Social Order*, trans. Mary Hottinger (New York: Harper & Brothers, 1945), 23.

5. 2 Chron. 19:6–7.

6. Brunner, *Justice and the Social Order*, 7.

7. Ibid., 89.

8. Karen Lebacqz, *Six Theories of Justice: Perspectives from Philosophical and Theological Ethics* (Minneapolis: Augsburg, 1986), 73.

9. Cf. also Deut. 25:13–16; Prov. 11:1; 20:10; Ezek. 45:10; Amos 8:5.

10. Lebacqz, *Six Theories of Justice*, 28.

11. See the helpful discussion in Dennis P. Hollinger, *Choosing the Good: Christian Ethics in a Complex World* (Grand Rapids: Baker, 2002), 226–34.

12. David Hollenbach, *Justice, Peace, and Human Rights: American Catholic Social Ethics in a Pluralistic Context* (New York: Crossroad, 1988), 81.

13. Robert Nozick, quoted in Lebacqz, *Six Theories of Justice*, 55.

14. For example, Ronald H. Nash, *Freedom, Justice and the State* (Lanham, MD: University Press of America, 1980), 43–75; Doug Bandow, *Beyond Good Intentions: A Biblical View of Politics* (Westchester, IL: Crossway, 1988), 87; E. Calvin Beisner, *Prosperity and Poverty: The Compassionate Use of Resources in a World of Scarcity* (Westchester, IL: Crossway, 1988), 54. It is important to note that these evangelicals all agree that Christians must help the poor. The debate is over the role of the state.

15. Closely related to this debate about procedural and distributive justice is the heated twentieth-century debate about human rights. Are they primarily civil/political or primarily socioeconomic or both? See chapter 6 below.

16. *Theological Dictionary of the Old Testament* [hereafter, *TDOT*] (Grand Rapids: Eerdmans, 1971–99), 9:87.

17. *TDOT*, 12:250, 253.

18. Roland de Vaux, *Ancient Israel* (New York: McGraw-Hill, 1965), 2:72–73.

19. The following lengthy section comes from Ronald J. Sider, *Just Generosity: A New Vision for Overcoming Poverty in America* (Grand Rapids: Baker, 1999), 56; and Stephen J. Mott and Ronald J. Sider, "Economic Justice: A Biblical Paradigm," in David P. Gushee, ed., *Toward a Just and Caring Society* (Grand Rapids: Baker, 1999), 26.

20. Mott's translation. Cf. also Pss. 40:10; 43:1–2; 65:6; 71:1–2, 24; 72:1–4; 116:5–6; 119:123; Isa. 45:8; 46:12–13; 59:11, 17; 61:10; 62:1–2; 63:7–8 (LXX).

21. Cf. Job 29:12, 14; Prov. 24:11.

22. *Triumphs* in the NRSV translates the word for *justice* (*tsedaqah*) in the plural—i.e., "acts of justice" (cf. NIV, "righteous acts").

23. Cf. Ps. 107; 113:7–9.

24. Literally! See the collection (about two hundred pages of biblical texts) in Ronald J. Sider, *For They Shall Be Fed* (Dallas: Word, 1997).

25. Cf. Norman H. Snaith, *The Distinctive Ideas of the Old Testament* (London: Epworth, 1944), 68, 71–72; James H. Cone, *God of the Oppressed* (New York: Seabury, 1975), 70–71.

26. This is not to ignore the fact that there are many causes of poverty—including laziness and other sinful choices (see Sider, *Rich Christians in an Age of Hunger*, chap. 7). God wants people who are poor because of their own sinful choices to repent and be changed by the power of the Holy Spirit.

27. Ps. 72:1–4; Prov. 31:8–9; Isa. 1:10, 17, 23, 26; Jer. 22:2–3, 14–15; Dan. 4:27.

28. The following section is adapted from Ronald J. Sider, *Genuine Christianity* (Grand Rapids: Zondervan, 1996), 137–41.

29. See further, Stephen Charles Mott, "The Partiality of Biblical Justice," *Transformation*, January–March 1993, 24.

30. This section comes from Mott and Sider, "Economic Justice," in Gushee, ed., *Toward a Just and Caring Society*, 31–33.

31. Mott's translation.

32. Rights are the privileges of membership in the communities to which we belong; cf. Max L. Stackhouse, *Creeds, Society, and Human Rights: A Study in Three Cultures* (Grand Rapids: Eerdmans, 1984), 5, 44, 104–5.

33. C. Spicq, *Les Épîtres Pastorales, Études Bibliques* (Paris: Gabalda, 1969), 190 (on 1 Tim. 6:8).

34. Cf. Job 22 where injustice includes sins of omission—i.e., failure to provide drink for the weary and bread for the hungry (v. 7; cf. 31:17), as well as the exploitative use of

economic power (v. 6a). In 31:19 the omission is failure to provide clothing. Cf. the important modern statement of benefit rights by Pope John XXIII, in his encyclical, *Pacem in Terris*, in which he says that each person has the right "to the means necessary for the proper development of life, particularly food, clothing, shelter, medical care, rest, and finally, the necessary social services." Pope John XXIII, *Pacem in Terris*, 11, in *Papal Encyclicals, Vol. 5: 1958–1981*, ed. C. Carlen (n.p.: Consortium, 1981), 108.

35. Cf. Stephen C. Mott, "The Contribution of the Bible to Economic Thought," *Transformation*, June–September/October–December 1987, 31.

36. Eryl W. Davies, *Prophecy and Ethics: Isaiah and the Ethical Traditions of Israel* (Sheffield: Sheffield Academic Press, 1981), 69, 116.

37. Leslie Poles Hartley, *Facial Justice* (New York: Doubleday, 1960).

38. See Roland de Vaux, *Ancient Israel: Its Life and Institutions*, trans. John McHugh (London: Darton, Longman and Todd, 1961), I, 164.

39. H. Eberhard von Waldow, "Social Responsibility and Social Structure in Early Israel," *Catholic Biblical Quarterly* 32 (1970), 195.

40. See the discussion and the literature cited in Mott, *Biblical Ethics and Social Change*, 65–66; and Stephen Charles Mott, "Egalitarian Aspects of the Biblical Theory of Justice," in the *American Society of Christian Ethics, Selected Papers 1978*, ed. Max Stackhouse (Newton, MA: American Society of Christian Ethics, 1978), 8–26.

41. In his study of early Israel, Norman Gottwald concluded that Israel was "an egalitarian, extended-family, segmentary tribal society with an agricultural-pastoral economic base . . . characterized by profound resistance and opposition to the forms of political domination and social stratification that had become normative in the chief cultural and political centers of the ancient Near East." *The Tribes of Yahweh: A Sociology of the Religion of Liberated Israel 1250–1050 BCE* (London: SCM Press, 1979), 10.

42. See the somewhat parallel view in the Catholic thinker, John Ryan, in *Economic Justice*, ed., Beckley, xv–xvi.

43. For a survey of the literature on Leviticus 25, see R. Gnuse, "Jubilee Legislation in Leviticus: Israel's Vision of Social Reform," *Biblical Theological Bulletin* 15 (1983): 43–48.

44. See in this connection the fine article by Paul G. Schrotenboer, "The Return of Jubilee," *International Reformed Bulletin*, Fall 1973, 19ff. (esp. 23–24).

45. On the centrality of the land in Israel's self-understanding, see further Christopher J. H. Wright, *An Eye for an Eye: The Place of Old Testament Ethics Today* (Downers Grove, IL: InterVarsity, 1983), esp. chaps. 3 and 4. Walter Brueggemann, *The Land* (Philadelphia: Fortress Press, 1977), is also a particularly important work on this topic.

46. See Jer. 34 for a fascinating account of God's anger at Israel for their failure to obey this command.

47. Some modern commentators think that Deut. 15:1–11 provides for a one-year suspension of repayment of loans rather than an outright remission of them. See, for example, Christopher J. H. Wright, *God's People in God's Land* (Grand Rapids: Eerdmans, 1990), 148; and S. R. Driver, *Deuteronomy*, International Critical Commentary, 3rd ed. (Edinburgh: T&T Clark, 1895), 179–80. But Driver's argument is basically that remission would have been *impractical*. He admits that verse 9 seems to point toward remission of loans. Also, Gerhard von Rad, *Deuteronomy* (Philadelphia: Westminster, 1966), 106.

48. See de Vaux, *Ancient Israel*, 1:174–75, for discussion of the law's implementation. In the Hellenistic period, there is clear evidence that it was put into effect.

49. The following paragraphs are adapted from Ronald J. Sider, *Fixing the Moral Deficit* (Downers Grove, IL: InterVarsity, 2012), 57–59.

50. See especially John Mason's excellent article, "Assisting the Poor: Assistance Programmes in the Bible," *Transformation*, April–June, 1987, 1–14.

51. Ibid., 7.

52. See ibid., 8.

53. Ibid., 9.

54. Ibid., 14n39. Mason comments: "Two Hebrew words are used for 'rights' or 'cause': the predominant word is *mishpat*, which is used elsewhere to refer to the laws and judgments of God; at Ps. 140:12 (with *mishpat*), Prov. 29:7, 31:9 and Jer. 22:16 the word is *din* and means most likely 'righteous judgment' or 'legal claim'" (*TDOT* 3:190–91; R. Harris, et al., *Theological Workbook of the Old Testament* [Chicago: Moody, 1980], 2:752–55, 947–49).

55. Mason, "Assisting the Poor," 9.

56. For a much longer discussion of both the passages in Acts and Paul's collection, see Sider, *Rich Christians in an Age of Hunger*, 79–89.

Chapter 6 Human Rights, Democracy, and Capitalism

1. Allen D. Hertzke, *Freeing God's Children: The Unlikely Alliance for Global Human Rights* (Lanham, MD: Rowman & Littlefield, 2004).

2. David Hollenbach, *Claims in Conflict: Retrieving and Renewing the Catholic Human Rights Tradition* (New York: Paulist Press, 1979), 144; *Reformed Ecumenical Synod Testimony on Human Rights* (Grand Rapids: Reformed Ecumenical Synod, 1983). The Reformed Ecumenical Synod's excellent book on human rights claims that not just individuals but also institutions (e.g., churches, families, economic institutions, etc.) have human rights. As chapters 4 and 5 show, I agree strongly that there are many institutions in society that exist between the individual and the state, and these different institutions have their own independent rights. But I think one can affirm that crucial point without abandoning the standard understanding that the term *human rights* refers to individuals.

3. Marshall, "Universal Human Rights," in Luis Lugo, ed., *Sovereignty at the Crossroads?* (Lanham, MD: Rowman & Littlefield, 1996), 161.

4. Monsma, *Pursuing Justice in a Sinful World*, 40. That is not to say that rights and duties are always the mere converse of each other; see "Justice and Peace" in *New Dictionary of Christian Ethics and Pastoral Theology*, 16–17.

5. Max L. Stackhouse, *Creeds, Society, and Human Rights: A Study in Three Cultures* (Grand Rapids: Eerdmans, 1984), x.

6. See Hollenbach's comment: "The Roman Catholic tradition answers the question of the foundation of human rights with a single phrase: the dignity of the human person." Hollenbach, *Claims in Conflict* (New York: Paulist Press, 1979), 90. I disagree with Paul Marshall's attempt to ground human rights in a theory of the just state rather than in the inherent rights of individuals. Paul Marshall, "Universal Human Rights," in Lugo, ed., *Sovereignty at the Crossroads?* 156ff., esp. 171. See Joseph Boyle's critique, "On the Importance of Natural Rights," *Sovereignty at the Crossroads?* 177–83, and his insistence on grounding human rights in a natural right of persons grounded finally in the Creator.

7. See the parallel argument in *Reformed Ecumenical Synod Testimony on Human Rights* (Grand Rapids: Reformed Ecumenical Synod, 1983), 96–99.

8. John Locke, *Second Treatise on Civil Government*, in Ernest Barker, ed., *Social Contract: Essays by Locke, Hume, and Rousseau* (New York: Oxford University Press, 1962), 4; cited in Hollenbach, *Claims in Conflict*, 14.

9. Mary Ann Glendon, *Rights Talk: The Impoverishment of Political Discourse* (New York: Free Press, 1991), x–xi, 14, 109–10.

10. Joan O'Donovan, "Rights, Law and Political Community: A Theological and Historical Perspective," *Transformation* 20, no. 1 (January 2003): 37.

11. See my discussion in chapter 5.

12. Glenn Tinder, *Political Thinking: The Perennial Questions*, 6th ed. (New York: Harper Collins, 1995), chap. 3, esp. 61–75.

13. See the helpful discussion in Wogaman, *Christian Perspectives on Politics*, 156–58.

14. Moltmann, *God for a Secular Society*, 79.

15. Obviously I can do this only briefly here. A full treatment would require many volumes.

16. I have chosen to follow the breakdown used by the United Nations. In addition to the United Nations Universal Declaration of Human Rights, the United Nations has two covenants that some but not all countries have ratified: The International Covenant on Civil and Political Rights and The International Covenant on Economic, Social and Cultural Rights. See *Human Rights: A Compilation of the International Instruments of the United Nations* (New York: United Nations Publications, 1973). There are other helpful ways to categorize human rights; see, for example, Hollenbach, *Claims in Conflict*.

17. Pacifist and just-war Christians disagree on this issue.

18. Moltmann, *God for a Secular Society*, 84.

19. Matt. 13:37–39.

20. For the interesting role of Richard Overton, a Leveller influenced by Dutch Mennonites, see Glen Stassen, *Just Peacemaking: Transforming Initiatives for Justice and Peace* (Louisville: Westminster John Knox, 1992), 141–55.

21. E.g., Exod. 19:7–8; 1 Sam. 10:24.

22. This right is closely connected with, but not identical to, the right to productive assets. Knowledge is not private property, but it is a crucial productive asset.

23. Brunner, *Justice and the Social Order*, 59.

24. One of the best Christian statements on work is John Paul II's encyclical, *Laborem exercens*, 1981.

25. Marshall, "Universal Human Rights," in Lugo, ed., *Sovereignty at the Crossroads?* 165–68; Raymond Plant, *Politics, Theology, and History* (Cambridge: Cambridge University Press, 2001), 237–55.

26. See Marshall, "Universal Human Rights," 168–69; and Plant, *Politics, Theology, and History*, 254–55.

27. For the Reformed tradition, see the *Reformed Ecumenical Synod Testimony on Human Rights*; for the Catholic tradition, see Boyle's response to Paul Marshall in "On the Importance of Natural Rights," in Lugo, ed., *Sovereignty at the Crossroads?* 181; and Hollenbach, *Claims in Conflict*. For mainline Protestants see the United Church of Christ's "Pronouncement on Human Rights," in Stackhouse, *Creeds*, appendix IV, 295–300.

28. By liberals here, I mean the broad Western political tradition going back to Locke. It includes people who are popularly called both liberals (e.g., Democrats in the United States) and conservatives (Republicans).

29. Hollenbach, *Claims in Conflict*, 200.

30. Amartya Sen, *Freedom as Development* (New York: Knopf, 1999), 16, 51–53, 155–57, 170–75.

31. Hollenbach, *Claims in Conflict*, 204. Hollenbach's whole book has a superb discussion of competing claims.

32. See the distinction between "individualist" liberal democracy, which places little emphasis on these non-state institutions, and "personalist Christian Democracy," which affirms and nurtures them. Timothy R. Sherratt and Ronald P. Mahurin, *Saints as Citizens* (Grand Rapids: Baker, 1995), 108.

33. See the helpful discussion in chapter 9 of Wogaman, *Christian Perspectives on Politics*.

34. Reinhold Niebuhr, *The Children of Light and the Children of Darkness: A Vindication of Democracy and a Critique of Its Traditional Defense* (New York: Scribner & Sons, 1972), xiii.

35. From a speech in The House of Commons (November 11, 1947), quoted in Roy Frank, ed., *Quotationery* (New York: Random House, 2001), 174.

36. See the helpful essay by Richard John Neuhaus, "Christianity and Democracy" (the founding document of the Institute on Religion and Democracy) available at www.ird-renew.org.

37. There are two quite different definitions of *socialism*. I use *socialism* to mean state ownership of the means of production and state control of wages and prices. In principle one could have democratic socialism. The second definition of *socialism* (common in Western Europe) refers to situations where the means of production are largely privately owned but the state (e.g., in Sweden) operates a much larger system of welfare and social protection programs than is the case in the United States.

38. See the evidence in Sider, *Rich Christians in an Age of Hunger*, 136–38.

39. For an elaboration of these points, see ibid., 138–43; and Sider, *Fixing the Moral Deficit*, esp. chap. 2.

40. See Sider, *Rich Christians in an Age of Hunger*, 233–36 and the articles cited there in nn. 36–42.

Chapter 7 The Sanctity of Human Life

1. National Right to Life Campaign, November 30, 2006, www.nrlc.org.

2. Peter Singer, "Sanctity of Life or Quality of Life?" *Pediatrics* 72, no. 1 (July 1983): 129.

3. Gen. 1:26–27.

4. Nigel M. de S. Cameron, "The Sanctity of Life in the Twenty-first Century," in Sider and Knippers, eds., *Toward an Evangelical Public Policy*, 216.

5. Ibid., 224.

6. Moltmann, *God for a Secular Society*, 84.

7. This wording is used to set aside, for the moment, the question of whether taking human life in capital punishment or just war is permitted.

8. "Report of the Committee to Study the Matter of Abortion," in Minutes of the Thirty-eighth General Assembly, The Orthodox Presbyterian Church, Philadelphia, May 24–29, 1971, 146.

9. See the discussion of Exod. 21:22–24 in Ronald J. Sider, *Completely Pro-Life: Building a Consistent Stance* (Downers Grove, IL: InterVarsity, 1987), 46–47.

10. See further, ibid., 45.

11. *California Medicine* 113, no. 3 (1979), quoted in John Jefferson Davis, *Abortion and the Christian* (Phillipsburg, NJ: Presbyterian and Reformed, 1984), 22.

12. The following two paragraphs are from Sider, *Completely Pro-Life*, 49.

13. This section is adapted from ibid., 54–55.

14. I would support legislation that permits abortion when the physical life of the mother is genuinely at risk. I would not oppose legislation that permitted abortion in the case of rape or incest.

15. See, for example, the basic distinction made in the *Catechism of the Catholic Church* between "direct euthanasia," which involves "putting an end to the lives of handicapped, sick or dying persons," which is always wrong, and "discontinuing medical procedures that are burdensome, dangerous, extraordinary or disproportionate to the expected outcome," which can be morally legitimate. In the latter case, "one does not will to cause death; one's inability to impede it is merely accepted." *Catechism of the Catholic Church* (New York: Doubleday, 1995), sec. 2277, 2278.

16. Cameron, "The Sanctity of Human Life," in Sider and Knippers, eds., *Toward an Evangelical Public Policy*, 222.

17. "For the Health of the Nation," in Sider and Knippers, eds., *Toward an Evangelical Public Policy*, 371.

18. See Cameron, "Sanctity of Human Life," 221.

19. Oxfam America, "Fast for a World Harvest."

20. World Health Organization, *World Health Organization Report on Infectious Disease: Removing Obstacles to Healthy Development*, http://www.who.int/infectious-disease-report/pages/textonly.html.

21. See the data in Sider, *Rich Christians in an Age of Hunger*, 13.

22. World Bank, *World Bank Development Report 2003* (Washington, DC: International Bank for Reconstruction and Development, 2002), 3.

23. See Ronald J. Sider, *Rich Christians in an Age of Hunger*, 5th ed. (2005), for a detailed agenda on how to do this.

24. "Annual Smoking—United States, 1997–2001," *Morbidity and Mortality Weekly Reports*, Centers for Disease Control 54, no. 25 (July 2005).

25. "Why Is Smoking a Public Health Priority?" *World Health Organization Tobacco Free Initiative*, accessed November 30, 2006, http://www.who.int/tobacco/health_priority/en/index.htm.

26. "Annual Smoking—United States, 1997–2001."

27. See Sider, *Completely Pro-Life*, 191.

28. See the Centers for Disease Control's "Best Practices for Comprehensive Tobacco Control Programs, August 1999" fact sheet as part of their *Tobacco Information and Prevention Source* database at the CDC website, www.cdc.gov, for statistics and more information.

29. Colson, however, has changed his mind. See Charles W. Colson, "Capital Punishment: A Personal Statement," *OldSpeak* (November 11, 2002): http://www.rutherford.org/Oldspeak/Articles/Religion/oldspeak-capitalpunishment.html.

30. See Sider, *The Early Church on Killing: A Comprehensive Sourcebook on War, Abortion, and Capital Punishment* (Grand Rapids: Baker, 2012).

31. See the interesting discussion in Lowell O. Erdahl, *Pro-Life/Pro-Peace: Life-Affirming Alternatives to Abortion, War, Mercy Killing and the Death Penalty* (Minneapolis: Augsburg, 1986), 113–19.

32. John Paul II, *Evangelium Vitae*, 56.2, in George Weigel, *Witness to Hope: The Biography of Pope John Paul II (1920–2005)* (New York: Harper Perennial, 2005), 758.

33. Ron Sider, *Completely Pro-Life* (Downers Grove, IL: InterVarsity, 1987).

34. http://www.manhattandeclarartion.org/pdfs/ManhattanDeclaration.pdf.

35. Michael J. Gorman, *Abortion and the Early Church* (Downers Grove, IL: InterVarsity, 1982), 90.

36. From a speech entitled "A Consistent Ethic of Life: Continuing the Dialogue," given at St. Louis University, March 11, 1984, published in Joseph Bernardin, *The Seamless Garment* (Kansas City: National Catholic Reporter, 1984).

Chapter 8 Marriage and Family

1. See the detailed statistics and documentation in Ronald J. Sider, *Just Generosity: A New Vision for Overcoming Poverty in America*, 2nd ed. (Grand Rapids: Baker, 2007), chap. 5.

2. David P. Gushee, *Getting Marriage Right* (Grand Rapids: Baker, 2004), 30.

3. See Sider, *Just Generosity*, chap. 5, fig. 7.

4. Ibid., 160n54.

5. Ibid., 161n61.

6. Gushee, *Getting Marriage Right*, 92.

7. Again, that is not to deny the value and goodness of singleness. But singles, just as much as married people, need societies with wholesome marriages and families for their own well-being (for example, as happy aunts and uncles).

8. Gushee, *Getting Marriage Right*, 100.

9. See Gushee's longer discussion of these four principles of marriage, ibid., 94–100.

10. For the issue of homosexual sex, see Richard Hays, *Moral Vision of the New Testament*, 379–406.

11. See also Hays's masterful discussion of divorce in ibid., 347–48; and Craig Keener, *And Marries Another* (Peabody, MA: Hendrickson, 1991).

12. Matt. 19:4–9.

13. Brunner, *Justice and the Social Order*, 146.

14. For a somewhat larger discussion of the history, see Gushee, *Getting Marriage Right*, 43–55.

15. *Just Generosity*, chap. 5, n32.

16. Ibid., 154.

17. Ibid., chap. 5, n26.

18. David Popenoe, "The Controversial Truth," *New York Times*, December 26, 1992.

19. Sylvia Ann Hewlett and Cornel West, *The War Against Parents* (New York: Houghton Mifflin, 1998), 242.

20. Gushee, *Getting Marriage Right*, 223.

21. Ibid., 224. See all of Gushee, chapter 10 (and the references to other literature) for a longer discussion of how to reshape public law.

22. See the longer discussion in Ronald J. Sider, "Bearing Better Witness," *First Things*, December 2010, 47–50.

23. See Robert A. J. Gagnon, *The Bible and Homosexual Practice: Texts and Hermeneutics* (Nashville: Abingdon, 2001); and Richard B. Hays, *The Moral Vision of the New Testament* (San Francisco: HarperSanFrancisco, 1996), chap. 16.

24. Sider, "Bearing Better Witness," 47–50.

25. I am among the almost 500,000 people who have signed this declaration. See http://www.manhattandeclaration.org/pdfs/ManhattanDeclaration.pdf.

26. In countries where polygamy has been accepted throughout history, public law should both accept the current marriages of polygamists and refuse any new polygamous marriages.

Chapter 9 Religious Freedom, Church, and State

1. Dennis P. Hollinger, "The Purpose of Government," in Timothy J. Demy and Gary P. Stewart, eds., *Politics and Public Policy: A Christian Response* (Grand Rapids: Kregel, 2000), 30.

2. See, for example, Franklin Hamlin Littell, *The Anabaptist View of the Church* (Boston: Starr King, 1958).

3. See Glen H. Stassen, *Just Peacemaking* (Louisville: Westminster John Knox, 1992), 141–55.

4. Overton had joined a Baptist group in Holland just after it merged with a Mennonite congregation. Stassen, *Just Peacemaking*, 141.

5. Ibid., 146.

6. Noll, *One Nation Under God?* 65.

7. The first American colony to have legislation prescribing religious toleration was Maryland, but the 1649 Act of Toleration was repealed a few years later.

8. See Skillen, *Reshaping*, 114–17.

9. See Paul Marshall and Lela Gilbert, *Their Blood Cries Out* (Dallas: Word, 1997), for a careful account of how widespread religious persecution (and martyrdom) still is today.

10. See Wogaman, *Christian Perspectives on Politics*, 193–94.

11. Thomas Jefferson, quoted in Wogaman, *Christian Perspectives on Politics*, 193.

12. See John Fea, *Was America Founded as a Christian Nation?* (Louisville: Westminster John Knox, 2011).

13. See James Skillen's brief insightful comments in "An American Covenant with God," *Capital Commentary*, December 12, 2003.

14. See John Howard Yoder's different but partially parallel list in Craig A. Carter, *Politics of the Cross* (Grand Rapids: Brazos, 2001), 221; see John Howard Yoder, *The Christian Witness to the State* (Newton, KS: Faith and Life, 1964), 16–22.

15. Karl Barth, *Community, State, and Church*, 136.

16. See ibid., 186, and Yoder, *Politics of Jesus*, 152–57.

17. David Gitari, *In Season and Out of Season: Sermons to a Nation* (Oxford: Regnum, 1996).

18. There may be special historical circumstances where sidestepping this rule is temporarily necessary; for example, there was a time in American history when the black pastor was the only black person largely free of white control.

19. Carl H. Esbeck, "Church-State Relations in America: What's at Stake and What's Not," *Liberty* 100, no. 3 (May–June 2005), 3, 29.

20. Neither state nor federal governments may pass laws that "aid one religion, aid all religions." *Everson v. Board of Education*, 1947. See Stephen V. Monsma, *When Sacred and Secular Mix* (Lanham, MD: Rowman & Littlefield, 1996), 30–31.

21. Ibid., chap. 3.

22. See Carl Esbeck, "The Neutral Treatment of Religion," in Derek H. Davis and Barry Harkins, eds., *Welfare Reform and Faith-Based Organizations* (Waco, TX: J. M. Dawson Institute of Church-State Studies, 1999), especially 175–77. See also Ira C. Lupu, "To

Control Faction and Protect Liberty: A General Theory of the Religion Clause," *Journal of Contemporary Legal Issues* 7 (1996), 357–84.

23. See Carl H. Esbeck, Stanley Carlson-Thies, and Ronald J. Sider, *The Freedom of Faith-Based Organizations to Staff on a Religious Basis* (Washington, DC: Center for Public Justice, 2004).

24. See Heidi Rolland Unruh and Ronald J. Sider, *Saving Souls, Serving Society* (New York: Oxford University Press, 2005), chap. 6 for a more detailed classification.

25. The last two paragraphs are from Sider and Unruh, "An (Ana)Baptist Theological Perspective on Church-State Cooperation," in Davis and Harkins, eds., *Welfare Reform*, 116. See also Ronald J. Sider, "The Case for 'Discrimination,'" *First Things*, June/July 2002, 19–21; and "Evaluating the Faith-Based Initiative: Is Charitable Choice Good Public Policy?" *Theology Today* 61, no. 4 (January 2005): 485–98.

Chapter 10 Peacemaking, Just War, and Nonviolence

1. R. J. Rummel, *Statistics of Democide: Genocide and Mass Murder Since 1900* (Piscatway, NJ: Transaction Publishers, 1997), chap. 2.

2. Jonathan Glover, *Humanity: A Moral History of the Twentieth Century* (New Haven: Yale University Press, 2000), 47.

3. R. J. Rummel, "War Isn't This Century's Biggest Killer," *Wall Street Journal*, July 7, 1986; see also his *Statistics of Democide*.

4. Mennonite Old Testament scholar Millard C. Lind suggests that if Israel had obediently trusted Yahweh, he might have protected them without Israel engaging in war. *Yahweh Is a Warrior* (Scottdale, PA: Herald Press, 1980).

5. The next several pages are adapted from Ronald J. Sider and Richard K. Taylor, *Nuclear Holocaust and Christian Hope* (Downers Grove, IL: InterVarsity, 1982), 97ff.

6. See also Isa. 32:15–18; 52:7; 60:17–18.

7. His discussion of *eirēnē* in Gerhard Kittel and Gerhard Friedrich, eds., *Theological Dictionary of the New Testament* (Grand Rapids: Eerdmans, 1964), 2:405.

8. Werner Foerster says this text means that the promise of eschatological peace is fulfilled in Jesus. Eschatological salvation is now present. *Theological Dictionary of the New Testament*, 2:413.

9. Origen, *Contra Celsus*, 5.33, quoted in Richard McSorley, *New Testament Basis of Peacemaking* (Washington: Center for Peace Studies, Georgetown University, n.d.), 75. See also the many other texts in Sider, *The Early Church on Killing*.

10. Palestinian Targum on Genesis 49:10; quoted in Martin Hengel, *Victory Over Violence* (London: SPCK, 1975), 69.

11. Hengel, *Victory Over Violence*, 69.

12. For example, see C. E. B. Cranfield, *The Gospel according to Mark*, The Cambridge Greek New Testament Commentary (Cambridge: Cambridge University Press, 1963), 353–54.

13. Culbert G. Rutenber, *The Dagger and the Cross* (New York: Fellowship, 1950), 39.

14. Hengel, *Victory Over Violence*, 76.

15. John Piper, *Love Your Enemies* (Cambridge: Cambridge University Press, 1979), 21–48.

16. Ibid., 33.

17. Eduard Schweizer, *The Good News according to Matthew* (Atlanta: John Knox, 1975), 132; also Piper, *Love Your Enemies*, 40–41.

18. There are explicit quotations (Matt. 8:17; 12:17–21; Luke 22:37; John 12:38; Acts 8:32–33) and numerous allusions. See W. Zimmerli and J. Jeremias, *The Servant of God*, Studies in Biblical Theology, no. 20 (Naperville, IL: Allenson, 1957), 88ff.

19. Ibid., 99ff.

20. See Sider, *Early Church on Killing*, 163ff.

21. Roland H. Bainton, *Christian Attitudes toward War and Peace* (New York: Abingdon, 1960), 53.

22. Ramsey, *War and the Christian Conscience: How Shall Modern War Be Conducted Justly?* (Durham, NC: Duke University Press, 1961), xv.

23. Ibid., xvi.

24. See Sider, *Early Church on Killing*, 185ff.

25. Bainton, *Christian Attitudes*, 68.

26. Ibid., 68–69.

27. Sider, *Early Church on Killing*, 185ff.

28. Ramsay MacMullen, *Soldier and Civilian in the Later Roman Empire* (Cambridge: Harvard University Press, 1963), *v*.

29. Sider, *Early Church on Killing*, 177–78.

30. Bainton, *Christian Attitudes*, 77.

31. *On the Garland*, 11.2; quoted in McSorley, *New Testament Basis of Peacemaking*, 78.

32. *Against Celsus*, 8.73; 5.33; quoted in McSorley, *New Testament Basis*, 75.

33. *Dialogue with Trypho*, 110; quoted in John Ferguson, *The Politics of Love* (Cambridge: James Clarke, n.d.), 57.

34. Sider, *Early Church on Killing*, 163ff.

35. It is important to note that the just-war tradition is really a number of overlapping traditions. See, for instance, LeRoy B. Walters Jr., "Five Classic Just War Theories: A Study in the Thought of Thomas Aquinas, Vitoria, Suarez, Gentili and Grotius" (PhD diss., Yale University, 1971); Frederick H. Russell, *The Just War in the Middle Ages* (New York: Cambridge University Press, 1975). Among the most significant modern attempts to work in the just-war tradition are Michael Walzer's *Just and Unjust Wars*; and the many works of Paul Ramsey, especially *War and the Christian Conscience*, and his major collection of pamphlets and articles, *The Just War: Force and Political Responsibility* (New York: Scribner & Sons, 1968); and James T. Johnson, *The Just War Tradition and the Restraint of War: A Moral and Historical Inquiry* (Princeton, NJ: Princeton University Press, 1981).

36. Edward L. Long, *War and Conscience in America* (Philadelphia: Westminster, 1968), 22–33. See also R. B. Potter, *The Moral Logic of War* (Philadelphia: United Presbyterian Church, n.d.); James F. Childress, "Just War Theories: The Bases, Interrelations, Priorities, and Functions of Their Criteria," *Theological Studies* 39 (September 1978): 427–45.

37. This section is adapted from Sider and Taylor, *Nuclear Holocaust and Christian Hope*, 61–62.

38. Long, *War and Conscience*, 24.

39. Ibid.

40. Ibid., 27.

41. Ibid.

42. Ibid., 28.

43. Ibid., 29.

44. Justus George Lawler, "The Council Must Speak," in *Peace, the Churches and the Bomb*, ed. James Finn (New York: The Council on Religion and International Affairs, 1965), 33–34.

45. See J. Bryan Hehir, "The Just War Ethic and Catholic Theology," in *War or Peace? The Search for New Answers*, ed. Thomas A. Shannon (Maryknoll, NY: Orbis Books, 1980), 19.

46. See, for example, John Howard Yoder, *When War Is Unjust: Being Honest in Just-War Thinking* (Minneapolis: Augsburg, 1984).

47. Paul Alexander, *Peace to War: Shifting Allegiances in the Assemblies of God* (Scottdale, PA: Herald Press, 2009).

48. See, for example, Ronald J. Sider, *Non-Violence: The Invincible Weapon?* (Dallas: Word, 1989); and Daniel Buttry, *Christian Peacemaking* (Valley Forge, PA: Judson, 1994), chap. 4.

49. Sider, *Non-Violence*, 76.

50. Ibid., chap. 3.

51. Ibid., chap. 2.

52. See Arthur G. Gish, *Hebron Journal: Stories of Nonviolent Peacemaking* (Scottdale, PA: Herald Press, 2001); and Tricia Gates Brown, *Getting in the Way: Stories from Christian Peacemaker Teams* (Scottdale, PA: Herald Press, 2005), 69–100.

53. See the longer discussion in Ronald J. Sider, "Courageous Nonviolence," *Christianity Today*, December 2007, 44–45.

54. See Glenn Stassen, ed., *Just Peacemaking: Ten Practices for Abolishing War* (Cleveland: Pilgrim, 1998); Glenn Stassen, *Just Peacemaking: Transforming Initiatives for Justice and Peace* (Louisville: Westminster John Knox, 1992); and, more briefly, Stassen, "The Ethics of War and Peacemaking," in Sider and Knippers, eds., *Toward an Evangelical Public Policy*, 302–6.

55. Stassen, "The Ethics of War and Peacemaking," 302.

56. Ibid., 303.

57. Ibid.

58. Ibid.

59. Ibid.

60. Ibid., 304.

61. Ibid.

62. Ibid.

63. Ibid., 305.

64. International Monetary Fund, "Kohler Wolfensohn Calls Attention to Imbalances in World Economy and between Rich and Poor," *IMSURVEY* 32, no. 17 (Fall 2003): 268.

65. Ibid., 305.

66. Sider and Knippers, eds., *Toward an Evangelical Public Policy*, 368.

67. Ibid., 374.

Chapter 11 Creation Care

1. When Congress or the Executive Branch wants to know what the best scientific evidence and conclusions have to say regarding policy decisions, they turn to the National Academy of Sciences, our country's most prestigious and authoritative scientific body. In May 2010 they issued their latest report on the science of climate change, in which they

state the following: "Climate change is occurring, is caused largely by human activities, and poses significant risks for—and in many cases is already affecting—a broad range of human and natural systems" (p. 21). The report regards both global warming and that human activities are the primary cause as "settled facts" (p. 17). It goes on to state, "The ultimate magnitude of climate change and the severity of its impacts depend strongly on the actions that human societies take to respond to these risks" (p. 22). See National Academy of Sciences (NAS), National Research Council, *Advancing the Science of Climate Change* (National Academies Press: May 2010): http://books.nap.edu/openbook.php?record_id=12782&page=R1#.

Internationally, the major reports of the Nobel prize–winning Intergovernmental Panel on Climate Change (IPCC), considered the world's most authoritative body on the subject, have provided the scientific basis upon which the world's governments have collectively made their decisions about climate change. The IPCC's summary reports are approved line by line in open meetings by representatives from nearly all the governments of the world (except some of the smallest ones). The latest IPCC report (2007) involved over 3,750 scientific experts from more than 130 countries. It concluded that "Warming of the climate system is unequivocal," and that there is "*very high confidence* [at least a 9 out of 10 chance] that global average net effect of human activities since 1750 has been one of warming . . . its rate of increase during the industrial era is *very likely* [90% or greater probability] to have been unprecedented in more than 10,000 years" (IPCC, AR4, WG1, SPM, pp. 5, 3). Furthermore, "Most of the observed increase in global average temperatures since the mid-20th century is *very likely* [90% or greater probability] due to the observed increase in anthropogenic [human caused] greenhouse gas concentrations" (p. 10). See Intergovernmental Panel on Climate Change, Fourth Assessment Report (AR4), Working Group One (WG1), Summary for Policymakers (SPM). IPCC reports can be found at their website, www.ipcc.ch.

In its last year in office the Bush Administration issued a major report on climate change that affirmed these findings of the IPCC. See National Science and Technology Council (NSTC), *Scientific Assessment of the Effects of Global Change on the United States*, Executive Office of the President and US Climate Change Science Program (May 2008: Washington, DC): http://www.whitehouse.gov/files/documents/ostp/NSTC%20Reports/Scientific%20Assessment%20FULL%20Report.pdf. See especially pp.1–7.

For a book written by Christians for Christians that explains the science of climate change for the average layperson and addresses many of the questions raised by those who are skeptical, see Katharine Hayhoe and Andrew Farley, *A Climate for Change: Global Warming Facts for Faith-based Decisions* (FaithWorks: New York, 2009): http://climateforchangethebook.com/. Dr. Hayhoe is a highly respected climate scientist and Rev. Farley is an evangelical pastor.

See also Jim Ball, *Global Warming and the Risen Lord: Christian Discipleship and Climate Change* (Washington, DC: Evangelical Environmental Network, 2010).

2. Grudem, *Politics according to the Bible* (Grand Rapids: Zondervan, 2010), 371. His italics.

3. Ibid., 368.

4. Ibid.

5. Ibid., 380.

6. The following paragraphs are adapted from Sider, *Rich Christians in an Age of Hunger*, 246–48.

7. For more information about the "What Would Jesus Drive?" education campaign, see http://www.whatwouldjesusdrive.org.

8. Sider and Knippers, eds., *Toward an Evangelical Public Policy*, 374.

Chapter 12 Nation-States and International Affairs

1. See Scott M. Thomas, *The Global Resurgence of Religion and the Transformation of International Relations* (New York: Palgrave Macmillan, 2005).

2. In their promotion of global human rights (especially religious freedom) in the last decade, American evangelicals have done that; see Allen D. Hertzke, *Freeing God's Children* (Lanham, MD: Rowman & Littlefield, 2004).

3. See Daniel Philpott, *Revolutions in Sovereignty: How Ideas Shaped Modern International Relations* (Princeton, NJ: Princeton University Press, 2001).

4. See James W. Skillen, *With or against the World? America's Role among the Nations* (Lanham, MD: Rowman & Littlefield, 2005), especially 72–78.

5. Albert Beveridge, quoted in Richard T. Hughes, *Myths America Lives By* (Urbana: University of Illinois Press, 2003), 37. (Chapter 1 deals with the myth of the "chosen nation.")

6. George Bush, quoted in Skillen, *With or Against the World?* 97.

7. Skillen, ibid., 104.

8. Germain Grisez, *The Way of the Lord Jesus; Volume Two: Living a Christian Life* (Quincy, IL: Franciscan, 1993), 837–38.

9. Skillen, *With or Against the World?* 132; Daniel Philpott, "On the Cusp of Sovereignty," in Luis E. Lugo, ed., *Sovereignty at the Crossroads?* (Lanham, MD: Rowman & Littlefield, 1996), 56.

10. See Sider, *Rich Christians in an Age of Hunger*, 55–56.

11. *Populorum Progressio* (1967), sec. 48; Michael Walsh and Brian Davies, eds., *Proclaiming Justice and Peace: Documents from John XXIII to John Paul II* (Mystic, CT: Twenty-Third Publications, 1984), 154–55.

12. *Populorum Progressio* (1967), sec. 62; Walsh and Davies, *Proclaiming Justice and Peace*, 158.

13. *Pacem in terris* (1963), sec. 132; Walsh and Davies, *Proclaiming Justice and Peace*, 68.

14. Quoted in O'Donovan and O'Donovan, *Sourcebook in Christian Political Thought*, 13.

15. This point is made well by Duane K. Friesen, *Christian Peacemaking and International Conflict* (Scottdale, PA: Herald Press, 1986), 44.

16. George Weigel, "Idealism without Illusions," in Lugo, ed., *Sovereignty at the Crossroads?* 198.

17. Max L. Stackhouse, *Public Theology and Political Economy* (Grand Rapids: Eerdmans, 1987), 108.

18. Acts 17:26 does not mean that God wills and ordains specific national boundaries (that would mean that God wanted Hitler and Stalin to overrun and annex other nations), but rather that there is just one God who is Creator and Lord of history.

19. For the last, see Sider, *Rich Christians in an Age of Hunger*, chap. 9.

20. "A Pastoral Letter Concerning Migration from the Catholic Bishops of Mexico and the United States," January 22, 2003, secs. 28–33. See also *Pacem in terris*, secs. 105, 106.

21. See the careful arguments and the vast citation of contemporary thinkers in Justin Cooper, "The State, Transnational Relations, and Justice," in Lugo, ed., *Sovereignty at the*

Crossroads? 3–28; and Lawrence Adams, "Foundations for Post–Cold War International Justice," in Demy and Stewart, eds., *Politics and Public Policy*, 297–316.

22. See Daniel Philpott and Timothy Shah, "Faith, Freedom, and Federation: The Role of Religious Ideas and Institutions in European Political Convergence," in Timothy Byrnes and Peter Katzenstein, eds., *Religion in an Expanding Europe* (Cambridge: Cambridge University Press, 2006).

23. See *The Responsibility to Protect* (December 2001), a report of the International Commission on Intervention and State Sovereignty (published by the International Development Research Centre, P.O. Box 8500, Ottawa, ON K1G 3H9).

24. See Philpott, *Revolutions in Sovereignty*, 39–43.

25. Ibid., 262.

26. Adams, "Foundations for Post–Cold War International Justice," 306.

27. *Pacem in terris*, sec. 141; Walsh and Davies, *Proclaiming Justice and Peace*, 70.

28. See, for example, *Forging a World of Liberty under Law: US National Security in the 21st Century* (Final Paper of the Princeton Project on National Security codirected by G. John Ikenberry and Anne-Marie Slaughter), September 27, 2006.

29. Ibid., 7.

Chapter 13 Biblical Balance, Historic Opportunity

1. Sider and Knippers, eds., *Toward an Evangelical Public Policy*, 366.

2. See the helpful discussion in Wogaman, *Christian Perspectives on Politics*, 200–208; and Neuhaus, *Christian Faith and Public Policy*, 34–57.

3. Wogaman, *Christian Perspectives on Politics*, 200.

4. Personal correspondence and conversation with Michael Cromartie, 1989.

5. Personal conversation with Ed Dobson, March 1, 2000.

6. See H. M. Kuitert, *Everything Is Politics: But Politics Is Not Everything*, trans. John Bowden (Grand Rapids: Eerdmans, 1986), 151.

7. The US Catholic bishops did this effectively in the 1980s with their pastoral letters on peace and economic justice.

8. Kuitert, *Everything Is Politics*, 151.

9. Monsma, *Pursuing Justice in a Sinful World*, 82.

10. David P. Gushee, *The Future of Faith in American Politics* (Waco, TX: Baylor University Press, 2008), 87.

11. See Pontifical Council for Justice and Peace, *Compendium of the Social Doctrine of the Church* (Washington, DC: US Conference of Catholic Bishops, 2004).

12. See *American Piety in the 21st Century: New Insights to the Depth and Complexity of Religion in the US*, reporting on a September 2006 Baylor Religion Survey done by the Baylor Institute for Studies of Religion, 7–12.

Subject Index

fair procedures, 69
fair trial, 106
faith-based initiatives, 7, 155
fall, 40–41, 57, 58, 112
Falwell, Jerry, 3–4, 8
family, 56, 64, 68, 70, 129–39, 193
fatalism, 37
fetus, 119–20
First Amendment, 146–47, 152, 153–54
Foerster, Werner, 231n8
food, as right, 107
fornication, 131
Forrester, Duncan, 52, 218n41
"For the Health of the Nation," 67, 170, 193, 199
Fox, Matthew, 173
freedom, 57, 69, 103, 141. *See also* religious freedom
  and democracy, 112
  and market economies, 114
  and private property, 108
  and responsibilities, 90
freedom of speech, 106
Freston, Paul, 4–5
Freud, Sigmund, 20
fundamentalists
  enclaves of, 6
  political activity of, 3–4
future, 51–52

Gandhi, Mahatma, 72, 73, 167, 169
gay marriage, 9, 138–39
genetic engineering, 122–23
genocide, 157
Gerson, Michael, xv
Gitari, David, 150
Glendon, Mary Ann, 103
global political structures, 187–90
global warming, 171–72, 177–78
globalization, 182
Glover, Jonathan, 157
God
  covenant with America, 149
  as just, 77–78, 82
  partial to poor, 84–85, 86
  transcendence and immanence of, 172
good life, 52
good Samaritan, 162
Gorman, Michael J., 126
Gottwald, Norman, 224n41
government, 28. *See also* state
Gregory, Eric, xiv

Grudem, Wayne, xvi–xvii, 171
Guinness, Os, 6
Gushee, David, xiv, 8, 9, 137, 199

hand, as power, 87
Harper, Lisa Sharon, xv
health care, 108
Helms, Jesse, 7, 124
Heltzel, Peter Goodwin, xiv
Hengel, Martin, 162
Henry, Carl F. H., xiv, 218n10
Henry, Paul, 5
heretics, execution of, 145
Hewlett, Sylvia Ann, 135
history, 42
history of salvation, 31–32
Hitler, Adolf, 8, 16
Hollenbach, David, 110–12, 225n6
Hollinger, Dennis, 9
homosexual practice, 131, 138
hope, 52
  for creation, 175–76
human flourishing, 17, 57
humanitarian intervention, 188
human laws, 77–78
human rights, 101–15, 169, 193, 225n2
humans, interdependence with creation, 173
Hume, David, 21
humility, in politics, 197–98
Hunter, James Davison, xiii

ideal monarch, 60–61
image of God, 24, 33–34, 39–40, 177
  and dominion, 173
  and equality, 104
  and human rights, 102
  and sanctity of human life, 117–18
  and social institutions, 56–57
  and work, 43
immigration policy, 186–87
incarnation, 144
indignity, 88
individual, and image of God, 34–35
individualism, 36, 40, 81, 103–4, 133
industrial world, 133
infanticide, 20, 117
injustice, 88
  of market economies, 114–15
Innes, D. C., xv
institutions. *See* social institutions
Intergovernmental Panel on Climate Change, 234n1

Scripture Index

245

New Testament

Ancient Christian Writings

Ronald J. Sider (PhD, Yale University) is professor of theology, holistic ministry, and public policy as well as director of the Sider Center on Ministry and Public Policy at Palmer Theological Seminary of Eastern University. He is also president of Evangelicals for Social Action. A widely known evangelical speaker and writer, Sider has spoken on six continents and published more than thirty books and scores of articles. His *Rich Christians in an Age of Hunger* was recognized by *Christianity Today* as being among the one hundred most influential books in religion of the twentieth century. His most recent books are *Just Generosity: A New Vision for Overcoming Poverty in America*, *Churches That Make a Difference: Reaching Your Community with Good News and Good Works* (with Phil Olson and Heidi Unruh), *The Scandal of the Evangelical Conscience: Why Are Christians Living Just Like the Rest of the World?*, *Fixing the Moral Deficit: A Balanced Way to Balance the Budget*, and *The Early Church on Killing: A Comprehensive Sourcebook on War, Abortion, and Capital Punishment*. Sider is publisher of *PRISM* magazine and a contributing editor for *Christianity Today* and *Sojourners*. He has lectured at scores of colleges and universities around the world, including Yale, Harvard, Princeton, and Oxford.